Big Data MBA

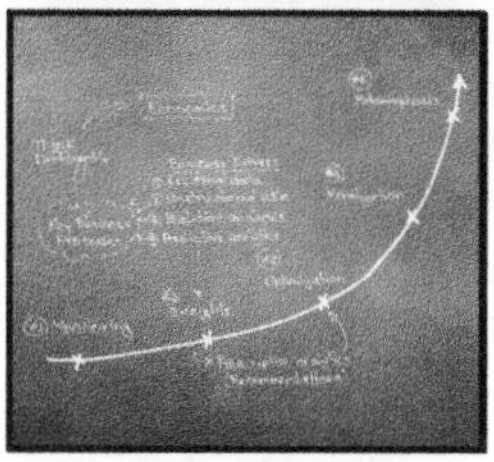

Big Data MBA

Driving Business Strategies with Data Science

Bill Schmarzo

WILEY

Big Data MBA: Driving Business Strategies with Data Science

Published by
John Wiley & Sons, Inc.
10475 Crosspoint Boulevard
Indianapolis, IN 46256
www.wiley.com

Published by John Wiley & Sons, Inc., Indianapolis, Indiana

Published simultaneously in Canada

ISBN: 978-1-119-18111-8
ISBN: 978-1-119-23884-3 (ebk)
ISBN: 978-1-119-18138-5 (ebk)

Manufactured in the United States of America

10 9 8 7 6 5 4 3 2 1

Library of Congress Control Number: 2015955444

About the Author

Bill Schmarzo is the Chief Technology Officer (CTO) of the Big Data Practice of EMC Global Services. As CTO, Bill is responsible for setting the strategy and defining the big data service offerings and capabilities for EMC Global Services. He also works directly with organizations to help them identify where and how to start their big data journeys. Bill is the author of *Big Data: Understanding How Data Powers Big Business,* writes white papers, is an avid blogger, and is a frequent speaker on the use of big data and data science to power an organization's key business initiatives. He is a University of San Francisco School of Management (SOM) Fellow, where he teaches the "Big Data MBA" course.

Bill has over three decades of experience in data warehousing, business intelligence, and analytics. He authored EMC's Vision Workshop methodology and co-authored with Ralph Kimball a series of articles on analytic applications. Bill has served on The Data Warehouse Institute's faculty as the head of the analytic applications curriculum. Previously, he was the Vice President of Analytics at Yahoo! and oversaw the analytic applications business unit at Business Objects, including the development, marketing, and sales of their industry-defining analytic applications.

Bill holds a master's degree in Business Administration from the University of Iowa and a Bachelor of Science degree in Mathematics, Computer Science, and Business Administration from Coe College. Bill's recent blogs can be found at `http://infocus.emc.com/author/william_schmarzo/`. You can follow Bill on Twitter @schmarzo and LinkedIn at `www.linkedin.com/in/schmarzo`.

About the Technical Editor

Jeffrey Abbott leads the EMC Global Services marketing practice around big data, helping customers understand how to identify and take advantage of opportunities to leverage data for strategic business initiatives, while driving awareness for a portfolio of services offerings that accelerate customer time-to-value. As a content developer and program lead, Jeff emphasizes clear and concise messaging on persona-based campaigns. Prior to EMC, Jeff helped build and promote a cloud-based ecosystem for CA Technologies that combined an online social community, a cloud development platform, and an e-commerce site for cloud services. Jeff also spent several years within CA's Thought Leadership group, creating and promoting executive-level messaging and social-media programs around major disruptive trends in IT. Jeff has held various other product marketing roles at firms such as EMC, Citrix, and Ardence and spent a decade running client accounts at numerous boutique marketing firms. Jeff studied small business management at the University of Vermont and resides in Sudbury, MA, with his wife, two boys, and dog. Jeff enjoys skiing, backpacking, photography, and classic cars.

Credits

Project Editor
Adaobi Obi Tulton

Technical Editor
Jeffrey Abbott

Production Editor
Barath Kumar Rajasekaran

Copy Editor
Chris Haviland

Manager of Content Development & Assembly
Mary Beth Wakefield

Production Manager
Kathleen Wisor

Marketing Director
David Mayhew

Marketing Manager
Carrie Sherrill

Professional Technology & Strategy Director
Barry Pruett

Business Manager
Amy Knies

Associate Publisher
Jim Minatel

Project Coordinator, Cover
Brent Savage

Proofreader
Nicole Hirschman

Indexer
Nancy Guenther

Cover Designer
Wiley

Cover Image
©STILLFX/iStockphoto

Acknowledgments

Acknowledgments are dangerous. Not dangerous like wrestling an alligator or an unhappy Chicago Cubs fan, but dangerous in the sense that there are so many people to thank. How do I prevent the Acknowledgments section from becoming longer than my book? This book represents the sum of many, many discussions, debates, presentations, engagements, and late night beers and pizza that I have had with so many colleagues and customers. Thanks to everyone who has been on this journey with me.

So realizing that I will miss many folks in this acknowledgment, here I go…

I can't say enough about the contributions of Jeff Abbott. Not only was Jeff my EMC technical editor for this book, but he also has the unrewarding task of editing all of my blogs. Jeff has the patience to put up with my writing style and the smarts to know how to spin my material so that it is understandable and readable. I can't thank Jeff enough for his patience, guidance, and friendship.

Jen Sorenson's role in the book was only supposed to be EMC Public Relations editor, but Jen did so much more. There are many chapters in this book where Jen's suggestions (using the Fairy-Tale Theme Parks example in Chapter 6) made the chapters more interesting. In fact, Chapter 6 is probably my favorite chapter because I was so over my skis on the data science algorithms material. But Jen did a marvelous job of taking a difficult topic (data science algorithms) and making it come to life.

Speaking of data science, Pedro DeSouza and Wei Lin are the two best data scientists I have ever met, and I am even more grateful that I get to call them friends. They have been patient in helping me to learn the world of data science over the past several years, which is reflected in many chapters in the book (most notably Chapters 5 and 6). But more than anything else, they taught me a very valuable life lesson: being humble is the best way to learn. I can't even express in words my admiration for them and how they approach their profession.

Joe Dossantos and Josh Siegel may be surprised to find their names in the acknowledgments, but they shouldn't be. Both Joe and Josh have been with me on many steps in this big data journey, and both have contributed tremendously to my understanding of how big data can impact the business world. Their fingerprints are all over this book.

Adaobi Obi Tulton and Chris Haviland are my two Wiley editors, and they are absolutely marvelous! They have gone out of their way to make the editing process as painless as possible, and they understand my voice so well that I accepted over 99 percent of all of their suggestions. Both Adaobi and Chris were my editors on my first book, so I guess they forgot how much of a PITA (pain in the a**) I can be when they agreed to be the editors on my second book. Though I have never met them face-to-face, I feel a strong kinship with both Adaobi and Chris. Thanks for all of your patience and guidance and your wonderful senses of humor!

A very special thank you to Professor Mouwafac Sidaoui, with whom I co-teach the Big Data MBA at the University of San Francisco School of Management (USF SOM). I could not pick a better partner in crime—he is smart, humble, demanding, fun, engaging, worldly, and everything that one could want in a friend. I am a Fellow at the USF SOM because of Mouwafac's efforts, and he has set me up for my next career—teaching.

I also what to thank Dean Elizabeth Davis and the USF MBA students who were willing to be guinea pigs for testing many of the concepts and techniques captured in this book. They helped me to determine which ideas worked and how to fix the ones that did not work.

Another special thank you to EMC, who supported me as I worked at the leading edge of the business transformational potential of big data. EMC has afforded me the latitude to pursue new ideas, concepts, and offerings and in many situations has allowed me to be the tip of the big data arrow. I could not ask for a better employer and partner.

The thank you list should include the excellent and creative people at EMC with whom I interact on a regular basis, but since that list is too long, I'll just mention Ed, Jeff, Jason, Paul, Dan, Josh, Matt, Joe, Scott, Brandon, Aidan, Neville, Bart, Billy, Mike, Clark, Jeeva, Sean, Shriya, Srini, Ken, Mitch, Cindy, Charles, Chuck, Peter, Aaron, Bethany, Susan, Barb, Jen, Rick, Steve, David, and many, many more.

I want to thank my family, who has put up with me during the book writing process. My wife Carolyn was great about grabbing Chipotle for me when I had a tough deadline, and my sons Alec and Max and my daughter Amelia were supportive throughout the book writing process. I've been blessed with a marvelous family (just stop stealing my Chipotle in the refrigerator!).

My mom and dad both passed away, but I can imagine their look of surprise and pride in the fact that I have written two books and am teaching at the University of San Francisco in my spare time. We will get the chance to talk about that in my next life.

But most important, I want to thank the EMC customers with whom I have had the good fortune to work. Customers are at the frontline of the big data transformation, and where better to be situated to learn about what's working and what's not working then arm-in-arm with EMC's most excellent customers at those frontlines. Truly the best part of my job is the chance to work with our customers. Heck, I'm willing to put up with the airline travel to do that!

Contents at a Glance

Contents

Introduction

I never planned on writing a second book. Heck, I thought writing one book was enough to check this item off my bucket list. But so much has changed since I wrote my first book that I felt compelled to continue to explore this once-in-a-lifetime opportunity for organizations to leverage data and analytics to transform their business models. And I'm not just talking the "make me more money" part of businesses. Big data can drive significant "improve the quality of life" value in areas such as education, poverty, parole rehabilitation, health care, safety, and crime reduction.

My first book targeted the Information Technology (IT) audience. However, I soon realized that the biggest winner in this big data land grab was the business. So this book targets the business audience and is based on a few key premises:

- Organizations do not need a big data strategy as much as they need a business strategy that incorporates big data.
- The days when business leaders could turn analytics over to IT are over; tomorrow's business leaders must embrace analytics as a business discipline in the same vein as accounting, finance, management science, and marketing.
- The key to data monetization and business transformation lies in unleashing the organization's creative thinking; we have got to get the business users to "think like a data scientist."
- Finally, the business potential of big data is only limited by the creative thinking of the business users.

I've also had the opportunity to teach "Big Data MBA" at the University of San Francisco (USF) School of Management since I wrote the first book. I did well enough that USF made me its first School of Management Fellow. What I experienced while working with these outstanding and creative students and Professor Mouwafac Sidaoui compelled me to undertake the challenge of writing this second book, targeting those students and tomorrow's business leaders.

One of the topics that I hope jumps out in the book is the power of data science. There have been many books written about data science with the goal of helping people to become data scientists. But I felt that something was missing—that instead of trying to create a world of data scientists, we needed to help tomorrow's business leaders think like data scientists.

So that's the focus of this book—to help tomorrow's business leaders integrate data and analytics into their business models and to lead the cultural transformation by unleashing the organization's creative juices by helping the business to "think like a data scientist."

Overview of the Book and Technology

The days when business stakeholders could relinquish control of data and analytics to IT are over. The business stakeholders must be front and center in championing and monetizing the organization's data collection and analysis efforts. Business leaders need to understand where and how to leverage big data, exploiting the collision of new sources of customer, product, and operational data coupled with data science to optimize key business processes, uncover new monetization opportunities, and create new sources of competitive differentiation. And while it's not realistic to convert your business users into data scientists, it's critical that we teach the business users to *think like data scientists* so they can collaborate with IT and the data scientists on use case identification, requirements definition, business valuation, and ultimately analytics operationalization.

This book provides a business-hardened framework with supporting methodology and hands-on exercises that not only will help business users to identify where and how to leverage big data for business advantage but will also provide guidelines for operationalizing the analytics, setting up the right organizational structure, and driving the analytic insights throughout the organization's user experience to both customers and frontline employees.

How This Book Is Organized

The book is organized into four sections:

- **Part I: Business Potential of Big Data.** Part I includes Chapters 1 through 4 and sets the business-centric foundation for the book. Here is where I introduce the Big Data Business Model Maturity Index and frame the big data discussion around the perspective that "organizations do not need a big data strategy as much as they need a business strategy that incorporates big data."

- **Part II: Data Science**. Part II includes Chapters 5 through 7 and covers the principle behind data science. These chapters introduce some data science basics and explore the complementary nature of Business Intelligence and data science and how these two disciplines are both complementary and different in the problems that they address.
- **Part III: Data Science for Business Stakeholders**. Part III includes Chapters 8 through 12 and seeks to teach the business users and business leaders to "think like a data scientist." This part introduces a methodology and several exercises to reinforce the data science thinking and approach. It has a lot of hands-on work.
- **Part IV: Building Cross-Organizational Support**. Part IV includes Chapters 13 through 15 and discusses organizational challenges. This part covers envisioning, which may very well be the most important topic in the book as the business potential of big data is only limited by the creative thinking of the business users.

Here are some more details on each of the chapters in the book:

- **Chapter 1: The Big Data Business Mandate**. This chapter frames the big data discussion on how big data is more about business transformation and the economics of big data than it is about technology.
- **Chapter 2: Big Data Business Model Maturity Index**. This chapter covers the Big Data Business Model Maturity Index (BDBM), which is the foundation for the entire book. Take the time to understand each of the five stages of the BDBM and how the BDBM provides a road map for measuring how effective your organization is at integrating data and analytics into your business models.
- **Chapter 3: The Big Data Strategy Document**. This chapter introduces a CXO level document and process for helping organizations identify where and how to start their big data journeys from a business perspective.
- **Chapter 4: The Importance of the User Experience**. This is one of my favorite topics. This chapter challenges traditional Business Intelligence reporting and dashboard concepts by introducing a more simple but direct approach for delivering actionable insights to your key business stakeholders—frontline employees, channel partners, and end customers.
- **Chapter 5: Differences Between Business Intelligence and Data Science**. This chapter explores the different worlds of Business Intelligence and data science and highlights both the differences and the complementary nature of each.

- **Chapter 6: Data Science 101**. This chapter (my favorite) reviews 14 different analytic techniques that my data science teams commonly use and in what business situations you should contemplate using them. It is accompanied by a marvelous fictitious case study using Fairy-Tale Theme Parks (thanks Jen!).
- **Chapter 7: The Data Lake**. This chapter introduces the concept of a data lake, explaining how the data lake frees up expensive data warehouse resources and unleashes the creative, fail-fast nature of the data science teams.
- **Chapter 8: Thinking Like a Data Scientist**. The heart of this book, this chapter covers the eight-step "thinking like a data scientist" process. This chapter is pretty deep, so plan on having a pen and paper (and probably an eraser as well) with you as you read this chapter.
- **Chapter 9: "By" Analysis Technique.** This chapter does a deep dive into one of the important concepts in "thinking like a data scientist"—the "By" analysis technique.
- **Chapter 10: Score Development Technique.** This chapter introduces how scores can drive collaboration between the business users and data scientist to create actionable scores that guide the organization's key business decisions.
- **Chapter 11: Monetization Exercise**. This chapter provides a technique for organizations that have a substantial amount of customer, product, and operational data but do not know how to monetize that data. This chapter can be very eye-opening!
- **Chapter 12: Metamorphosis Exercise**. This chapter is a fun, out-of-the-box exercise that explores the potential data and analytic impacts for an organization as it contemplates the Business Metamorphosis phase of the Big Data Business Model Maturity Index.
- **Chapter 13: Power of Envisioning**. This chapter starts to address some of the organizational and cultural challenges you may face. In particular, Chapter 13 introduces some envisioning techniques to help unleash your organization's creative thinking.
- **Chapter 14: Organizational Ramifications**. This chapter goes into more detail about the organizational ramifications of big data, especially the role of the Chief Data (Monetization) Officer.
- **Chapter 15: Stories**. The book wraps up with some case studies, but not your traditional case studies. Instead, Chapter 15 presents a technique for creating "stories" that are relevant to your organization. Anyone can find case studies, but not just anyone can create a story.

Who Should Read This Book

This book is targeted toward business users and business management. I wrote this book so that I could use it in teaching my Big Data MBA class, so included all of the hands-on exercises and templates that my students would need to successfully earn their Big Data MBA graduation certificate.

I think folks would benefit by also reading my first book, *Big Data: Understanding How Data Powers Big Business*, which is targeted toward the IT audience. There is some overlap between the two books (10 to 15 percent), but the first book sets the stage and introduces concepts that are explored in more detail in this book.

Tools You Will Need

No special tools are required other than a pencil, an eraser, several sheets of paper, and your creativity. Grab a chai tea latte, some Chipotle, and enjoy!

What's on the Website

You can download the "Thinking Like a Data Scientist" workbook from the book's website at `www.wiley.com/go/bigdatamba`. And oh, there might be another surprise there as well! Hehehe!

What This Means for You

As students from my class at USF have told me, this material allows them to take a problem or challenge and use a well-thought-out process to drive cross-organizational collaboration to come up with ideas they can turn into actions using data and analytics. What employer wouldn't want a future leader who knows how to do that?

Part

I

Business Potential of Big Data

Chapters 1 through 4 set the foundation for driving business strategies with data science. In particular, the Big Data Business Model Maturity Index highlights the realm of what's possible from a business potential perspective by providing a road map that measures the effectiveness of your organization to leverage data and analytics to power your business models.

In This Part

CHAPTER

1

The Big Data Business Mandate

Having trouble getting your senior management team to understand the business potential of big data? Can't get your management leadership to consider big data to be something other than an IT science experiment? Are your line-of-business leaders unwilling to commit themselves to understanding how data and analytics can power their top initiatives?

If so, then this "Big Data Senior Executive Care Package" is for you!

And for a limited time, you get an unlimited license to share this care package with as many senior executives as you desire. But you must act NOW! Become the life of the company parties with your extensive knowledge of how new customer, product, and operational insights can guide your organization's value creation processes. And maybe, just maybe, get a promotion in the process!!

NOTE **All company material referenced in this book comes from public sources and is referenced accordingly.**

Big Data MBA Introduction

The days when business users and business management can relinquish control of data and analytics to IT are over, or at least for organizations that want to survive beyond the immediate term. The big data discussion now needs to focus on how organizations can couple new sources of customer, product, and operational data with advanced analytics (data science) to power their key business processes and elevate their business models. Organizations need to understand that they *do not need a big data strategy as much as they need a business strategy that incorporates big data.*

The *Big Data MBA* challenges the thinking that data and analytics are ancillary or a "bolt on" to the business; that data and analytics *are* someone else's problem. In a growing number of leading organizations, data and analytics are critical to business success and long-term survival. Business leaders and business users reading this book will learn why they must take responsibility for identifying where and how they can apply data and analytics to their businesses—otherwise they put their businesses at risk of being made obsolete by more nimble, data-driven competitors.

The *Big Data MBA* introduces and describes concepts, techniques, methodologies, and hand-on exercises to guide you as you seek to address the big data *business mandate.* The book provides hands-on exercises and homework assignments to make these concepts and techniques come to life for your organization. It provides recommendations and actions that enable your organization to start today. And in the process, *Big Data MBA* teaches you to "think like a data scientist."

The Forrester study "Reset on Big Data" (Hopkins et al., 2014)[1] highlights the critical role of a business-centric focus in the big data discussion. The study argues that technology-focused executives within a business will think of big data as a technology and fail to convey its importance to the boardroom.

Businesses of all sizes must reframe the big data conversation with the business leaders in the boardroom. The critical and difficult big data question that business leaders must address is:

> *How effective is our organization at integrating data and analytics into our business models?*

Before business leaders can begin these discussions, organizations must understand their current level of big data maturity. Chapter 2 discusses in detail the "Big Data Business Model Maturity Index" (see Figure 1-1). The Big Data Business Model Maturity Index is a measure of how effective an organization is at integrating data and analytics to power their business model.

---

[1] Hopkins, Brian, Fatemeh Khatibloo with Kyle McNabb, James Staten, Andras Cser, Holger Kisker, Ph.D., Leslie Owens, Jennifer Belissent, Ph.D., Abigail Komlenic, "Reset On Big Data: Embrace Big Data to Engage Customers at Scale," Forrester Research, 2014.

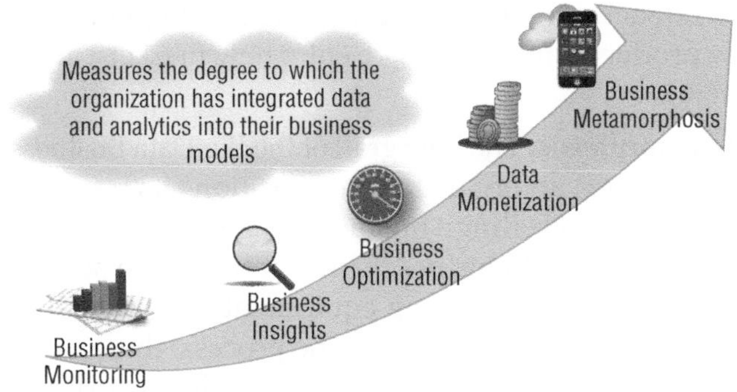

Figure 1-1: Big Data Business Model Maturity Index

The Big Data Business Model Maturity Index provides a road map for how organizations can integrate data and analytics into their business models. The Big Data Business Model Maturity Index is composed of the following five phases:

- **Phase 1: Business Monitoring.** In the Business Monitoring phase, organizations are leveraging data warehousing and Business Intelligence to monitor the organization's performance.
- **Phase 2: Business Insights.** The Business Insights phase is about leveraging predictive analytics to uncover customer, product, and operational insights buried in the growing wealth of internal and external data sources. In this phase, organizations aggressively expand their data acquisition efforts by coupling all of their detailed transactional and operational data with internal data such as consumer comments, e-mail conversations, and technician notes, as well as external and publicly available data such as social media, weather, traffic, economic, demographics, home values, and local events data.
- **Phase 3: Business Optimization.** In the Business Optimization phase, organizations apply prescriptive analytics to the customer, product, and operational insights uncovered in the Business Insights phase to deliver actionable insights or recommendations to frontline employees, business managers, and channel partners, as well as customers. The goal of the Business Optimization phase is to enable employees, partners, and customers to optimize their key decisions.
- **Phase 4: Data Monetization.** In the Data Monetization phase, organizations leverage the customer, product, and operational insights to create new sources of revenue. This could include selling data—or insights—into new markets (a cellular phone provider selling customer behavioral data to advertisers), integrating analytics into products and services to create

"smart" products, or re-packaging customer, product, and operational insights to create new products and services, to enter new markets, and/or to reach new audiences.

- **Phase 5: Business Metamorphosis.** The holy grail of the Big Data Business Model Maturity Index is when an organization transitions its business model from selling products to selling "business-as-a-service." Think GE selling "thrust" instead of jet engines. Think John Deere selling "farming optimization" instead of farming equipment. Think Boeing selling "air miles" instead of airplanes. And in the process, these organizations will create a platform enabling third-party developers to build and market solutions on top of the organization's business-as-a-service business model.

Ultimately, big data only matters if it helps organizations make more money and improve operational effectiveness. Examples include increasing customer acquisition, reducing customer churn, reducing operational and maintenance costs, optimizing prices and yield, reducing risks and errors, improving compliance, improving the customer experience, and more.

No matter the size of the organization, *organizations don't need a big data strategy as much as they need a business strategy that incorporates big data.*

Focus Big Data on Driving Competitive Differentiation

I'm always confused about how organizations struggle to differentiate between technology investments that drive competitive parity and those technology investments that create unique and compelling competitive differentiation. Let's explore this difference in a bit more detail.

Competitive parity is achieving similar or same operational capabilities as those of your competitors. It involves leveraging industry best practices and pre-packaged software to create a baseline that, at worst, is equal to the operational capabilities across your industry. Organizations end up achieving competitive parity when they buy foundational and undifferentiated capabilities from enterprise software packages such as Enterprise Resource Planning (ERP), Customer Relationship Management (CRM), and Sales Force Automation (SFA).

Competitive differentiation is achieved when an organization leverages people, processes, and technology to create applications, programs, processes, etc., that differentiate its products and services from those of its competitors in ways that add unique value for the end customer and create competitive differentiation in the marketplace.

Leading organizations should seek to "buy" foundational and undifferentiated capabilities but "build" what is differentiated and value-added for their customers. But sometimes organizations get confused between the two.

Let's call this the *ERP effect*. ERP software packages were sold as a software solution that would make everyone more profitable by delivering operational excellence. But when everyone is running the same application, what's the source of the competitive differentiation?

Analytics, on the other hand, enables organizations to uniquely optimize their key business processes, drive a more engaging customer experience, and uncover new monetization opportunities with unique insights that they gather about their customers, products, and operations.

Leveraging Technology to Power Competitive Differentiation

While most organizations have invested heavily in ERP-type operational systems, far fewer have been successful in leveraging data and analytics to build strategic applications that provide unique value to their customers and create competitive differentiation in the marketplace. Here are some examples of organizations that have invested in building differentiated capabilities by leveraging new sources of data and analytics:

- Google: PageRank and Ad Serving
- Yahoo: Behavioral Targeting and Retargeting
- Facebook: Ad Serving and News Feed
- Apple: iTunes
- Netflix: Movie Recommendations
- Amazon: "Customers Who Bought This Item," 1-Click ordering, and Supply Chain & Logistics
- Walmart: Demand Forecasting, Supply Chain Logistics, and Retail Link
- Procter & Gamble: Brand and Category Management
- Federal Express: Critical Inventory Logistics
- American Express and Visa: Fraud Detection
- GE: Asset Optimization and Operations Optimization (Predix)

None of these organizations bought these strategic, business-differentiating applications off the shelf. They understood that it was necessary to provide differentiated value to their internal and external customers, and they leveraged data and analytics to build applications that delivered competitive differentiation.

History Lesson on Economic-Driven Business Transformation

More than anything else, the driving force behind big data is the economics of big data—it's 20 to 50 times cheaper to store, manage, and analyze data than it is to use traditional data warehousing technologies. This 20 to 50 times economic impact is courtesy of commodity hardware, open source software, an explosion of new open source tools coming out of academia, and ready access to free online training on topics such as big data architectures and data science. A client of mine in the insurance industry calculated a 50X economic impact. Another client in the health care industry calculated a 49X economic impact (they need to look harder to find that missing 1X).

History has shown that the most significant technology innovations are ones that drive economic change. From the printing press to interchangeable parts to the microprocessor, these technology innovations have provided an unprecedented opportunity for the more agile and more nimble organizations to disrupt existing markets and establish new value creation processes.

Big data possesses that same economic potential whether it be to create smart cities, improve the quality of medical care, improve educational effectiveness, reduce poverty, improve safety, reduce risks, or even cure cancer. And for many organizations, the first question that needs to be asked about big data is:

> *How effective is my organization at leveraging new sources of data and advanced analytics to uncover new customer, product, and operational insights that can be used to differentiate our customer engagement, optimize key business processes, and uncover new monetization opportunities?*

Big data is nothing new, especially if you view it from the proper perspective. While the popular big data discussions are around "disruptive" technology innovations like Hadoop and Spark, the real discussion should be about the economic impact of big data. New technologies don't disrupt business models; it's what organizations do with these new technologies that disrupts business models and enables new ones. Let's review an example of one such economic-driven business transformation: the steam engine.

The steam engine enabled urbanization, industrialization, and the conquering of new territories. It literally shrank distance and time by reducing the time required to move people and goods from one side of a continent to the other. The steam engine enabled people to leave low-paying agricultural jobs and move into cities for higher-paying manufacturing and clerical jobs that led to a higher standard of living.

For example, cities such as London shot up in terms of population. In 1801, before the advent of George Stephenson's Rocket steam engine, London had 1.1 million residents. After the invention, the population of London more than doubled to 2.7 million residents by 1851. London transformed the nucleus of society from small tight-knit communities where textile production and agriculture were prevalent into big cities with a variety of jobs. The steam locomotive provided quicker transportation and more jobs, which in turn brought more people into the cities and drastically changed the job market. By 1861, only 2.4

percent of London's population was employed in agriculture, while 49.4 percent were in the manufacturing or transportation business. The steam locomotive was a major turning point in history as it transformed society from largely rural and agricultural into urban and industrial.[2]

Table 1-1 shows other historical lessons that demonstrate how technology innovation created economic-driven business opportunities.

Table 1-1: Exploiting Technology Innovation to Create Economic-Driven Business Opportunities

TECHNOLOGY INNOVATION	ECONOMIC IMPACT
Printing Press	Expanded literacy (simplified knowledge capture and enabled knowledge dissemination and the education of the masses)
Interchangeable Parts	Drove the standardization of manufacturing parts and fueled the industrial revolution
Steam Engine (Railroads and Steamboats)	Sparked urbanization (drove transition from agricultural to manufacturing-centric society)
Internal Combustion Engine	Triggered suburbanization (enabled personal mobility, both geographically and socially)
Interstate Highway System	Foundation for interstate commerce (enabled regional specialization and wealth creation)
Telephone	Democratized communications (by eliminating distance and delays as communications issues)
Computers	Automated common processes (thereby freeing humans for more creative engagement)
Internet	Gutted cost of commerce and knowledge sharing (enabled remote workforce and international competition)

This brings us back to big data. All of these innovations share the same lesson: it wasn't the technology that was disruptive; it was how organizations leveraged the technology to disrupt existing business models and enabled new ones.

[2] http://railroadandsteamengine.weebly.com/impact.html

Critical Importance of "Thinking Differently"

Organizations have been taught by technology vendors, press, and analysts to think faster, cheaper, and smaller, but they have not been taught to "think *differently*." The inability to think differently is causing organizational alignment and business adoption problems with respect to the big data opportunity. Organizations must throw out much of their conventional data, analytics, and organizational thinking in order to get the maximum value out of big data. Let's introduce some key areas for thinking differently that will be covered throughout this book.

Don't Think Big Data Technology, Think Business Transformation

Many organizations are infatuated with the technical innovations surrounding big data and the three Vs of data: volume, variety, and velocity. But starting with a technology focus can quickly turn your big data initiative into a science experiment. You don't want to be a solution in search of a problem.

Instead, focus on the four Ms of big data: *Make Me More Money* (or if you are a non-profit organization, maybe that's *Make Me More Efficient*). Start your big data initiative with a business-first approach. Identify and focus on addressing the organization's key business initiatives, that is, what the organization is trying to accomplish from a business perspective over the next 9 to 12 months (e.g., reduce supply chain costs, improve supplier quality and reliability, reduce hospital-acquired infections, improve student performance). Break down or decompose this business initiative into the supporting decisions, questions, metrics, data, analytics, and technology necessary to support the targeted business initiative.

CROSS-REFERENCE **This book begins by covering the Big Data Business Model Maturity Index in Chapter 2. The Big Data Business Model Maturity Index helps organizations address the key question:**

How effective is our organization at leveraging data and analytics to power our key business processes and uncover new monetization opportunities?

The maturity index provides a guide or road map with specific recommendations to help organizations advance up the maturity index. Chapter 3 introduces the big data strategy document. The big data strategy document provides a framework for helping organizations identify where and how to start their big data journey from a business perspective.

Don't Think Business Intelligence, Think Data Science

Data science is different from Business Intelligence (BI). Resist the advice to try to make these two different disciplines the same. For example:

- Business Intelligence focuses on reporting what happened (descriptive analytics). Data science focuses on predicting what is likely to happen (predictive analytics) and then recommending what actions to take (prescriptive analytics).
- Business Intelligence operates with schema on load in which you have to pre-build the data schema before you can load the data to generate your BI queries and reports. Data science deals with schema on query in which the data scientists custom design the data schema based on the hypothesis they want to test or the prediction that they want to make.

Organizations that try to "extend" their Business Intelligence capabilities to encompass big data will fail. That's like stating that you're going to the moon, then climbing a tree and declaring that you are closer. Unfortunately, you can't get to the moon from the top of a tree. Data science is a new discipline that offers compelling, business-differentiating capabilities, especially when coupled with Business Intelligence.

CROSS-REFERENCE **Chapter 5 ("Differences Between Business Intelligence and Data Science") discusses the differences between Business Intelligence and data science and how data science can complement your Business Intelligence organization. Chapter 6 ("Data Science 101") reviews several different analytic algorithms that your data science team might use and discusses the business situations in which the different algorithms might be most appropriate.**

Don't Think Data Warehouse, Think Data Lake

In the world of big data, Hadoop and HDFS is a game changer; it is fundamentally changing the way organizations think about storing, managing, and analyzing data. And I don't mean Hadoop as yet another data source for your data warehouse. I'm talking about Hadoop and HDFS as the *foundation* for your data and analytics environments—to take advantage of the massively parallel processing, cheap scale-out data architecture that can run hundreds, thousands, or even tens of thousands of Hadoop nodes.

We are witnessing the dawn of the age of the *data lake*. The data lake enables organizations to gather, manage, enrich, and analyze many new sources of data, whether structured or unstructured. The data lake enables organizations to treat data as an organizational asset to be gathered and nurtured versus a cost to be minimized.

Organizations need to treat their reporting environments (traditional BI and data warehousing) and analytics (data science) environments differently. These two environments have very different characteristics and serve different purposes. The data lake can make both of the BI and data science environments more agile and more productive (Figure 1-2).

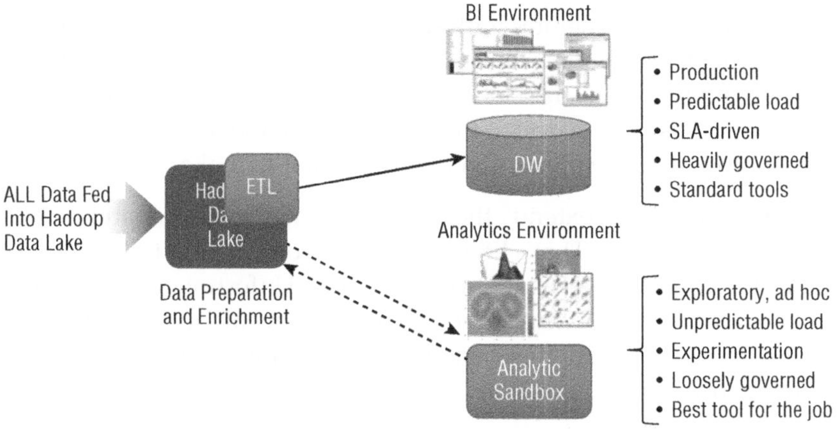

Figure 1-2: Modern data/analytics environment

CROSS-REFERENCE **Chapter 7 ("The Data Lake") introduces the concept of a data lake and the role the data lake plays in supporting your existing data warehouse and Business Intelligence investments while providing the foundation for your data science environment. Chapter 7 discusses how the data lake can un-cuff your data scientists from the data warehouse to uncover those variables and metrics that might be better predictors of business performance. It also discusses how the data lake can free up expensive data warehouse resources, especially those resources associated with Extract, Transform, and Load (ETL) data processes.**

Don't Think "What Happened," Think "What Will Happen"

Business users have been trained to contemplate business questions that monitor the current state of the business and to focus on retrospective reporting on what happened. Business users have become conditioned by their BI and data warehouse environments to only consider questions that report on current business performance, such as "How many widgets did I sell last month?" and "What were my gross sales last quarter?"

Unfortunately, this retrospective view of the business doesn't help when trying to make decisions and take action about future situations. We need to get business users to "think differently" about the types of questions they can ask. We need to move the business investigation process beyond the performance monitoring questions to the predictive (e.g., What will likely happen?) and prescriptive (e.g., What should I do?) questions that organizations need to address in order to optimize key business processes and uncover new monetization opportunities (see Table 1-2).

Table 1-2: Evolution of the Business Questions

WHAT HAPPENED? (DESCRIPTIVE/BI)	WHAT WILL HAPPEN? (PREDICTIVE ANALYTICS)	WHAT SHOULD I DO? (PRESCRIPTIVE ANALYTICS)
How many widgets did I sell last month?	How many widgets will I sell next month?	Order [5,0000] units of Component Z to support widget sales for next month
What were sales by zip code for Christmas last year?	What will be sales by zip code over this Christmas season?	Hire [Y] new sales reps by these zip codes to handle projected Christmas sales
How many of Product X were returned last month?	How many of Product X will be returned next month?	Set aside [$125K] in financial reserve to cover Product X returns
What were company revenues and profits for the past quarter?	What are projected company revenues and profits for next quarter?	Sell the following product mix to achieve quarterly revenue and margin goals
How many employees did I hire last year?	How many employees will I need to hire next year?	Increase hiring pipeline by 35 percent to achieve hiring goals

CROSS-REFERENCE **Chapter 8 ("Thinking Like a Data Scientist") differentiates between descriptive analytics, predictive analytics, and prescriptive analytics. Chapters 9, 10, and 11 then introduce several techniques to help your business users identify the predictive ("What will happen?") and prescriptive ("What should I do?") questions that they need to more effectively drive the business. Yeah, this will mean lots of Post-it notes and whiteboards, my favorite tools.**

Don't Think HIPPO, Think Collaboration

Unfortunately, today it is still the HIPPO—the Highest Paid Person's Opinion—that determines most of the business decisions. Reasons such as "We've always done things that way" or "My years of experience tell me …" or "This is what the CEO wants …" are still given as reasons for why the HIPPO needs to drive the important business decisions.

Unfortunately, that type of thinking has led to siloed data fiefdoms, siloed decisions, and an un-empowered and frustrated business team. Organizations need to think differently about how they empower all of their employees. Organizations need to find a way to promote and nurture creative thinking and groundbreaking ideas across all levels of the organization. There is no edict that states that the best ideas only come from senior management.

The key to big data success is empowering cross-functional collaboration and exploratory thinking to challenge long-held organizational rules of thumb, heuristics, and "gut" decision making. The business needs an approach that is inclusive of all the key stakeholders—IT, business users, business management, channel partners, and ultimately customers. The business potential of big data is only limited by the creative thinking of the organization.

CROSS-REFERENCE **Chapter 13 ("Power of Envisioning") discusses how the BI and data science teams can collaborate to brainstorm, test, and refine new variables that might be better predictors of business performance. We will introduce several techniques and concepts that can be used to drive collaboration between the business and IT stakeholders and ultimately help your data science team uncover new customer, product, and operational insights that lead to better business performance. Chapter 14 ("Organizational Ramifications") introduces organizational ramifications, especially the role of Chief Data Monetization Officer (CDMO).**

Summary

Big data is interesting from a technology perspective, but the real story for big data is how organizations of different sizes are leveraging data and analytics to power their business models. Big data has the potential to uncover new customer, product, and operational insights that organizations can use to optimize key business processes, improve customer engagement, uncover new monetization opportunities, and re-wire the organization's value creation processes.

As discussed in this chapter, organizations need to understand that big data is about business transformation and business model disruption. There will be winners and there will be losers, and having business leadership sit back and wait for IT to solve the big data problems for them quickly classifies into which group your organization will likely fall. Senior business leadership needs to determine where and how to leverage data and analytics to power your business models before a more nimble competitor or a hungrier competitor disintermediates your business.

To realize the financial potential of big data, business leadership must make big data a top business priority, not just a top IT priority. Business leadership must actively participate in determining where and how big data can deliver business value, and the business leaders must be front and center in leading the integration of the resulting analytic insights into the organization's value creation processes.

For leading organizations, big data provides a once-in-a-lifetime business opportunity to build key capabilities, skills, and applications that optimize key business processes, drive a more compelling customer experience, uncover new monetization opportunities, and drive competitive differentiation. Remember: buy for parity, but build for competitive differentiation.

At its core, big data is about economic transformation. Big data should not be treated like just another technology science experiment. History is full of lessons of how organizations have been able to capitalize on economics-driven business transformations. Big data provides one of those economic "Forrest Gump" moments where organizations are fortunate to be at the right place at the right time. Don't miss this opportunity.

Finally, organizations have been taught to think cheaper, smaller, and faster, but they have not been taught to think differently, and that's exactly what's required if you want to exploit the big data opportunity. Many of the data and analytics best practices that have been taught over the past several decades no longer hold true. Understand what has changed and learn to think differently about how your organization leverages data and analytics to deliver compelling business value.

In summary, business leadership needs to lead the big data initiative, to step up and make big data a top business mandate. If your business leaders don't take the lead in identifying where and how to integrate big data into your business models, then you risk being disintermediated in a marketplace where more agile, hungrier competitors are learning that data and analytics can yield compelling competitive differentiation.

Homework Assignment

Use the following exercises to apply what you learned in this chapter.

> **Exercise #1:** Identify a key business initiative for your organization, something the business is trying to accomplish over the next 9 to 12 months. It might be something like improve customer retention, optimize customer

acquisition, reduce customer churn, optimize predictive maintenance, reduce revenue theft, and so on.

Exercise #2: Brainstorm and write down what (1) customer, (2) product, and (3) operational insights your organization would like to uncover in order to support the targeted business initiative. Start by capturing the different types of descriptive, predictive, and prescriptive questions you'd like to answer about the targeted business initiative. Tip: Don't worry about whether or not you have the data sources you need to derive the insights you want (yet).

Exercise #3: Brainstorm and write down data sources that might be useful in uncovering those key insights. Look both internally and externally for interesting data sources that might be useful. Tip: Think outside the box and imagine that you could access any data source in the world.

CHAPTER

2

Big Data Business Model Maturity Index

Organizations do not understand how far big data can take them from a business transformation perspective. Organizations don't have a way of understanding what the ultimate big data end state would or could look like or answering questions such as:

- Where and how should I start my big data journey?
- How can I create new revenue or monetization opportunities?
- How do I compare to others with respect to my organization's adoption of big data as a business enabler?
- How far can I push big data to power—even transform—my business models?

To help address these types of questions, I've created the *Big Data Business Model Maturity Index*. Not only can organizations can use this index to understand where they sit with respect to other organizations in exploiting big data and advanced analytics to power their business models, but the index provides a road map to help organizations accelerate the integration of data and analytics into their business models.

The Big Data Business Model Maturity Index is a critical foundational concept supporting the *Big Data MBA* and will be referenced regularly throughout the book. It's important to lay a strong base foundation in how organizations can use the Big Data Business Model Maturity Index to answer this fundamental big data business question: "How effective is my organization at integrating data and analytics into our business models?"

CHAPTER 2 OBJECTIVES

- **Introduce the Big Data Business Model Maturity Index as a framework for organizations to measure how effective they are at leveraging data and analytics to power their business models**
- **Discuss the objectives and characteristics of each of the five phases of the Big Data Business Model Maturity Index: Business Monitoring, Business Insights, Business Optimization, Data Monetization, and Business Metamorphosis**
- **Discuss how the *economics of big data* and the four *big data value drivers* can enable organizations to cross the *analytics chasm* and advance past the Business Monitoring phase into the Business Insights and Business Optimization phases**
- **Review lessons learned that help organizations advance through the phases of the Big Data Business Model Maturity Index**

Introducing the Big Data Business Model Maturity Index

Organizations are moving at different paces with respect to where and how they are adopting big data and advanced analytics to create business value. Some organizations are moving very cautiously, as they are unclear as to where and how to start and which of the bevy of new technology innovations they need to deploy in order to start their big data journeys. Others are moving at a more aggressive pace by acquiring and assembling a big data technology foundation built on many new big data technologies such as Hadoop, Spark, MapReduce, YARN, Mahout, Hive, HBase, and more.

However, a select few are looking beyond just the technology to identify where and how they should be integrating big data into their existing business processes. These organizations are aggressively looking to identify and exploit opportunities to optimize key business processes. And these organizations are seeking new monetization opportunities; that is, seeking out business opportunities where they can

- Package and sell their analytic insights to others
- Integrate advanced analytics into their products and services to create "intelligent" products
- Create entirely new products and services that help them enter new markets and target new customers

These are the folks who realize that they don't need a big data strategy as much as they need a business strategy that incorporates big data. And when organizations "flip that byte" on the focus of their big data initiatives, the business potential is almost boundless.

Organizations can use the Big Data Business Model Maturity Index as a framework against which they can measure where they sit today with respect to their adoption of big data. The Big Data Business Model Maturity Index provides a road map for helping organizations to identify where and how they can leverage data and analytics to power their business models (see Figure 2-1).

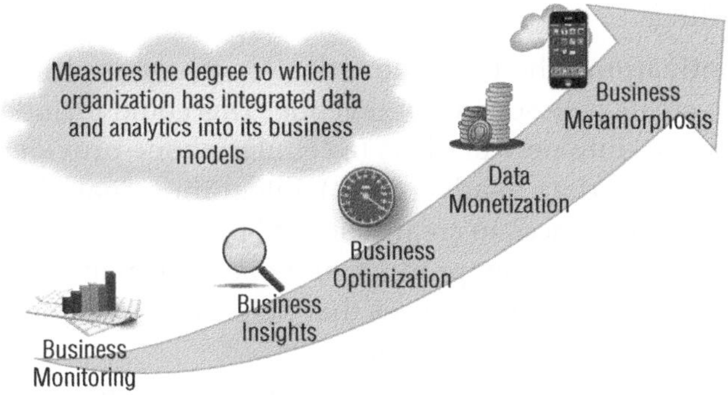

Figure 2-1: Big Data Business Model Maturity Index

Organizations tend to find themselves in one of five phases on the Big Data Business Model Maturity Index:

- **Phase 1: Business Monitoring.** In the Business Monitoring phase, organizations are applying data warehousing and Business Intelligence techniques and tools to monitor the organization's business performance (also called Business Performance Management).
- **Phase 2: Business Insights.** In the Business Insights phase, organizations aggressively expand their data assets by amassing *all* of their detailed transactional and operational data and coupling that transactional and operational data with new sources of internal data (e.g., consumer comments, e-mail conversations, technician notes) and external data (e.g., social media, weather, traffic, economic, data.gov) sources. Organizations in the Business Insights phase then use predictive analytics to uncover customer, product, and operational insights buried in and across these data sources.
- **Phase 3: Business Optimization.** In the Business Optimization phase, organizations build on the customer, product, and operational insights uncovered in the Business Insights phase by applying prescriptive

analytics to optimize key business processes. Organizations in the Business Optimization phase push the analytic results (e.g., recommendations, scores, rules) to frontline employees and business managers to help them optimize the targeted business process through improved decision making. The Business Optimization phase also provides opportunities for organizations to push analytic insights to their customers in order to influence customer behaviors. An example of the Business Optimization phase is a retailer that delivers analytic-based merchandising recommendations to the store managers to optimize merchandise markdowns based on purchase patterns, inventory, weather conditions, holidays, consumer comments, and social media postings.

- **Phase 4: Data Monetization.** The Data Monetization phase is where organizations seek to create new sources of revenue. This could include selling data—or insights—into new markets (a cellular phone provider selling customer behavioral data to advertisers), integrating analytical insights into products and services to create "smart" products and services, and/or re-packaging customer, product, and operational insights to create entirely new products and services that help them enter new markets and target new customers or audiences.
- **Phase 5: Business Metamorphosis.** The holy grail of the Big Data Business Model Maturity Index is when an organization leverages data, analytics, and insights to metamorphose its business. This metamorphosis necessitates a major shift in the organization's core business model (e.g., processes, people, products and services, partnerships, target markets, management, promotions, rewards and incentives) driven by the insights gathered as the organization traversed the Big Data Business Model Maturity Index. One example is organizations that metamorphose from selling products to selling "business-as-a-service." Think GE selling "thrust" instead of selling jet engines. Think John Deere selling "farming optimization" instead of selling farming equipment. Think Boeing selling "air miles" instead of airplanes. Another example is an organization creating a data and analytics platform that enables the growing body of third-party developers to build and market value-added applications on the organization's business-as-a-service platform.

Let's explore each of these phases in more detail.

Phase 1: Business Monitoring

The Business Monitoring phase is the phase where organizations are deploying Business Intelligence (BI) and data warehousing solutions to *monitor* ongoing business performance. Sometimes called Business Performance Management, organizations in the Business Monitoring phase create reports and dashboards that monitor the current state of the business, flag under- and/or over-performance areas of the business, and alert key business stakeholders with pertinent information whenever special "out of bound" performance situations occur.

The Business Monitoring phase is a great starting point for most big data journeys. As part of their Business Intelligence and data warehousing efforts, organizations have invested significant time, money, and effort to identify and document their key business processes; that is, those business processes that make their organizations unique and successful. They have assembled, cleansed, normalized, enriched, and integrated the key operational data sources; have painstakingly constructed a supporting data model and data architecture; and have built countless reports, dashboards, and alerts around the key activities and metrics that support that business process. Lots of great assets have already been created, and these assets provide the launching pad for starting our big data journey.

Unfortunately, moving beyond the Business Monitoring phase is a significant challenge for many organizations. The inertia established from years and decades of BI and data warehouse efforts work against the "think differently" approach that is necessary to fully exploit big data for business value. Plus the big financial payoff isn't typically realized until the organization pushes through the Business Insights phase into the Business Optimization phase. So let's discuss how organizations can leverage the economics of big data to cross the analytics chasm.

Phase 2: Business Insights

The Business Insights phase couples the organization's growing wealth of internal and external structured and unstructured data with predictive analytics to uncover *customer, product, and operational insights* buried in the data. This means uncovering occurrences in the data that are unusual (or outside normal behaviors, trends, and patterns) and worthy of business investigation.

This is the phase of the Big Data Business Model Maturity Index where organizations need to exploit the economics of big data; that is, big data technologies are 20 to 50 times cheaper than traditional data warehouses in storing, managing, and analyzing data. The economics of big data enable organizations to think differently about how they gather, integrate, manage, analyze, and act upon data and provide the foundation for how organizations can advance beyond the Business Monitoring phase and cross the analytics chasm. The economics of big data enable four new capabilities that will help the organization cross the analytics chasm and move beyond the Business Monitoring phase into the Business Insights phase. These four big data value drivers are:

1. **Access to *All* of the Organization's Transactional and Operational Data.** In big data, we need to move beyond the summarized and aggregated data that is housed in the data warehouse and be prepared to store and analyze the organization's complete history of detailed transactional and operational data. Think 25 years of detailed point of sale (POS) transactional data, not just the 13 to 25 months of aggregated POS data stored in the data warehouse.

   Imagine the business potential of being able to analyze each POS transaction at the individual customer level (courtesy of loyalty programs) for the past 15 to 25 years. For example, grocers could see when individual customers start to struggle financially because they are likely to change their purchase behaviors and product preferences (i.e., buying lower-quality products, replacing branded products with private label products, increasing the use of discounts and coupons). You can't see those individual customer behaviors and purchase tendencies in the aggregated data stored in the data warehouse. With big data, organizations have the ability to collect, analyze, and act on the entire history of every purchase occasion by Bill Schmarzo—what products he bought in what combinations, what prices he paid, what coupons he used, what and when he bought on discount, which stores he frequented on what time of day and day of the week, what were the outside weather conditions during those purchase occasions, what were the local economic conditions, etc.

   When you can analyze transactional and operational data at the individual customer (or patient, student, technician, teacher, wind turbine, ATM, truck, jet engine, etc.) level, you can uncover insights about individual customer or product behaviors, tendencies, propensities, preferences, and usage patterns. It is on these individual customer or product insights that organizations can take action. It's very difficult to create actionable insights at the aggregated level of store, zip code, or customer behavioral categories.

2. **Access to Internal and External Unstructured Data.** Data warehouses don't like unstructured data. Data warehouses want structured data. Since data warehouses have been built on relational database management systems (RDMBS), the data warehouse wants its data in rows and columns. As a consequence, organizations and their business users have been taught that they really don't need access to unstructured data.

   But big data challenges this issue by giving all organizations a cost-effective way to ingest, store, manage, and analyze vast varieties of unstructured data. And the integration of the organization's unstructured data with the organization's detailed structured data provides the opportunity to uncover new customer, product, and operational insights.

While most of the excitement about unstructured data seems to be about the potential of external unstructured data (e.g., social, blogs, newsfeeds, annual reports, mobile, third-party, publicly available), the gold for many organizations lies in their internal unstructured data (e.g., consumer comments, e-mail conversations, doctor/teacher/technician notes, work orders, service requests). For example, in a project to improve the predictive maintenance of wind turbines, it was discovered that when a technician scales a wind turbine to replace a ball bearing, he or she makes other observations while at the top of the turbine, observations such as "It smells weird in here" or "It's warmer than normal" or "There are dust particles in the air." Each of these types of unstructured comments could provide invaluable insights into the predictive maintenance of the wind turbine, especially when coupled with the operational sensor readings, error codes, and vibrations that are coming off that particular wind turbine.

3. **Exploiting Real-Time Analytics.** New big data technologies provide organizations the technical capabilities to flag and act on special or unusual situations in real-time. Data warehouses have traditionally been batch environments and struggled to uncover and support the real-time opportunities in the data. For example, "trickle feeding" data into the data warehouse has been a long-time data warehouse challenge because the minute new data enters the data warehouse, all the supporting indices, aggregate tables, and materialized views need to be updated with the new data. That's hardly conducive to real-time analysis.

   Most organizations do not have a long list of use cases that require a real-time analytics environment (e.g., real-time bidding, fraud detection, digital ad placement, pricing, yield optimization). However, there are many use cases for "right-time" analytics, where the opportunity time is measured not in seconds but in minutes or hours or even days. For example, nurses and admissions personnel in a hospital likely have 4 to 5 minutes to score the likelihood of a patient catching a hospital-acquired infection (staph infection) during the patient's admission process. Another example is location-based services that target shoppers that meet certain demographic and/or behavioral characteristics as they walk by a store.

   The best approach for uncovering these right-time analytic opportunities is to break the targeted key business initiative into the data events that compose that business initiative. Then identify those data events where knowing about that event sooner (minutes sooner, hours sooner, maybe even a day sooner) *could* provide a monetization opportunity.

4. **Integrating Predictive Analytics.** Finally, we can use predictive analytics to mine the wealth of structured and unstructured data to identify areas of "unusualness" in the data; that is, use predictive analytics to uncover occurrences in the data that are outside normal behaviors or engagement patterns. Organizations can apply predictive analytics and data mining techniques to uncover customer, product, and operational insights or areas of "unusualness" buried in the massive volumes of detailed structured and unstructured data.

   These insights uncovered during the Business Insights phase need to be reviewed by the business users (the subject matter experts) to determine if these insights pass the S.A.M. test; that is, the insights are:

- Strategic—the insight is important or strategic to what the business is trying to accomplish with respect to the targeted business initiative.
- Actionable—the insight is something that the organization can act on when engaging with its key business entities.
- Material—the value or benefit of acting on the insight is greater than the costs associated with acting on that insight (e.g., cost to gather and integrate the data, cost to build and validate the analytic model, cost to integrate the analytic results into the operational systems).

  For example, organizations could apply basis statistics, data mining, and predictive analytics to their growing wealth of structured and unstructured data to identify insights such as:

- Marketing campaigns that are performing two to three times better than the average campaign performance in certain markets on certain days of the week
- Customers that are reacting two to three standard deviations outside the norm in their purchase patterns for certain product categories in certain weather conditions
- Suppliers whose components are operating outside the upper or lower limits of a control chart in extreme cold weather situations

CROSS-REFERENCE **For the predictive analytics to be effective, organizations need to build detailed analytic profiles for each individual business entity—customers, patients, students, wind turbines, jet engines, ATMs, etc. The creation and role of analytic profiles is a topic covered in Chapter 5, "Differences Between Business Intelligence and Data Science."**

Business Insights Phase Challenge

The Business Insights phase is the most difficult stage of the Big Data Business Model Maturity Index because it requires organizations to "think differently" about how they approach data and analytics. The rules, techniques, and approaches that worked in the Business Intelligence and data warehouse worlds do not necessary apply to the world of big data. This is truly the "crossing the analytics chasm" moment (see Figure 2-2).

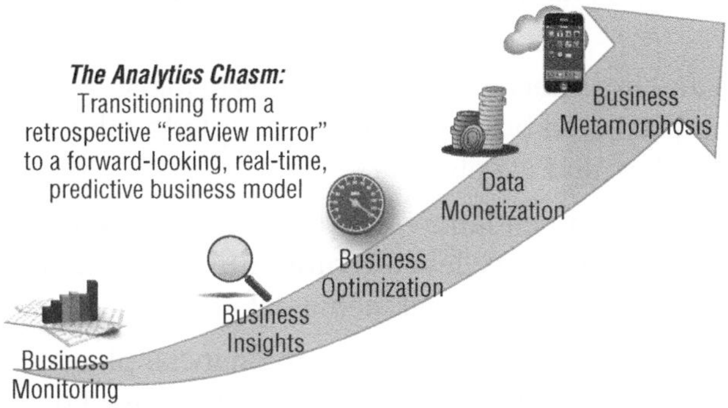

Figure 2-2: Crossing the analytics chasm

For example, Business Intelligence analysts were taught to "slice and dice" the data to uncover insights buried in the data. This approach worked fine when dealing with gigabytes of data, 5 to 9 dimensions, and 15 to 25 metrics. However, the "slice and dice" technique does not work well when dealing with petabytes of data, 40 to 60 dimensions, and hundreds of metrics.

Also, much of the big data financial payback or Return on Investment (ROI) is not realized until the organization reaches the Business Optimization phase. This is why it is important to focus your big data journey on a key business initiative; something that the business is trying to achieve over the next 9 to 12 months. The focus on a business initiative can provide the necessary financial and organizational motivation to push through the Business Insights phase and to realize the financial return and payback created in the Business Optimization phase.

Phase 3: Business Optimization

The Business Optimization phase is the stage of the Big Data Business Model Maturity Index where organizations develop the *predictive analytics* (predicts what is likely to happen) and the *prescriptive analytics* (recommends actions that should be taken) necessary to optimize the targeted key business process. This phase builds on the analytic insights uncovered during the Business Insights phase and constructs predictive and prescriptive analytic models around those insights that pass the S.A.M. criteria. One client called this the "Tell me what I need to do" phase.

While many believe that this is the part of the maturity index where organizations turn the optimization process over to the machines, in reality it is more likely that the Business Optimization phase delivers actionable insights (e.g., recommendations, scores, rules) to frontline employees and managers to help them make better decisions supporting the targeted business process. Examples include:

- Delivering resource scheduling recommendations to store managers based on purchase history, buying behaviors, seasonality, and local weather and events
- Delivering distribution and inventory recommendations to logistic managers given current and predicted buying patterns, coupled with local traffic, demographic, weather, and events data
- Delivering product pricing recommendations to product managers based on current buying patterns, inventory levels, competitive prices, and product interest insights gleaned from social media data
- Delivering financial investment recommendations to financial planners and agents based on a client's financial goals, current financial asset mix, risk tolerance, market and economic conditions, and savings objectives (e.g., house, college, retirement)
- Delivering maintenance, scheduling, and inventory recommendations to wind turbine technicians based on error codes, sensor readings, vibration readings, and recent comments captured by the technician during previous maintenance activities

The Business Optimization phase also seeks to influence customer purchase and engagement behaviors by analyzing the customer's past purchase patterns, behaviors, and tendencies in order to deliver relevant and actionable recommendations. Common examples include Amazon's "Customers Who Bought This Item Also Bought" recommendations, Netflix's movie recommendations, and Pandora's music recommendations. The key to the effectiveness of these recommendations is capturing and analyzing an individual customer's purchase, usage, and engagement activities to build analytic profiles that codify that customer's preferences, behaviors, tendencies, propensities, patterns, trends, interests, passions, affiliations, and associations.

Finally, the Business Optimization phase needs to integrate the customer, product, and operational prescriptive analytics or recommendations back into the operational systems (e.g., call center, sales force automation, direct marketing, procurement, logistics, inventory) and management applications (reports, dashboards) systems. For example, think of an "intelligent" store manager's dashboard, where instead of just presenting tables and charts of data, the intelligent dashboard goes one step further to actually deliver recommendations to the store manager to improve store operations.

CROSS-REFERENCE The potential user experience ramifications of pushing prescriptive analytics to both customers and frontline employees are discussed in Chapter 4, "Importance of the User Experience."

Phase 4: Data Monetization

The Data Monetization phase is the phase of the Big Data Business Model Maturity Index where organizations leverage the insights gathered from the Business Insights and Business Optimization phases to create new revenue opportunities. New monetization opportunities could include:

- Packaging data (with analytic insights) for sale to other organizations. In one example, a smartphone vendor could capture and package insights about customer behaviors, product performance, and market trends to sell to advertisers, marketers, and manufacturers. In another example, MapMyRun (which was purchased by Under Armour for $150M) could package the customer usage data from its smartphone application to create audience and product insights that it could sell to a variety of companies, including sports apparel manufacturers, sporting goods retailers, insurance companies, and health care providers (see Figure 2-3).

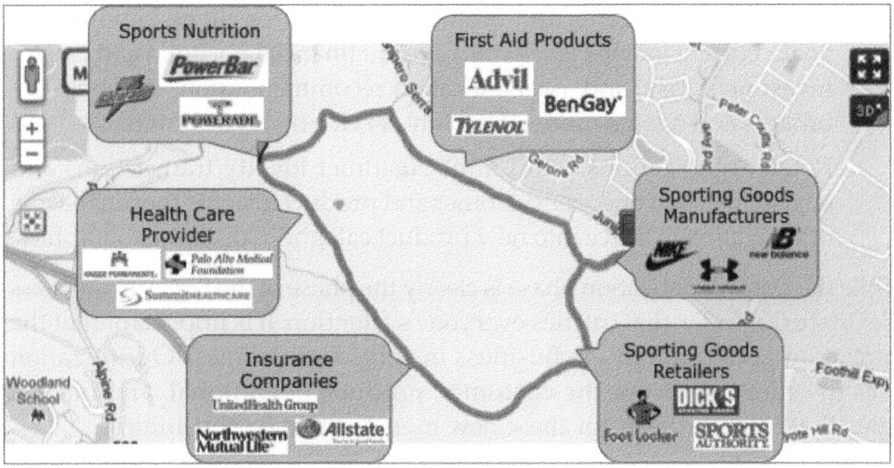

Figure 2-3: Packaging and selling audience insights

- Integrating analytic insights directly into an organization's products and services to create "intelligent" products or services, such as:
  - Cars that learn a customer's driving patterns and behaviors and adjust driver controls, seats, mirrors, brake pedals, suspension, steering, dashboard displays, etc. to match the customer's driving style

  - Televisions and DVRs that learn what types of shows and movies a customer likes and search across the different cable and Internet channels to find and automatically record similar shows for that customer
  - Ovens that learn how a customer likes certain foods prepared and cooks them in that manner automatically and also include recommendations for other foods and recipes that "others like you" enjoy
  - Jet engines that can ingest weather, elevation, wind speed, and other environmental data to make adjustments to blade angles, tilt, yaw, and rotation speeds to minimize fuel consumption during flight
- Repackaging insights to create entirely new products and services that help organizations to enter new markets and target new customers or audiences. For example, organizations can capture, analyze, and package customer, product, and operational insights across the overall market in order to help channel partners to more effectively market and sell to their customers, such as:
  - Online digital marketplaces (Yahoo, Google, eBay, Facebook) could leverage general market trends and other merchant performance data to provide recommendations to small merchants on inventory, ordering, merchandising, marketing, and pricing.
  - Financial services organizations could create a financial advisor dashboard for their agents and brokers that captures clients' investment goals, current income levels, and current financial portfolio and creates investment, risk, and asset allocation recommendations that help the brokers and agents more effectively service their customers.
  - Retail organizations could mine customer loyalty transactions and engagements to uncover customer and product insights that enable the organization to move into new product categories or new geographies.

While the Data Monetization phase is clearly the phase of the Big Data Business Model Maturity Index that catches everyone's attention, it is important that the organization goes through the Business Insights and Business Optimization phases in order to capture the customer, product, operational, and market insights that form the basis for these new monetization opportunities.

Phase 5: Business Metamorphosis

The Business Metamorphosis phase of the Big Data Business Model Maturity Index should be the ultimate goal for organizations. This is the phase of the maturity index where organizations seek to leverage the data, analytics, and analytic insights to metamorphosize or transform the organization's business model (e.g., processes, people, products and services, partnerships, target markets, management, promotions, rewards and incentives).

The Business Metamorphosis phase is where organizations integrate the insights that they captured about their customers' usage patterns, product performance behaviors, and overall market trends to transform their business models. This business model metamorphosis allows organizations to provide new services and capabilities to their customers in a way that is easier for the customers to consume and facilitates the organization engaging in higher-value and more strategic services.

For example, contemplate the data, analytics, and analytic insights that Boeing would need to transform its business from selling airplanes to selling air miles. Think of the data, analytics, and insights that Boeing would need to uncover about passengers, airlines, airports, routes, holidays, economic conditions, etc. in order to optimize its business models, processes, people, etc. to successfully execute this business change. Think of the business requirements necessary to encourage third-party developers to build and market value-add services and products on Boeing's new business model. This is a topic and example that is considered in more detail in Chapter 12, "Metamorphosis Exercise."

Other Business Metamorphosis phase examples could include:

- Energy companies moving into the "Home Energy Optimization" business by recommending when to replace appliances (based on predictive maintenance) and even recommending which appliance brands and models to buy based on the performance of different appliances taking into consideration your usage patterns, local weather, local water quality, and local environmental conditions such as local water conservation efforts and energy costs
- Retailers moving into the "Shopping Optimization" business by recommending specific products given customers' current buying patterns as compared with others like them, including recommendations for products that they may not even sell (think "Miracle on 43rd Street")
- Airlines moving into the "Travel Delight" business of not only offering discounts on air travel based on customers' travel behaviors and preferences but also proactively finding and recommending deals on hotels, rental cars, limos, sporting or musical events, and local sites, shows, restaurants, and shopping in the areas based on their areas of interest and preferences

While it is a significant challenge for organizations to ever reach the Business Metamorphosis phase, having that as the goal can both be motivating and provide an organizational catalyst to move more aggressively along the maturity index.

Big Data Business Model Maturity Index Lessons Learned

There are some interesting lessons that organizations will discover as they progress through the phases of the Big Data Business Model Maturity Index. Understanding these lessons ahead of time should help prepare organizations for their big data journey.

Lesson 1: Focus Initial Big Data Efforts Internally

The first three phases of the Big Data Business Model Maturity Index seek to extract more financial or business value out of the organization's internal processes or business initiatives. The first three phases drive business value and a Return on Investment (ROI) by seeking to integrate new sources of customer, product, operational, and market data with advanced analytics to improve the decisions that are made as part of the organization's key internal process and business initiatives (see Figure 2-4).

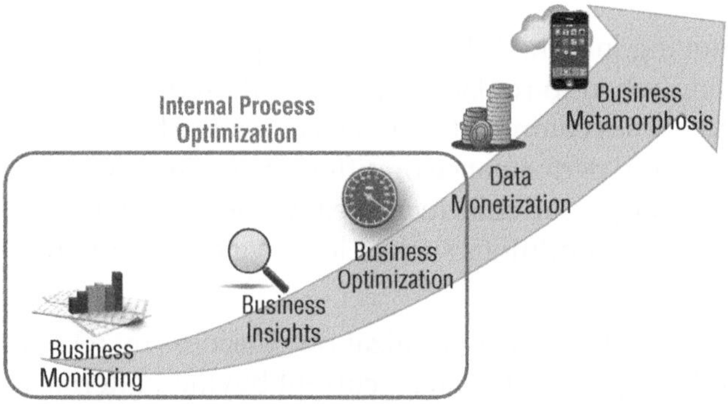

Figure 2-4: Optimize internal processes

The *internal process optimization* efforts start by seeking to leverage the organization's Business Intelligence and data warehouse assets. This includes building on the data warehouse's data sources, data extraction and enrichment algorithms, dimensions, metrics, key performance indicators, reports, and dashboards. The maturity process then applies the four big data value drivers to cross the analytics chasm from the Business Monitoring phase into the Business Insights and ultimately the Business Optimization phases.

THE FOUR BIG DATA VALUE DRIVERS

1. **Access to all the organization's detailed transactional and operational data at the lowest level of granularity (at the individual customer, machine, or device level).**
2. **Integration of unstructured data from both internal (consumer comments, e-mail threads, technician notes) and external sources (social media, mobile, publicly available) with the detailed transactional and operational data to provide new metrics and new dimensions against which to optimize key business processes.**
3. **Leverage real-time (or right-time) data analysis to accelerate the organization's ability to identify and act on customer, product, and market opportunities in a timelier manner.**
4. **Apply predictive analytics and data mining to uncover customer, product, and operational insights or areas of "unusualness" buried in the massive volumes of detailed structured and unstructured data that are worthy of further business investigation.**

Organizations must leverage these four big data value drivers to cross the analytics chasm by uncovering new customer, product, and operational insights that can be used to optimize key business processes—whether delivering actionable recommendations to frontline employees and business managers or delivering "Next Best Offer" or recommendations to delight customers and business partners.

Lesson 2: Leverage Insights to Create New Monetization Opportunities

The last two phases of the Big Data Business Model Maturity Index are focused on external market opportunities; opportunities to create new monetization or revenue opportunities based on the customer, product, and operational insights gleaned from the first three phases of the maturity index (see Figure 2-5).

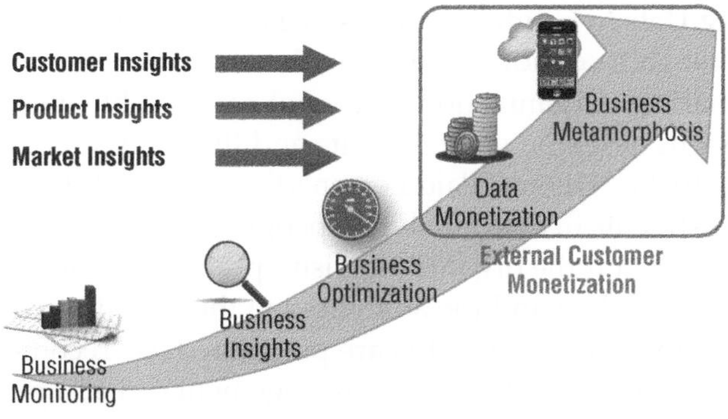

Figure 2-5: Create new monetization opportunities

This is the part of the big data journey that catches most organizations' attention: the opportunity to leverage the insights gathered through the optimization of their key business processes to create new revenue or monetization opportunities. Organizations are eager to leverage new corporate assets—data, analytics, and business insights—in order to create new sources of revenue. This is the "4 Ms" phase of the Big Data Business Model Maturity Index where organizations focus on leveraging data and analytics to create new opportunities to *"Make Me More Money!"*

Lesson 3: Preparing for Organizational Transformation

To fully exploit the big data opportunity, subtle organizational and cultural changes will be necessary for the organization to advance along the maturity index. If organizations are serious about integrating data and analytics into their business models, then three organizational or cultural transformations will need to take place:

1. **Treat Data as an Asset.** Organizations must start to treat data as an asset to be nurtured and grown, not a cost to be minimized. Organizations must develop an insatiable appetite for more and more data—even if they are unclear as to how they will use that data. This is a significant cultural change from the data warehouse days where we treated data as a cost to be minimized.
2. **Legally Protect Your Analytics Intellectual Property.** Organizations must put into place formal processes and procedures to capture, track, refine, and even legally protect their analytic assets (e.g., analytic models, data enrichment algorithms, and analytic results such as scores, recommendations, and association rules) as key organizational intellectual property. While the underlying technologies may change over time, the resulting data and analytic assets will survive those changes if the organizations can institute a well-managed and enforced process to capture, store, share, and protect those analytic assets.
3. **Get Comfortable Using Data to Guide Decisions.** Business management and business users must gain confidence in using data and analytics to guide their decision making. Organizations must get comfortable with making business decisions based on what the data and the analytics tell them versus defaulting to the "Highest Paid Person's Opinion" (HIPPO). The organization's investments in data, analytics, people, processes, and technology will be for naught if the organization isn't prepared to make decisions based on what the data and the analytics tell them. With that said, it's important that the analytic insights are positioned as "recommendations" that business users and business management can accept, reject, or modify. In that way, organizations can leverage analytics to establish organizational accountability.

Summary

Businesses of all sizes must reframe the big data conversation with business leaders. The Big Data Business Model Maturity Index provides a framework that enables business and IT leaders to discuss and debate the question "How effective is our organization at integrating data and analytics into our business model?"

The business possibilities seem almost endless with respect to where and how organizations can leverage big data and advanced analytics to drive their business model. The Big Data Business Model Maturity Index provides a road map—a how-to guide—to direct the business and IT stakeholders from the Business Monitoring phase through the Business Insights and Business Optimization phases, to the ultimate goals in the Data Monetization and Business Metamorphosis phases to create new business models (see Table 2-1).

Table 2-1: Big Data Business Model Maturity Index Summary

BUSINESS MONITORING	BUSINESS INSIGHTS	BUSINESS OPTIMIZATION	DATA MONETIZATION	BUSINESS METAMORPHOSIS
Monitor key business processes and report on business performance using data warehousing and Business Intelligence techniques	Pool *all* detailed operational and transactional data with internal unstructured data and external (third-party, publicly available) data; integrate with advanced analytics to uncover customer, product, and operational insights buried in the data	Deliver actionable recommendations and scores to frontline employees to optimize customer engagement; deliver actionable recommendations to end customers based on their product and usage preferences, propensities, and tendencies	Monetize the customer, product, and operational insights coming out of the optimization process to create new services and products, capture new markets and audiences, and create "smart" products and services	Reconstitute customer, product, and operational insights to metamorphose the very fabric of an organization's business model, including processes, people, compensation, promotions, products/services, target markets, and partnerships

Ultimately, big data only matters if it can help organizations generate more money through improved decision making (or improved operational effectiveness for non-profit organizations). Big data holds the potential to both optimize key business processes and create new monetization or revenue opportunities.

In summary:

- The Big Data Business Model Maturity Index provides a framework for organizations to measure how effective they are at leveraging data and analytics to power their business models.
- The five phases of the Big Data Business Model Maturity Index are Business Monitoring, Business Insights, Business Optimization, Data Monetization, and Business Metamorphosis.
- The economics of big data and the four big data value drivers can enable organizations to cross the analytics chasm.

The Big Data Business Model Maturity Index provides a road map for being successful with big data by beginning with an end in mind. Otherwise, *"if you don't know where you are going, you might end up someplace else"* (to quote Yogi Berra).

Homework Assignment

Use the following exercises to apply and reinforce the information presented in this chapter:

Exercise #1: List two or three of your organization's key business processes. That is, write down two or three business processes that uniquely differentiate your organization from your competition.

Exercise #2: List the four big data value drivers that are enabled by the economics of big data and describe how each might impact one of your organization's key business processes identified in Exercise #1.

Exercise #3: For the selected key business processes identified in Exercise #1, describe how each key business process might be improved as it transitions along the five phases of the Big Data Business Model Maturity Index. Identify the customer, product, and operational ramifications that each of the five phases might have on the selected key business process.

Exercise #4: List the cultural changes that your organization must address if it hopes to leverage big data to its fullest business potential. Flag the top two or three cultural challenges that might be the most difficult for your organization and list what you think the organization needs to do in order to address those challenges.

CHAPTER 3

The Big Data Strategy Document

One of the biggest challenges organizations face with respect to big data is identifying where and how to start. The *big data strategy document*, detailed in this chapter, provides a framework for linking an organization's business strategy and supporting business initiatives to the organization's big data efforts. The big data strategy document guides the organization through the process of breaking down its business strategy and business initiatives into potential big data business use cases and the supporting data and analytic requirements.

NOTE **The big data strategy document first appeared in my book *Big Data: Understanding How Data Powers Big Business*. Since then and courtesy of several client engagements, significant improvements have been made to help users to uncover big data use cases. In particular, the process has been enhanced to clarify the business value and implementation feasibility assessments of the different data sources and use case prioritization (see Figure 3-1).**

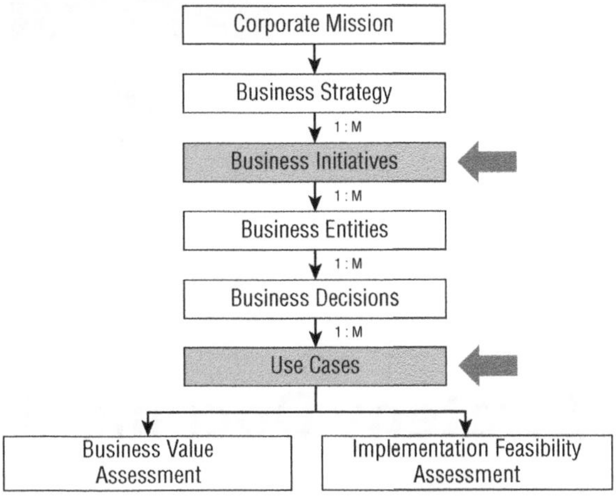

Figure 3-1: Big data strategy decomposition process

CHAPTER 3 OBJECTIVES

- Establish common terminology for big data.
- Examine the concept of a business initiative and provide some examples of where to find these business initiatives.
- Introduce the big data strategy document as a framework for helping organizations to identify the use cases that guide where and how they can start their big data journeys.
- Provide a hands-on example of the big data strategy document in action using Chipotle, a chain of organic Mexican food restaurants (and one of my favorite places to eat!).
- Introduce worksheets to help organizations to determine the business value and implementation feasibility of the data sources that come out of the big data strategy document process.
- Introduce the *prioritization matrix* as a tool that can drive business and IT alignment around prioritizing the use cases based on business value and implementation feasibility over a 9-to 12-month window.
- Finally, we will have some fun by applying the big data strategy document to the world of professional baseball and demonstrate how the big data strategy document could help a professional baseball organization win the World Series.

Establishing Common Business Terminology

Before we launch into the big data strategy document discussion, we need to define a few critical terms to ensure that we are using consistent terminology throughout the chapter and the book:

- **Corporate Mission.** *Why* the organization exists; defines what an organization is and the organization's reason for being. For example, The Walt Disney Company's corporate mission is "to be one of the world's leading producers and providers of entertainment and information."[1]
- **Business Strategy.** *How* the organization is going to achieve its mission over the next two to three years.
- **Strategic Business Initiatives.** *What* the organization plans to do to achieve its business strategy over the next 9 to 12 months; usually includes business objectives, financial targets, metrics, and time frames.
- **Business Entities.** The physical objects or entities (e.g., customers, patients, students, doctors, wind turbines, trucks) around which the business initiative will try to understand, predict, and influence behaviors and performance (sometimes referred to as the *strategic nouns* of the business).
- **Business Stakeholders.** Those business functions (sales, marketing, finance, store operations, logistics, and so on) that impact or are impacted by the strategic business initiative.
- **Business Decisions.** The decisions that the business stakeholders need to make in support of the strategic business initiative.
- **Big Data Use Cases.** The *analytic use cases* (decisions and corresponding actions) that support the strategic business initiative.
- **Data.** The structured and unstructured data sources, both internal and external of the organization, that will be identified throughout the big data strategy document process.

Introducing the Big Data Strategy Document

The big data strategy document helps organizations address the challenge of identifying where and how to start their big data journeys. The big data strategy document uses a single-page format that any organization can use (profit or

[1] `https://thewaltdisneycompany.com/investors`

non-profit) that links an organization's big data efforts to its business strategy and key business initiatives. The big data strategy document is effective for the following reasons:

- It's concise. It fits on a single page so that anyone in the organization can quickly review it to ensure he or she is working on the top priority items.
- It's clear. It clearly defines what the organization needs to do in order to achieve the organization's key business initiatives.
- It's business relevant. It starts by focusing on the business strategy and supporting initiatives before it dives into the data and technology requirements.

The big data strategy document is composed of the following sections (see Figure 3-2):

- Business strategy
- Key business initiatives
- Key business entities
- Key decisions
- Financial drivers (use cases)

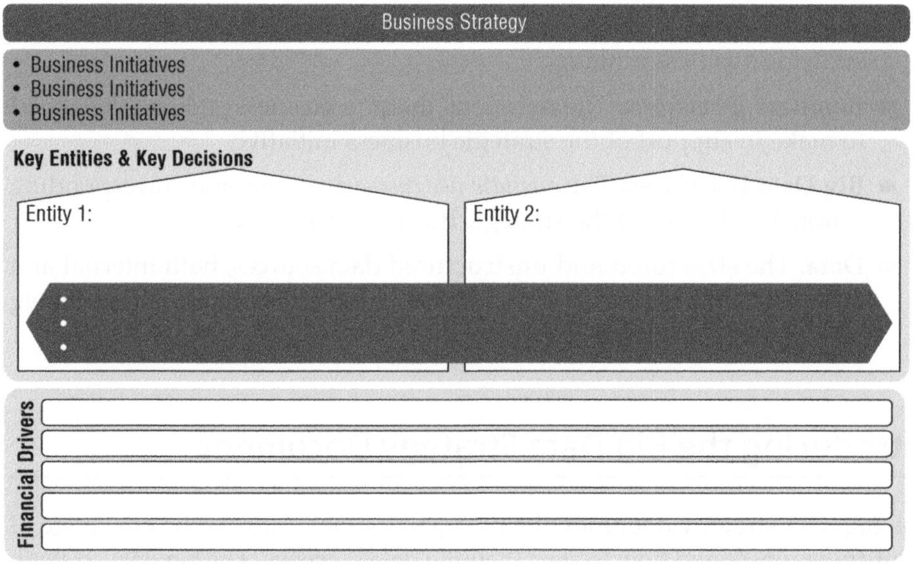

Figure 3-2: Big data strategy document

The rest of the chapter will detail each of these sections and provide guidelines for how the organization can triage the organization's business strategy into the financial drivers (or use cases) on which the organization can focus its big data efforts. We will use a case study around Chipotle Mexican Grills to reinforce the triage and analysis process.

Identifying the Organization's Key Business Initiatives

The starting point for the big data strategy document process is to identify the organization's business initiatives over the next 9 to 12 months. That is, what is the business trying to accomplish over the next 9 to 12 months? This 9-to 12-month time frame is critical, as it

- Focuses the organization's big data efforts on something that is of immediate value and relevance to the business
- Creates a sense of urgency for the organization to move quickly and diligently
- Gives the big data project a more realistic chance of delivering a positive Return on Investment (ROI) and a financial payback in 12 months or less

A business initiative supports the business strategy and has the following characteristics:

- Critical to immediate-term business and/or financial performance (usually 9-to 12-month time frame)
- Communicated (either internally or publicly)
- Cross-functional (involves more than one business function)
- Owned or championed by a senior business executive
- Has a measurable financial goal
- Has a well-defined delivery time frame
- Delivers compelling financial or competitive advantage

For example, a wireless provider might have a key business initiative to reduce the attrition rate among its most profitable customers by 20 percent over the next 12 months. Or a public utility might have a key business initiative to improve customer satisfaction by a certain number of basis points while reducing water consumption by 20 percent.

There are many places to uncover an organization's key business initiatives. If the company is public, then the organization's financial statements are a great starting point. For both private and non-profit organizations, there is a bevy of publicly available sources for identifying an organization's key business initiatives, including:

- Annual reports
- 10-K (filed annually)

- 10-Q (filed quarterly)
- Quarterly analyst calls
- Executive presentations and conferences
- Executive blogs
- News releases
- Social media sites
- SeekingAlpha.com
- Web searches using Google, Yahoo, and Bing

The best way to grasp the big data strategy document process is with a hands-on example. And what better place to test the big data strategy document than with one of my favorite restaurants, Chipotle!

What's Important to Chipotle?

Let's start the business strategy analysis process by reviewing Chipotle's annual report to determine what's important to the company from a business strategy perspective. Figure 3-3 shows an abbreviated version of the Chipotle President's Letter to Shareholders from the 2012 annual report.

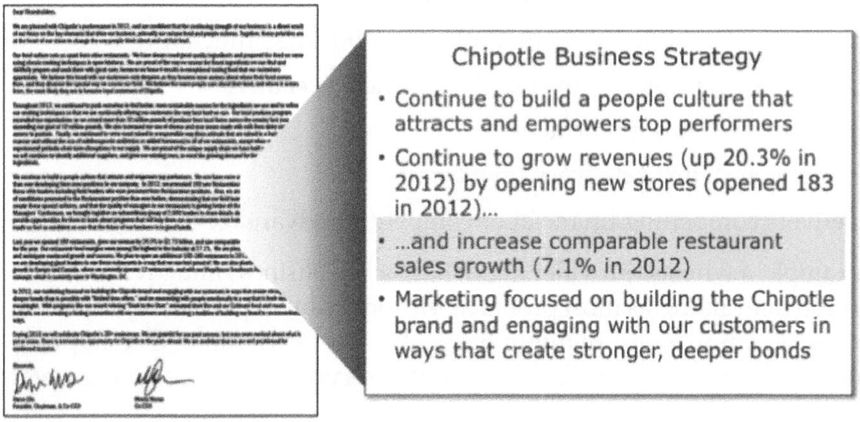

Figure 3-3: Chipotle's 2012 letter to the shareholders

From the President's Letter, we can identify at least four key business initiatives for the coming year:

- Improve employee (talent) acquisition, maturation, and retention (which is especially important for an organization where 90 percent of its management has come up through the ranks of the store).
- Continue double-digit revenue growth (up 20.3 percent in 2012) by opening new stores (opened 183 over 100 in 2012).
- Increase same store sales growth (7.1 percent growth in 2012).
- Improve marketing effectiveness on building the Chipotle brand and engaging with customers in ways that create stronger, deeper bonds.

While any four of these business initiatives are ripe for the big data strategy document, for the remainder of this exercise, we'll focus on the "increase same store sales" business initiative because increasing sales of a business entity or outlet is relevant across a number of different industries (i.e., hospitality, gaming, banking, insurance, retail, higher education, health care providers).

Identify Key Business Entities and Key Decisions

After identifying our targeted business initiative, the next step is to identify the key *business entities* that are important to the targeted business initiative ("increase same store sales"). Business entities are the strategic nouns around which the targeted business initiative must focus. You probably won't have more than three to five business entities, or strategic nouns, for any single business initiative.

NOTE **It is around these business entities that we are going to want to capture the behaviors, tendencies, patterns, trends, preferences, etc. at the individual entity level. For example, a credit card company would want to capture Bill Schmarzo's specific travel and buying patterns and tendencies in order to better detect fraud and improve merchant marketing offers.**

Figure 3-4 shows the template that we are going to use to support the big data strategy document process. We have already captured our targeted "increase same store sales" business initiative.

Take a moment to write down what you think might be the key business entities or strategic nouns for the "increase same store sales" business initiative:

-
-
-

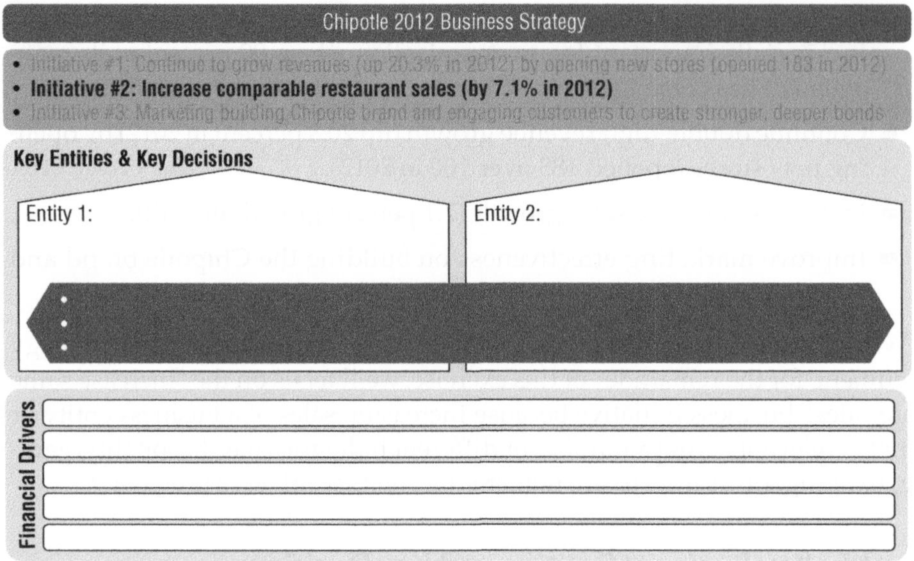

Figure 3-4: Chipotle's "increase same store sales" business initiative

Here are three business entities that I came up with:

- Stores
- Local events (sporting, entertainment, social)
- Local competitors

NOTE **I did not include "customers" as one of my business entities for Chipotle. Customers are typically a leading business entity candidate; however, as of the writing of this book, Chipotle did not have a customer loyalty program. The lack of a customer loyalty program would make it difficult for Chipotle to identify individual customer behaviors, tendencies, patterns, trends, and product preferences.**

Next, for each of the identified business entities, brainstorm the analytic insights that you might want to capture for each of the individual business entities. That is, what is it that you'd like to know about each individual business entity that could support the strategic business initiative? For each of the key business entities listed below, jot down some analytic insights that you would like to know about each:

- Stores
- Local events
- Local competitors

Here are some potential analytic insights that I would like to capture about each of the Chipotle business entities:

- **Stores**—For each individual store, understand in-store traffic patterns, nearby customer demographics, most popular market basket combinations, customer product preferences (by time of day, day of week, seasonality, and holidays), weather conditions, outside traffic conditions, local economic situation, local home values, nearby schools and colleges, Yelp rating, social media sentiment, and so forth.
- **Local Events**—For each individual local event, understand the type of event, the frequency of event, when event occurs (time of day, day of week, time of year), event start and stop times, the number of attendees, the demographics of participants and attendees (age, gender), event administrator/coordinator, event sponsors, and so on.
- **Local Competitors**—For each individual local competitor, understand type of competitor, size of competitor, chain or mom-and-pop competitor, distance from competitor, type of food served, type of service, price points, Yelp ratings, social media sentiment, length of time in service, customer demographics, etc.

Next, identify the key *business decisions* that need to be made about the key business entities in support of the targeted business initiative. That is, what *decisions* does Chipotle store and corporate management need to make about the business entities to support the "increase same store sales" business initiative? This is a great opportunity to brainstorm the decisions with your key business stakeholders, those people or workers who impact or are impacted by the key business initiative.

Here are examples of some key business decisions by business entity:

Business entity: Stores

- How much staffing, inventory, and ingredients do I need for the upcoming weekend given the local events?
- How much staffing, inventory, and ingredients do I need given upcoming holidays and seasonal events?
- How much staffing, inventory, and ingredients do I need for Friday local business catering?
- How much staffing, inventory, and ingredients do I need for local high school demand (school in-session versus school out-of-session)?
- What are the ideal hours of operations for the upcoming high school football season?

Business entity: Local events

- How much additional staffing will I need for which local events?
- How much additional inventory and ingredients will I need for which local events?
- Which local events do I want to sponsor and at what cost?
- What promotions do I want to offer in support of the local events?

Business entity: Local competitors

- What are the most effective offers or promotions to counter competitors that are taking customers away from me?
- What are my competitors' most effective promotions?
- What pricing and production changes do I need to make in light of key competitor activities?
- To which local competitors' promotions do I need to respond?
- What's the most effective response or promotion given competitors' promotional activities?

Take a shot below at brainstorming some additional business decisions that the store manager or corporate management might have to make about the key business entities to support the "increase same store sales" business initiative.

Business entity: Stores

- Decision:
- Decision:

Business entity: Local events

- Decision:
- Decision:

Business entity: Local competitors

- Decision:
- Decision:

NOTE **Some of the decisions will be very similar. That's good because it allows the organization to approach the decisions from multiple perspectives.**

Figure 3-5 shows is what the Chipotle big data strategy document looks at this point in the exercise with the addition of some of the business decisions.

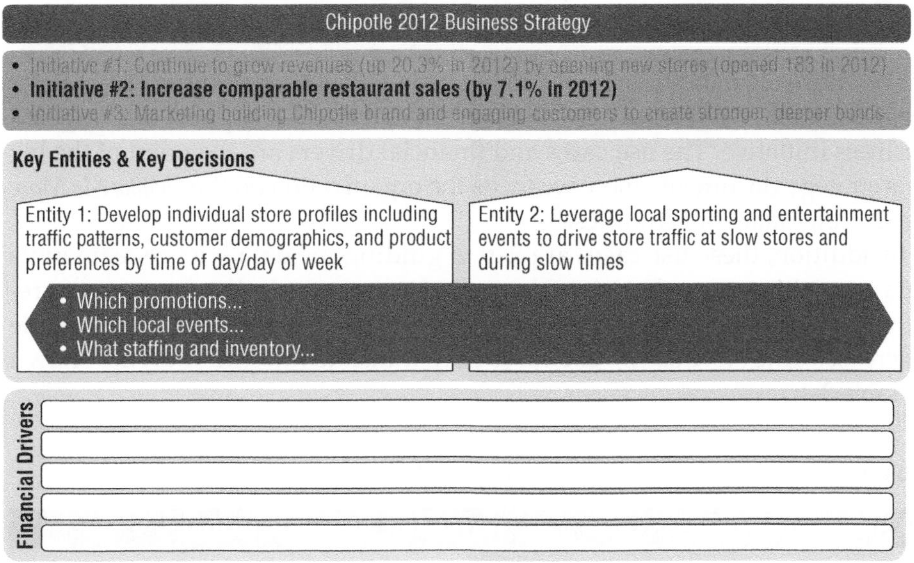

Figure 3-5: Chipotle key business entities and decisions

Identify Financial Drivers (Use Cases)

Next you want to group the decisions into common use cases or "common themes." That is, identify and cluster those decisions that seem similar in their business and financial objectives. The resulting use cases are the financial drivers or the "how do we make more money" opportunities for our targeted business initiative.

CROSS-REFERENCE **While it is hard to actually do this grouping process in a book, the use of facilitation techniques to help brainstorm and group these decisions will be covered in the Facilitation Techniques section of Chapter 13, "Power of Envisioning."**

For Chipotle's "increase same store sales" business initiative, the following are likely financial drivers or use cases:

- Increase store traffic (acquire new customers, increase frequency of repeat customers)
- Increase shopping bag revenue and margins (cross-sell complementary products, up-sell)

- Increase number of corporate events (catering, repeat catering events)
- Improve promotional effectiveness (Halloween Boo-ritto, Christmas gift cards, graduation, holiday, and special event gift cards)
- Improve new product introduction effectiveness (seasonal, holiday)

The entire big data strategy document process has been designed to uncover these use cases—to identify those financial drivers that support our targeted business initiative. The use cases and financial drivers are the point of the big data strategy document where we focus the organization on the "*Make Me More Money*" big data opportunities.

In addition, these use cases are key to guiding the data science team in its data acquisition, data cleansing, data enrichment, metric discovery, score creation, and analytic model development processes. For example, the Chipotle "increase same store sales" use cases may translate into the analytics shown in Table 3-1:

Table 3-1: Mapping Chipotle Use Cases to Analytic Models

CHIPOTLE USE CASES	POTENTIAL ANALYTIC MODELS
Increase Store Traffic	Store Marketing Effectiveness
	Store Layout Flow Analysis
	Store Remodeling Lift Analysis
	Store Customer Targeting
Increase Shopping Bag Revenue and Margin	In-store Merchandising Effectiveness
	Pricing Optimization
	Up-sell/Cross-sell Effectiveness
	Market Basket Analysis
Increase Number of Corporate Events	Campaign Effectiveness
	Pipeline and Sales Effectiveness
	Pricing Optimization
	Customer Lifetime Value Score
	Likelihood to Recommend Score

CHIPOTLE USE CASES	POTENTIAL ANALYTIC MODELS
Improve Promotional Effectiveness	Promotional Effectiveness
	Pricing Optimization
	Market Basket Analysis
	Up-sell/Cross-sell Effectiveness
Improve New Product Introductions	Pricing Optimization
	New Product Introductions Effectiveness
	Up-sell/Cross-sell Effectiveness

NOTE **You will discover that many of the analytic models developed for one use case will support other use cases. As organizations build out their analytic assets, you will find opportunities to leverage these analytic assets (data, data enrichment techniques, analytic models) to accelerate addressing additional big data use cases.**

Figure 3-6 shows what the final Chipotle big data strategy document looks like at this point in the exercise.

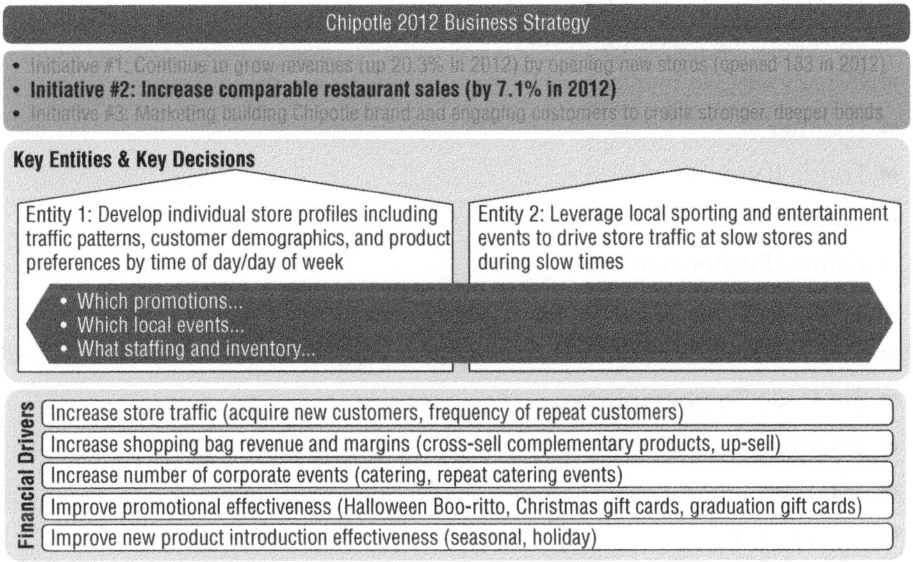

Figure 3-6: Completed Chipotle big data strategy document

Identify and Prioritize Data Sources

With the use cases and financial drivers identified, we are now ready to move into the data and metrics envisioning process. We want to brainstorm data sources (regardless of whether or not you currently have access to these data sources) that *might* yield new insights that support the targeted business initiative. We want to unleash the business and IT teams' creative thinking to brainstorm data sources that might yield new customer, product, store, campaign, and operational insights that could improve the effectiveness of the different use cases.

For example, Chipotle data sources that were identified as part of the envisioning exercises could include:

- Point of Sales Transactions
- Market Baskets
- Product Master
- Store Demographics
- Competitive Stores Sales
- Store Manager Notes
- Employee Demographics
- Store Manager Demographics
- Consumer Comments
- Weather
- Traffic Patterns
- Yelp
- Zillow/Realtor.com
- Twitter/Facebook/Instagram
- Twellow/Twellowhood
- Zip Code Demographics
- EventBrite
- MaxPreps
- Mobile App

But not all data sources are of equal business value or have equal implementation feasibility. The data sources need to be evaluated in light of

- The business value that data source could provide in support of the individual use case
- The feasibility (or ease) of acquiring, cleaning, aligning, normalizing, enriching, and analyzing those data sources

So we want to add two processes (worksheets) to the big data strategy document process that will evaluate the business value and implementation feasibility of each of the potential data sources.

Building on our Chipotle case study, let's first assess the potential business value of the different data sources vis-à-vis the identified use cases (see Figure 3-7).

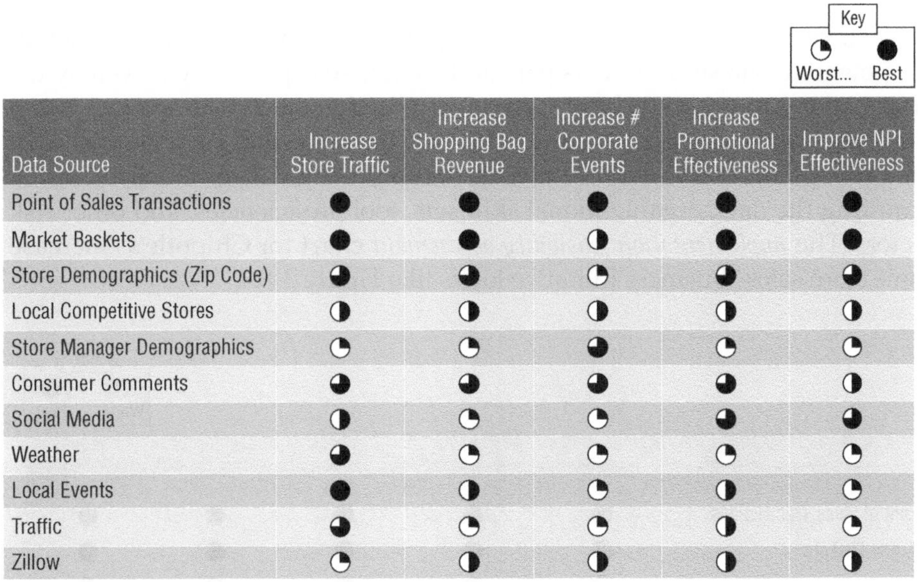

Figure 3-7: Business value of potential Chipotle data sources

You'd want to go through a group brainstorming process with the business stakeholders to assess the relative value of each data source with respect to each use case. The business users own the *business value* determination because they are best positioned to be able to understand and quantify the business value that each data source could provide to the use cases.

NOTE **I like using Harvey Balls (`http://en.wikipedia.org/wiki/Harvey_Balls`) in both the data value and the feasibility assessment charts. The Harvey Balls quickly and easily communicate the relative value of each data source with respect to each use case.**

Reviewing the data value assessment chart in Figure 3-7, you can quickly uncover some key observations, such as the following:

- Detailed point-of-sale data is important to all of the use cases.
- Insights from the Store Demographics data are important to four of the five use cases.

- Mining Consumer Comments has a surprising strong impact across four of the five use cases.
- Local events data is important to the "increase store traffic" and "improve promotional effectiveness" use cases but has little impact on the "increase shopping bag revenue," "increase number of corporate events," or "improve new product introduction effectiveness" use cases.

Next, you want to understand the implementation feasibility for each of the potential data sources. This part of the exercise is primarily driven by the IT organization since it is best positioned to understand the implementation challenges and risks associated with each of the data sources, such as ease of data acquisition, cleanliness of the data, data accuracy, data granularity, cost of acquiring the data, organizational skill sets, tool proficiencies, and other risk factors. The *implementation feasibility assessment* chart for Chipotle's "increase same store sales" business initiative looks like Figure 3-8.

Key: ◔ Worst... ● Best

Data Source	Ease of Acquiring	Cleanliness	Accuracy	Granularity	Cost
Point of Sales Transactions	●	●	●	●	●
Market Baskets	●	●	●	●	●
Store Demographics (Zip Code)	●	●	●	●	●
Competitive Stores Sales	◑	◑	◑	◑	◔
Store Manager Demographics	●	●	●	●	●
Consumer Comments	◑	◑	◔	◑	◕
Social Media	◔	◔	◔	◔	◔
Weather	◕	◕	◑	◑	◑
Local Events	◔	◑	◑	◑	◔
Traffic	◑	◑	◔	◕	◑
Zillow	◔	◔	◑	◑	◔

Figure 3-8: Implementation feasibility of potential Chipotle data sources

From the Chipotle implementation feasibility assessment chart in Figure 3-8, we can quickly make the following observations:

- Point of Sales, Market Baskets, and Store Manager Demographics data is readily available and easy to integrate (likely due to the master data management and data governance efforts necessary to load this data into a data warehouse).
- Consumer Comments data, which was very valuable in the business value assessment, has several implementation risks. Lack of organizational

experience in dealing with the unstructured data is likely the source of these risks, which manifest itself in the areas of data acquisition, standardization, integration, cleanliness, accuracy, granularity, skill sets, and tool proficiencies.

- Social Media data, which was rated about mid-value in the value assessment exercise, also looks to be a real challenge. Many of the same cleanliness, accuracy, and granularity issues exist, with the added issue that this is data that will need to be "acquired" through some means. Probably not the first data source you want to deal with in this use case.
- Local Events data, which was very important in the "increase store traffic" use case, also poses many challenges. Pulling data from sources such as EventBrite and MaxPreps may require screen scraping in order to get the level of detail needed about a particular local event. While these sites may provide APIs to ease the data acquisition process, many times the APIs don't provide the complete detail that the data science team may want. And screen scraping, while a very useful data scientist tool, poses all sorts of challenges in cleaning the data after scraping.

Introducing the Prioritization Matrix

The final step in the big data strategy document process is to take the business and IT stakeholders through a use case prioritization process. While we will cover the *prioritization matrix* in detail in Chapter 13, I want to introduce the concept here as the natural point of concluding the big data strategy document process.

As part of the big data strategy document, we have now done the work to identify the use cases that support the organization's key business initiative, brainstormed additional data sources, and determined the applicability of those data sources from a business value and implementation feasibility assessment. We are now ready to prioritize the use cases based on their relative business value and implementation feasibility over the next 9 to 12 months (see Figure 3-9).

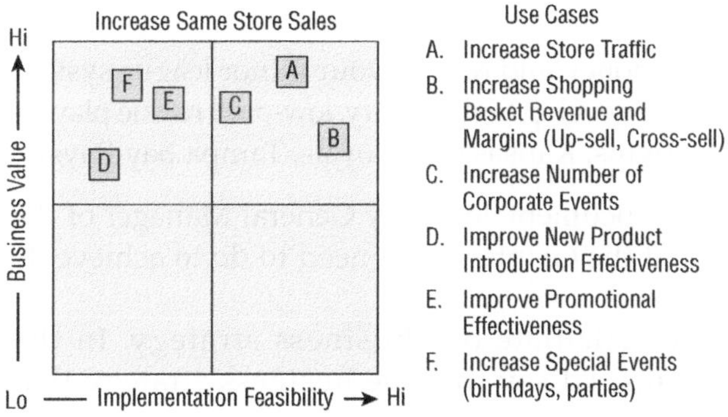

Figure 3-9: Chipotle prioritization of use cases

WARNING **It is critical to remember to use the next 9-to 12-month time frame as the basis for the prioritization process. The 9-to 12-month time frame ensures that the big data project is delivering immediate-term business value and business relevance with a sense of urgency, and it keeps the big data project from wandering into a "boil the ocean" type of project that is doomed to failure.**

Using the Big Data Strategy Document to Win the World Series

To test our competency with the big data strategy document, let's examine a fun case study. Let's say that you are the general manager of a professional baseball team. The corporate mission of the organization is to "Win the World Series" (On a personal note, I am convinced that there are teams where the goal is not to. "Win the World Series" but instead to just make profits without regard to the quality of play on the field, but that's the cynical Chicago Cubs fan in me coming out.)

As in any commercial business, there are multiple business strategies that a professional baseball organization could pursue in order to achieve the "Win the World Series" mission, including:

- Spend huge amounts of money for veteran, proven, top-performing players (New York Yankees, Boston Red Sox, Los Angeles Dodgers);
- Spend huge amounts of money for over-the-hill, inconsistent performing players (Chicago Cubs are moving away from this strategy, though the New York Mets seem to be trying to perfect this approach);
- Spend top money to have outstanding starting and relief pitching, and scrounge together enough timely hitting to win games (San Francisco Giants);
- Spend top money to have outstanding hitting and hope that you can piece together enough pitching to win games (Texas Rangers, Los Angeles Angels);
- Spend miserly amounts of money and rely on your minor league system and sabermetrics to draft and develop high-quality, low-paid rookie players (Oakland A's, Minnesota Twins, Kansas City Royals, Tampa Bay Rays).

So using the big data strategy document, let's play General Manager of the San Francisco Giants to see what the Giants would need to do to achieve its goal to "Win the World Series."

The first step is to clearly articulate our business strategy. In the case of the San Francisco Giants, I'd say that the business strategy that would support its "Win the World Series" corporate mission would be "Acquire and retain high-performing, sustainable, starting pitching coupled with small ball hitting to compete annually for the World Series."

Let's remember that a business strategy is typically two to three years or more on the horizon. If you change your business strategy annually, then that's not a strategy (sounds more like a fad). But companies do and should change their business strategies based on changing economic conditions, market forces, customer demographic trends, technology changes, and even new insights from big data analytics (which might reveal that strong pitching tends—from a statistical perspective—to beat strong hitting in the post season). This is exactly what the San Francisco Giants seem to have done as the team has moved away from a "long ball" baseball strategy in trying to reach the World Series (by surrounding Barry Bonds with other strong batters) to its current "superior starting pitching" business strategy.

So let's use the big data strategy document to see what we (the San Francisco Giants) need to do to execute against the "superior starting pitching to win the World Series" business strategy.

First, we want to decompose the business strategy into the supporting business initiatives. Remember, business initiatives are cross-functional plans, typically 9 to 12 months in length, with clearly defined financial or business metrics. For our baseball exercise, I'm only going to list two business initiatives (though I can think of two or three more that also need to be addressed in the case of the San Francisco Giants):

- Acquire and maintain top-tier starting pitching
- Perfect small ball offensive strategy

Next, I want to identify the *key business entities*, or strategic nouns, around which I need to capture analytic insights to support the targeted business initiatives. For our case study, this could include:

- **Pitchers.** Develop detailed knowledge and predictive insights into individual starting pitchers' in-game and situational pitching tendencies and performance as measured by quality starts (pitches at least six innings in a start), Earned Run Average (ERA), Walks and Hits per Inning Pitched (WHIP), strikeout-to-walk ratio, and number of homeruns per nine innings by competitors, by specific batters, by ball park, by weather conditions, by days rest, by number of games into the season, etc.
- **Batters.** Develop detailed knowledge and predictive insights into batter tendencies and behaviors as measured by On Base Percentage (OBP), batting average with runners in scoring position, stealing percentage, hit-and-run execution, and sacrifice hitting effectiveness by count, by number of outs, by competitive pitcher, by who's on base, by day versus night, etc.

We could also develop profiles for Coaches, Competitors, and maybe even Stadiums, but for reasons of time and simplicity, we'll just stick to the Pitchers and Batters business entities for this exercise.

Next, let's brainstorm the decisions and questions that we need to address about our key business entities to support our targeted business initiative:.

- Acquire and Maintain Top-Tier Starting Pitching
  - Who are my most effective starting pitchers?
  - Which starting pitchers do I re-sign and for how much money and length of contract?
  - Which free agent starting pitchers do I want to sign and for how much money and length of contract?
  - Which starting pitchers do I want to trade, and what is my expectation of the value that they will bring in the market?
  - Which competitors' starting pitchers do I want to try to acquire via trades and for how much?
  - Which of my minor league pitchers are projected to be my most effective big league starting pitchers over the next two to three years?
  - What is my starting pitching rotation?
  - Which starting pitchers are currently struggling, and what are the likely reasons for this struggling?
  - Which starting pitchers should I rest by having them miss a start?
- Perfect Small Ball Offensive Strategy
  - Which batters are most effective in getting on base?
  - Which batters are most effective in advancing runners?
  - Which batters are most effective in driving in runners from third base?
  - Which players are my best base stealers?
  - Who are my most timely hitters in late-in-the-game pressure situations?
  - Which minor league batters are most effective in getting on base?
  - Which minor league batters are most effective in advancing runners?
  - Which minor league batters are most effective in driving in runners from third base?
  - Which minor league players excel at base stealing?
  - Which free agent batters are most effective in getting on base?
  - Which free agent batters are most effective in advancing runners?

- Which free agent batters are most effective in driving in runners from third base?
- Which free agent players excel at base stealing?

If you are a baseball junkie like I am, take a moment to list some additional decisions and questions that you'd like to address for the two targeted business initiatives: top-tier starting pitching and small ball offense.

Now we can group the decisions (and questions in this exercise) into common *use cases* that could include:

- Improve starting pitching proficiency by optimizing trades, free agent signing, minor league promotions, and contract extensions (cost versus starting pitching performance effectiveness)
- Preserve starting pitching effectiveness throughout the regular season and playoffs by optimizing pitch counts, pitcher rotations, pitcher rests, etc.
- Improve batting and slugging proficiency by optimizing trades, free agent signings, minor league promotions, and contract extensions
- Increase in-game "small ball" runs scored effectiveness through the optimal combination of batters, hitting, stealing, base running, and sacrifice hitting strategies
- Accelerate minor league player development through player strength and conditioning training, game situations, and minor league assignments
- Optimize in-game pitch selection decisions through improved understanding of batter and pitcher matchups

Figure 3-10 shows the resulting big data strategy document.

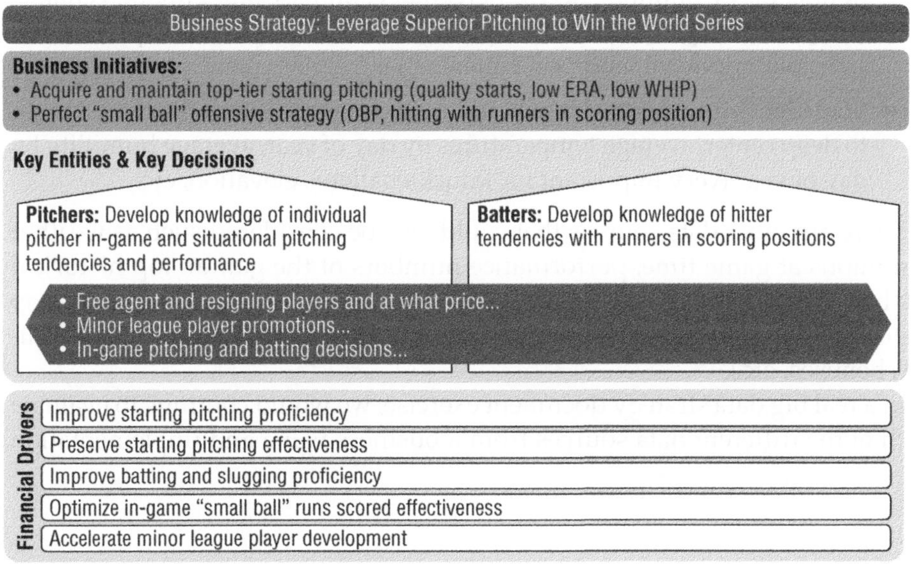

Figure 3-10: San Francisco Giants big data strategy document

Next, we would brainstorm the potential data sources to support the use cases, including:

- **Personnel Player Health.** This should include personal health history (weight, health, BMI, injuries, therapy, medications), physical performance metrics (60-foot dash time, long toss distances, fast ball velocity), and workout history (bench press, dead lift, crunches and pushups in 60 seconds, frequency and recency of workouts).
- **Starting Pitcher Performance.** This should include a detailed pitching history including number of pitches thrown, strike-to-ball ratio, strike outs-to-walk ratio, walks and hits per inning pitched, ERA, first pitch strikes, batting average against, and slugging percentage per time of year, per opponent, and per game.
- **Batter Performance.** This should include a detailed batting history including batting average, walks, on-base percentage, slugging percentage, strike outs, hitting into double plays, bunting success percentage, on-base slugging percentage, wins above replacement, and hitting with runners on base per time of year, per opponent, and per game.
- **Competitors' Pitching Performance.** This should include recent history of competitors' pitchers' performance including number of pitches thrown, strike-to-ball ratio, strike outs-to-walk ratio, walks and hits per inning pitched, ERA, first pitch strikes, batting average against, and slugging percentage against per time of year, per opponent, and per game.
- **Competitors' Hitting Performance.** This should include recent history of competitors' batters' hitting performance including batting average, walks, on-base percentage, slugging percentage, strike outs, hitting into double plays, bunting success percentage, on-base slugging percentage, wins above replacement, and hitting with runners on base per time of year, per opponent, and per game.
- **Stadium Information.** This should include length down the lines, length to deep center, average temperatures by day of year, average humidity by day of year (very important for knuckleballers), elevation, etc.

There are other data sources that could also be considered such as weather conditions at game time, performance numbers of the game's top historical pitchers (for benchmarking purposes), performance numbers for game's top historical batters (again, for benchmarking purposes), and economic costs (salary, bonuses, etc.).

In a real big data strategy document exercise, we would continue to evaluate each of the different data sources from a business value and implementation feasibility perspective vis-à-vis each of the identified use cases. Then we would go through a prioritization matrix process to ensure that both the business users (coaches, front office management) and IT agree on which use cases to start with.

So playing the San Francisco Giants' General Manager was a fun exercise that provided another perspective on how to use the big data strategy document not only to break down your organization's business strategy and key business initiatives into the key business entities and key decisions but to ultimately uncover the supporting data and analytic requirements.

Summary

This chapter focused on the big data strategy document and key related topics including:

- Introduced the concept of a business initiative and provided some examples of where to find these business initiatives
- Introduced the big data strategy document as a framework for helping organizations to identify the use cases that guide where and how they can start their big data journeys
- Provided a hands-on example of the big data strategy document in action using Chipotle, a chain of organic Mexican food restaurants
- Introduced worksheets to help organizations to determine the business value and implementation feasibility of the data sources that come out of the big data strategy document process
- Introduced the prioritization matrix as a tool to help drive business and IT alignment around the top priority use cases over a 9-to 12-month window
- Had some fun by applying the big data strategy document to the world of professional baseball

This chapter outlined the big data strategy document as a framework to help an organization identify where and how to start its big data journey in support of the organization's 9-to 12-month key business initiatives. The big data strategy document is a tool to ensure that your big data journey is valuable and relevant from a business perspective.

To swing back around to the Chipotle case study, Figure 3-11 shows some initial results of the company's success with its "increase same store revenues" business initiative. (For more information, see the article at `www.trefis.com/stock/cmg/articles/210221/chipotles-sales-surge-on-traffic-gains-high-food-costs-dent-margins/2013-10-21`.)

Chipotle's Sales Surge On Traffic Gains; High Food Costs Dent Margins

Oct 21 2013, 23:09 | 1 comment | about: CMG

BOOKMARK / READ LATER

Trefis

Articles (2,426)
Instablog (14)
StockTalks (3)
Comments (37)
Profile

2,006 Followers
2 Following

Follow
Send Message

About this author:

Strong sales, buoyed by higher traffic, helped Chipotle Mexican Grill (NYSE:CMG) post a strong set of third quarter numbers. Total revenues for the quarter rose 18.0% to $826.9 million while the operating income surged 17% to $137.1 million. Chipotle's net income jumped to $83.4 million, or $2.66 per share, up from $2.27 per share in the previous year quarter. Shares of the company were up 8% in the post market trading.

We have revised our price estimate for Chipotle to $416, following the third quarter earnings release.

Same-Store Sales Better Than Expected

Investors were surprised by the company's third same-store sales growth of 6.2%. Sales were boosted by higher traffic. The results highlight how the company's efforts to lure more customers through new menu additions and increased marketing are paying off. After a disappointing 1% rise in the same-store sales in the first quarter, the figure accelerated to 5.5% in the second quarter.

The restaurant chain added a new tofu like product called "sofritas" to its menu. At present, approximately 25% of the restaurants serve this product but the figure should increase to 40% by the year end. Chipotle's bet on introducing an unusual vegetarian item seems to be paying off as it already accounts for 4% of the sales at the restaurants at which it is served. (CMG Earnings Transcript) The menu item attracts a lot of

Figure 3-11: Chipotle's same store sales results

It's nice to see that our Chipotle use case actually has a real business story behind it. But then again, every big data initiative should have a real business story behind it. Remember, organizations don't need a big data strategy as much as they need a business strategy that incorporates big data.

Homework Assignment

Use the following exercises to apply the big data strategy document to your organization (or one of your favorite organizations).

Exercise #1: Start by identifying your organization's key business initiatives over the next 9 to 12 months.

Exercise #2: Select one of your business initiatives, and then brainstorm the key business entities or strategic nouns that impact that selected business initiative. As a reminder, it is around the individual business entities that we want to capture the behaviors, tendencies, patterns, trends, preferences, etc. at the individual business entity level.

Exercise #3: Next, brainstorm the key decisions that need to be made about each key business entity with respect to the targeted business initiative.

Exercise #4: Next we want to group the decisions into common use cases; that is, cluster those decisions that seem similar in their business or financial objectives.

Exercise #5: Then brainstorm the different data sources that you might need to support those use cases:

- Identify potential internal structured (transactional data sources, operational data sources) and unstructured (consumer comments, notes, work orders, purchase requests) data sources
- Identify potential external data sources (social media, blogs, publicly available, data.gov, websites, mobile apps) that you also might want to consider

Exercise #6: Use the data assessment worksheets to determine the relative business value and implementation feasibility of each of the identified data sources with respect to the different use cases.

Exercise #7: Finally, use the prioritization matrix to rank each of the use cases vis-à-vis business value and implementation feasibility over the next 9 to 12 months.

CHAPTER

4

The Importance of the User Experience

The user experience is one of the secrets to big data success, and one of my favorite topics. If organizations cannot deliver insights to its employees, managers, partners, and customers in a way that is actionable, then why even bother. One of the keys to success in the *Big Data MBA* is to "begin with an end in mind" with respect to understanding how the analytic results are going to be delivered to frontline employees, business managers, channel partners, and customers in a way that is actionable. The *Big Data MBA* seeks to "close the analytics loop" with respect to delivering insights to the key business stakeholders via an actionable user experience (UEX).

CHAPTER 4 OBJECTIVES

- **Review an example of an "unintelligent" user experience.**
- **Highlight the importance of "thinking differently" with respect to creating an actionable dashboard versus building a traditional Business Intelligence dashboard.**
- **Review a sample actionable dashboard targeting frontline store managers.**
- **Review another sample actionable dashboard (financial advisor dashboard) targeting business-to-business channel partners.**

This chapter will challenge the traditional Business Intelligence approaches to building dashboards by seeking to leverage analytic insights (e.g., recommendations, scores, rules) to create actionable dashboards that empower frontline employees, guide channel partners, and influence customer behaviors.

The Unintelligent User Experience

One of my favorite subjects against which I love to rail is the "unintelligent" user experience. This is a problem caused by, in my humble opinion, the lack of effort by organizations to understand their key business stakeholders well enough to be able to deliver actionable insights in support of the organizations' key business initiatives. And this user experience problem is often only exacerbated by big data.

Here is a real-world example of how NOT to leverage actionable analytics in your organization's engagements with your customers. The names have been changed to protect the guilty.

My daughter Amelia got the e-mail (see Figure 4.1) from our cell phone provider warning her that she was about to exceed her monthly data usage limit of 2GB. She was very upset that she was about to go over her limit, and it would start costing her (actually, me) an additional $10.00 per GB over the limit. (Note: The "Monday, August 13, 2012" date in the figure will play an important role in this story.)

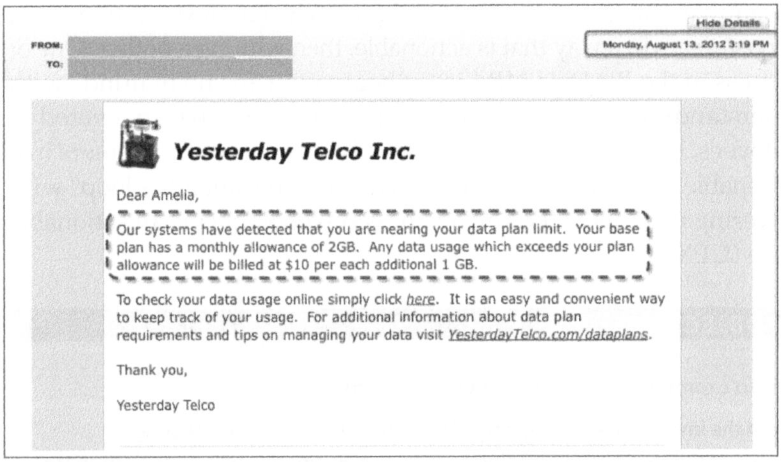
FROM:
TO:
Hide Details
Monday, August 13, 2012 3:19 PM

Yesterday Telco Inc.

Dear Amelia,

Our systems have detected that you are nearing your data plan limit. Your base plan has a monthly allowance of 2GB. Any data usage which exceeds your plan allowance will be billed at $10 per each additional 1 GB.

To check your data usage online simply click here. It is an easy and convenient way to keep track of your usage. For additional information about data plan requirements and tips on managing your data visit YesterdayTelco.com/dataplans.

Thank you,

Yesterday Telco

Figure 4-1: Original subscriber e-mail

I asked Amelia what information she thought she needed in order to make a ***decision*** about altering her Facebook, Pandora, Vine, Snapchat, and Instagram usage (since those are the main data hog culprits in her case) so that she would not exceed her data plan limits. She thought for a while and then said that she thought she needed the following information:

- How much of her data plan does she have left in the current month?
- When does her new month or billing period start?
- At her current usage rate, when will she run over for this month?

Capture the Key Decisions

This use case provides a good example of the process that organizations can employ to identify the key business ***decisions*** that the organization's key business stakeholders need to address in order to support the organization's key business initiatives. Here is an abbreviated process (that is similar to the process we just learned with the big data strategy document in Chapter 3):

Step 1: Understand your organization's key ***business initiatives*** or business challenge (in this example the initiative is "Don't exceed your monthly data usage plan").

Step 2: Identify your key ***business stakeholders*** (Amelia and me in this example).

Step 3: Capture the ***decisions*** that the key business stakeholders need to make in order to support the organization's key business initiatives (e.g., alter Facebook, Pandora, Vine, Snapchat, and Instagram usage).

Step 4: Brainstorm the ***questions*** that the key stakeholders need to answer to facilitate making the decisions (How much of my data plan do I have left? When does my new month start? When will I run over for my current period given my current usage?).

Support the User Decisions

Understanding the relationship between your business initiative and the supporting decisions and questions that need to be addressed is key to creating a user experience that provides the right information (or actionable insights) to the right user to make the right decisions at the right time.

So to continue the cellular provider story, I went online to research Amelia's key questions:

QUESTION	ANSWER
How much of my data plan do I have left?	Current usage as of August 13 is 65 percent
When does my new month start?	On August 14, which is 1 day from today
When am I likely to run over my data plan limit?	The probability of you overrunning your data plan is 0.00001 percent...or ***NEVER!!***

So given the results of my analysis, Amelia had nothing to worry about as she would have to consume nearly as much bandwidth in her final 24 hours as she had consumed the previous 30 days. The probability of that happening: near zero (or about the same probability of me beating Usain Bolt in the 100-meter dash). The bottom line is that the e-mail should have never been sent. There was nothing for Amelia to worry about, and it only caused unnecessary angst. Not the sort of user experience that organizations should be targeting.

Our cellular provider could have provided a user experience that highlighted the information and insights necessary to help Amelia make a decision about data usage. The user experience could have looked something like the e-mail message shown in Figure 4-2.

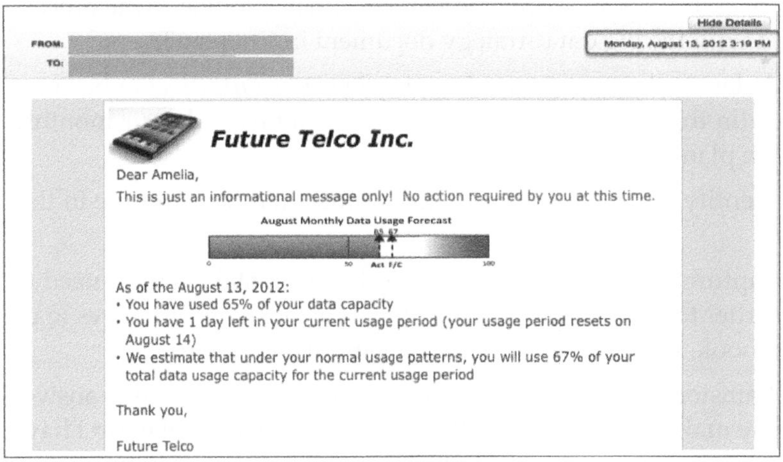

Figure 4-2: Improved subscriber e-mail

This sample e-mail has all the information that Amelia needs to make a decision about usage behaviors including:

- Actual usage to date (65 percent)
- A forecast of usage by the end of the period (67 percent)
- The date when the data plan will reset (in 1 day on August 14)

With this information, Amelia is now in a position to make the "right" decision about her data plan usage.

Consumer Case Study: Improve Customer Engagement

But let's take this case study one step further. Let's say that there actually was going to be a problem with Amelia's usage and her data plan. What if 82 percent of data usage had been consumed with 50 percent of usage period remaining?

How do we make the user experience and the customer engagement useful, relevant, and actionable?

The mock-up shown in Figure 4-3 offers one potential approach based on the same principles discussed earlier: provide enough information to help Amelia change her usage behaviors. However, Future Telco could also take the user experience and customer engagement one step further and offer her some recommendations to avoid the data plan overage.

For example, Future Telco could offer prescriptive advice about how to reduce data consumption such as:

- Transitioning to apps that are more data usage efficient (i.e., transitioning from Pandora to Rdio or iHeartRadio for streaming radio, assuming that Rdio and iHeartRadio are more efficient in their usage of the data bandwidth)
- Turning off apps in the background that are unnecessarily consuming data such as mapping apps (like Apple Map or Waze) or apps that are using GPS tracking

Future Telco could even offer Amelia options to avoid paying an overage penalty (see Figure 4-3) such as:

- Purchase a 1-month data usage upgrade for $2.00 (which is cheaper than the $10 overage penalty)
- Upgrade existing contract (covering 6 months) for $10.00

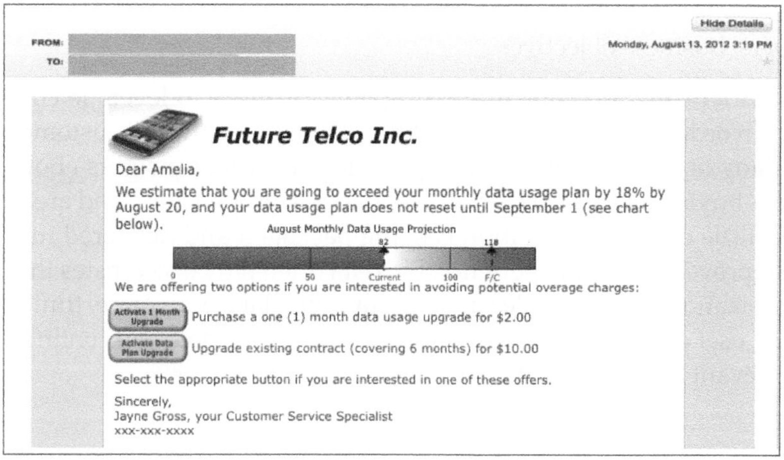

Figure 4-3: Actionable subscriber e-mail

But wait, there is even more that Future Telco could do to improve the customer experience. Future Telco could analyze Amelia's app usage tendencies and recommend new apps based on other apps that users like Amelia use, similar to what Amazon and Netflix do (see Figure 4-4).

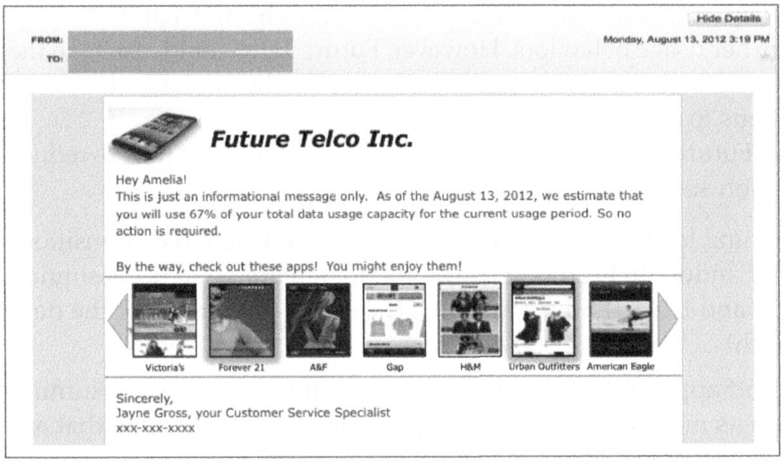

Figure 4-4: App recommendations

This level of customer intimacy can open up all sorts of new monetization opportunities such as:

- Leverage your customer's usage patterns and behaviors to recommend apps that move the user into a more profitable, high-retention user category
- Help app developers to be more successful while collecting referral fees, co-marketing fees, and other monetization ideas that align with the app developers' business objectives

Cellular providers are not alone in missing opportunities to leverage customer insights in order to provide a more relevant, more meaningful customer experience. Many organizations are sitting on gold mines of insights about their customers' buying and usage patterns, tendencies, propensities, and areas of interest, but little of that information is being packaged and delivered in a manner that improves the user experience. Big data often only exacerbates this problem. Organizations will either learn to leverage big data as an opportunity to improve their user experience, or they will get buried by the data and continue to provide irrelevant and even misleading customer experiences.

Business Case Study: Enable Frontline Employees

I had the opportunity to run a vision workshop for a grocery retailer. The goal of the session was to identify how the grocery chain could leverage big data and advanced analytics to deliver actionable insights (or recommendations) to store managers in order to help them improve store performance.

Big data can transform the business by enabling a completely new user experience (UEX) built around insight and recommendations versus just traditional Business Intelligence charts and tables. Retailers, like most organizations, can leverage detailed, historical transactional data—coupled with new sources of "right-time" data like local competitors' promotions (e.g., "best food days," which is the day when grocery stores post their weekly promotions), weather, and events—to uncover new insight about their customers, products, merchandising, competitors and operations. Big data provides organizations the ability to (1) rapidly ingest these new sources of customer, product, and operational data and then (2) leverage data science to yield real-time, actionable insights.

Let's walk through an example of integrating big data with a traditional BI dashboard to create a more actionable user experience that empowers frontline employees and managers.

Store Manager Dashboard

We start with a traditional Business Intelligence dashboard. This dashboard provides the key performance indicators (KPIs) and metrics against which the store manager measures the performance of the store. The dashboard can also present sales and margin trends and previous period comparisons for those KPIs. This is pretty standard Business Intelligence work (see Figure 4-5).

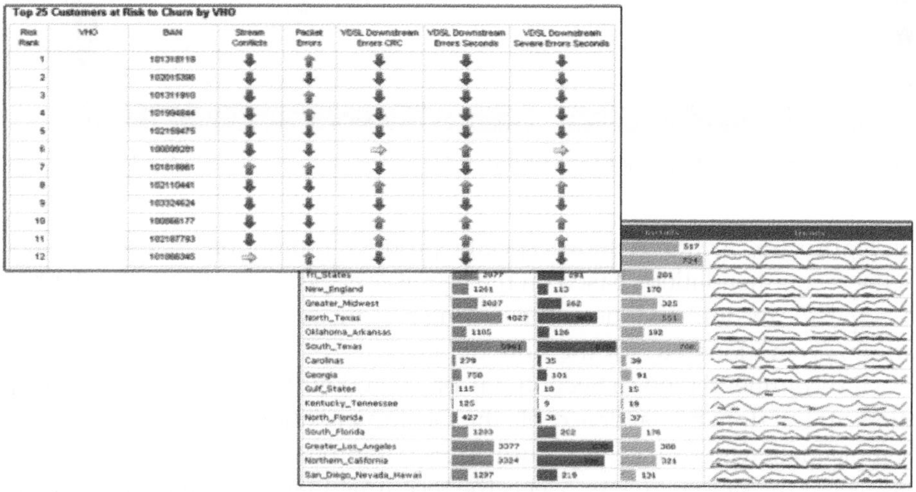

Figure 4-5: Traditional Business Intelligence dashboard

The challenge with these traditional BI dashboards is that unless you are an analyst, it's not clear what action the user is supposed to take. Arrows up, sideways, and down . . . I can see my performance, but the dashboard doesn't provide any insights to tell the store manager what actions to take.

The other challenge is that the store manager (like most frontline employees and managers) likely does not have a BI or an analytics background (likely worked his way up the ranks in the grocery store). As a result, UEX and the actionable insights and recommendations are critical because the store manager does not know how to drill into the BI reports and dashboards to uncover insights based on the raw data.

We can build on this traditional BI dashboard by including more predictive and prescriptive analytics. In Figure 4-6, the top part of the new actionable dashboard (Sections A and B) leverages predictive analytics and prescriptive analytics to provide recommendations that can help the store manager make more profitable business decisions.

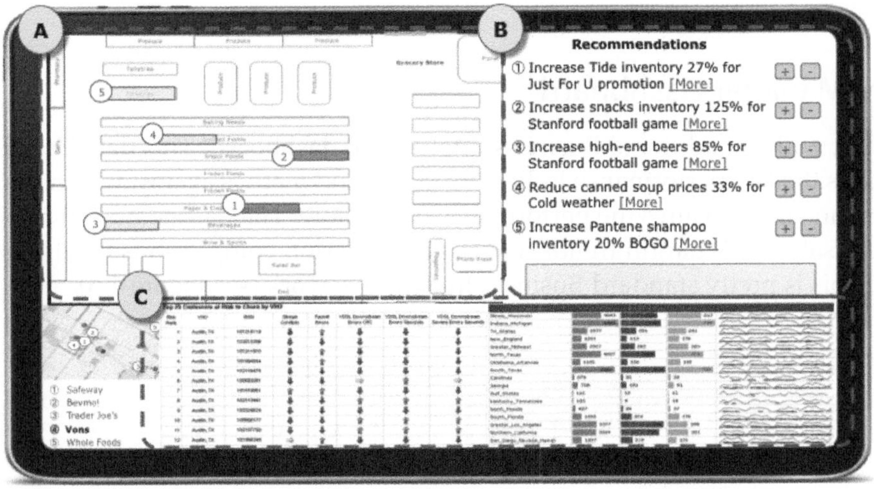

Figure 4-6: Actionable store manager dashboard

In Figure 4-6, Section A shows specific product, promotion, placement, and pricing recommendations based on the layout of a specific store. Section B provides specific recommendations concerning pricing, merchandising, inventory, staffing, promotions, etc. for the store manager.

Each recommendation in Section B is presented with Accept [+] or Reject [-] options. If the store manager accepts the recommendation by selecting [+], that recommendation is executed (e.g., raise prices, add promotion, add inventory, etc.). However, if the store manager rejects the recommendation, then the actionable dashboard captures the reason for the rejection so that the supporting analytic models can be constantly fine-tuned (see Figure 4-7).

Finally, the store manager can select the More option in Section B and modify the recommendation based on his own experience. Allowing the store manager to modify the recommendations based on his personal experiences allows the underlying analytic models to constantly learn what works and what doesn't work and build on the best practices and learnings from the organization's most effective and top-performing store managers.

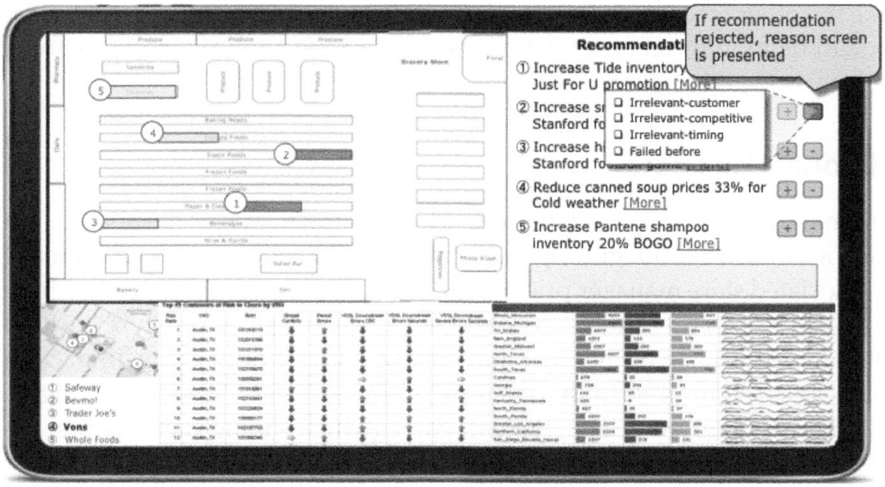

Figure 4-7: Store manager accept/reject recommendations

Sample Use Case: Competitive Analysis

One use case for the store manager dashboard enables the store manager to monitor local competitive activity and promotions. The grocery industry is very locally competitive. Competitors, for the most part, are within just a few miles or even blocks of each other. In this competitive analysis use case, the dashboard provides a map of the local grocery and beverage competitors (see Section C of Figure 4-7). Hovering over any particular competitor on the map immediately brings up its current marketing flyer. The store manager (or his business analyst) can browse through each of the competitors' flyers and make custom store recommendations around pricing, promotion, merchandising, inventory, and staffing based on the competitor's plans (see Figure 4-8).

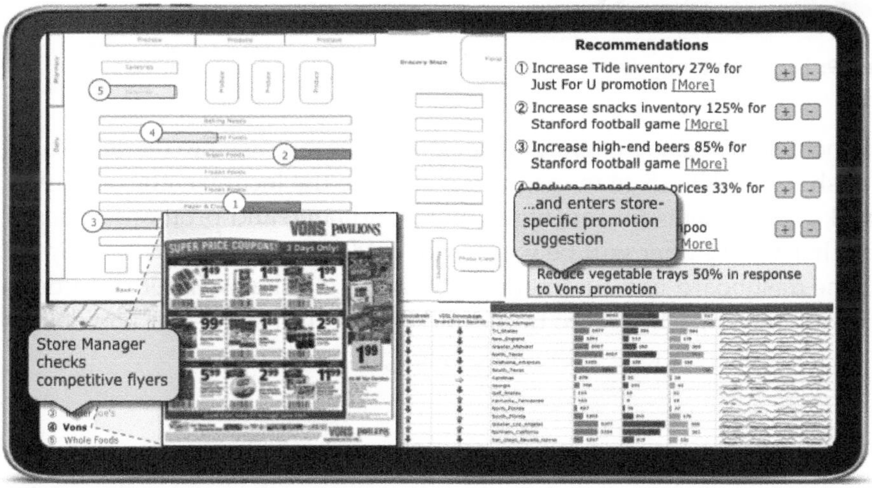

Figure 4-8: Competitive analysis use case

Like the other recommendations, the store manager's custom recommendations will be monitored for effectiveness so that the analytic models can be constantly updated and refined.

Additional Use Cases

Additional use cases can easily be added to the store manager dashboard. We can add a use case for integrating the local events calendar into the dashboard with associated store manager pricing, product, promotions, staffing, merchandising, and inventory recommendations. The store manager can analyze the local events calendar to flag events that may have a positive or negative impact on store sales (see Figure 4-9). In this example, the local events calendar highlights two events: (1) Stanford college football game (which should increase the sale of beer, chips, burgers, and other tailgating materials) and (2) farmers market (which should decrease the sale of fresh produce and fruits and other organic items). The analytics supporting the dashboard could automatically analyze the results of previous local events and leverage predictive analytics to predict how those events might impact store traffic and the sales of specific product categories.

Figure 4-9: Local events use case

Another use case is to integrate the local weather forecast into the store manager dashboard. The store manager can analyze the local weather forecasts and make adjustments for inventory, merchandising, and promotions based on whether the weather will be warmer or colder than expected (see Figure 4-10). The dashboard can automatically analyze similar weather conditions and predict the impact on store traffic and product category sales and deliver relevant recommendations to the store manager.

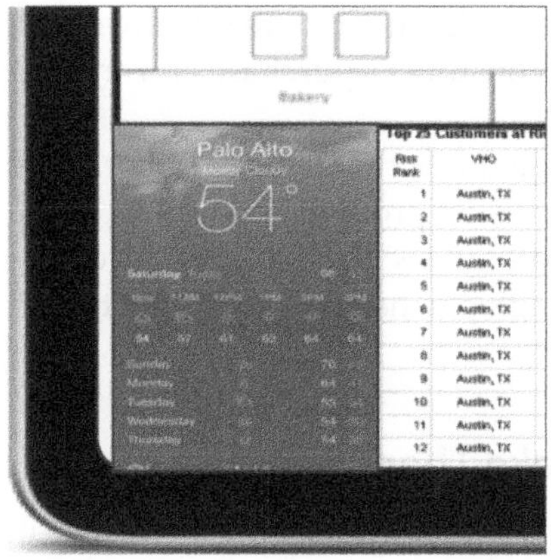

Figure 4-10: Local weather use case

The dashboard could even couple the competitive activities, local events, and weather data to predict what sort of impact the combination of these might have on store traffic and product category demand. These insights could yield new recommendations that drive the store manager's decisions about pricing, promotions, merchandising, staffing, and/or inventory.

B2B Case Study: Make the Channel More Effective

Over the course of my travels, I have met with several organizations that work through partners, brokers, agents, and advisors to get their products and services into the hands of the end consumer. These business-to-business (B2B) organizations face unique challenges:

- They have to work extra hard and be very creative in gathering data about how end consumers are buying and using their products.
- They need to find a way to mine the customer, product, and operational data to uncover insights and make recommendations that make their partners, brokers, and agents more effective.

This can be frustrating, especially in light of all the success stories from business-to-consumer (B2C) organizations such as retailers, mobile phone providers, credit card companies, travel, entertainment and hospitality companies, and other organizations that have direct engagement with the end consumer.

But not to fear, there are things that these B2B organizations can do to encourage their partners, brokers, agents, and advisors to share more of that valuable consumer data. There are also unique insights that these B2B organizations can provide to their partners and channels to make them more effective (and, hopefully, even more willing to share the end consumer's purchase and engagement data).

For purposes of this case study, I have created a fictitious financial services company called FSI. We'll assume that FSI sells its products and services via independent financial advisors. I hope that you can see the applicability of this use case to any industry that must work through partners, brokers, agents, and advisors to reach their end consumers.

The Advisors Are Your Partners—Make Them Successful

Many financial services advisors are small, specialized firms with 1 to 10 employees that provide financial advice to a small group of customers. Many lack the technical and analytic capabilities to analyze large amounts of data and develop predictive and prescriptive models based on their clients' financial goals, current financial situation, ongoing financial conversations, and deep history of financial transactions.

This provides a business opportunity for FSI to market customer, product, and market insights to these independent financial advisors. These insights could include:

- **Benchmarks:** What range of returns should a client expect from a certain type of portfolio? How does the client's portfolio performance compare to that of similar clients with similar financial objectives? What's the typical financial situation and asset base for other clients in similar financial conditions? What's the ideal portfolio mix given my client's age and specific financial goals?
- **Portfolio Mix:** How does my client's percentage of financial and investment contributions compare to that of others like him? How does my client's portfolio and financial asset mix compare to that of others like him?
- **Best Practices:** What are the best performing portfolios for someone with the same financial goals given his or her age and employment time frame? What are the best performing investment instruments for clients given the same retirement horizon as my client?
- **Industry Trends:** What current financial instruments provide the best return-to-risk ratio? How are these financial instruments projected to perform over the next 1, 5, and 10 years? What are the most specific contribution and investment risks for which my client needs to plan?

Financial Advisor Case Study

Okay, let's get to the fun stuff! Let's see how FSI could leverage the insights mentioned above to (1) make the independent financial advisors more effective in supporting their clients and (2) create a stronger, more profitable relationship between FSI and the financial advisors. Let's explore how FSI could deliver client-specific recommendations (prescriptive analytics) in a way that is actionable for both the advisor and the client. Let's also explore how FSI could create an actionable dashboard to drive further client engagement that could gather even more client financial data (financial goals, employment plans, spending patterns) that FSI could use to improve its predictive and prescriptive modeling.

The financial advisor dashboard should address the following functionality (see Figure 4-11):

- Report on client's current financial status and recent financial performance
- Assess client's financial status and progress against personal financial goals such as:
  - Buying a car
  - Buying a home
  - College education
  - Starting a business
  - Career or life change
  - Retirement
- Deliver recommendations to the financial advisors to improve the client's financial performance such as:
  - Modify financial contributions
  - Adjust investment strategies (short-term, long-term)
  - Reallocate financial portfolio
  - Change investment vehicles (stocks, bonds, mutual funds, etc.)

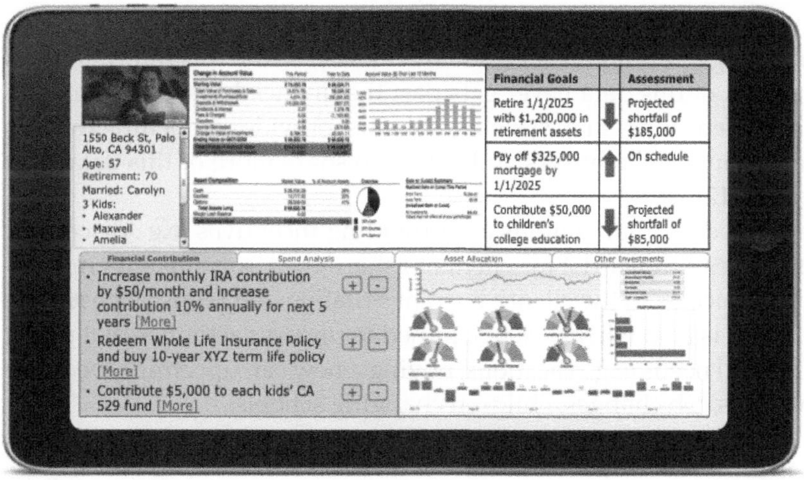

Figure 4-11: Financial advisor dashboard

The goal of the financial advisor dashboard is to uncover insights about the client's investment performance and provide client-specific recommendations that help these clients reach their financial goals. To generate actionable, accurate recommendations, we're going to need to know as much about the client as possible, including:

- Current and historical personal background information (e.g., marital status, spouse's financial and employment situation, number and age of children, outstanding mortgage on home(s) and any secondary real estate investments)
- Current financial investments and other assets (e.g., stocks, bonds, mutual funds, IRAs, 401-Ks, REITs)
- Current and historical income (and expenditures, if possible)
- Financial goals with specific timelines

We need to ensure that the financial advisor dashboard provides enough value to both the financial advisor and the advisor's clients in order to incent the clients to share as much of this data as possible.

Informational Sections of Financial Advisor Dashboard

Let's examine in more details the key informational sections of the financial advisor dashboard. These sections form the foundation for much of the analytics that will be developed to support the client's financial goals.

Client Personal Information: The first part of the dashboard presents relevant client personal and financial information. FSI wants to gather as much personal information as is relevant when the client first opens his accounts. But after the client opens his account, there needs to be a concerted effort to keep the data updated and capture new lifestyle, life stage, employment, and family information. Much of that client data can be captured via discussions and interactions that the financial advisor is having with the client (e.g., informational calls, e-mail dialogues, office visits, annual reviews). While this information is gold to FSI, much of this data never gets past the financial advisors' personal contact management and e-mail systems. FSI must provide compelling reasons to persuade the financial advisors and clients to share more of this data with FSI (see Figure 4-12).

Some leading-edge organizations are providing incentives (e.g., discounts, promotions, contests, rewards) for clients to share their social media interactions. Obviously, access to the client's current situation and plans as posted on social media sites is gold when it can be mined to uncover activities that might affect his financial needs (e.g., vacations, buying a new car, upcoming wedding plans, promotions, job changes, children changing schools).

Client Financial Status: The next section of the dashboard provides an overview of the client's current financial status. Again, the more data that can be gathered about the client's financial situation (e.g., investments, home, spending, debt), the more accurate and prescriptive the analytic models will be (see Figure 4-13).

Figure 4-12: Client personal information

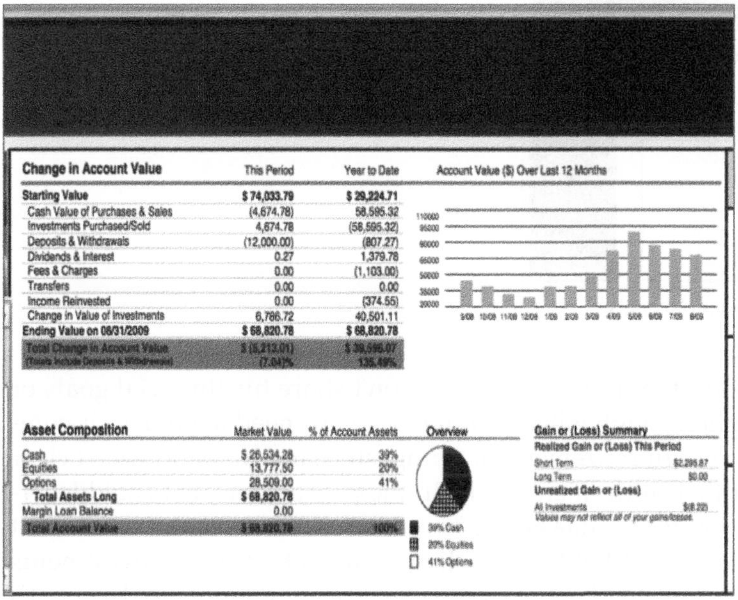

Figure 4-13: Client financial information

In this example, we have details on all the client's financial investments with FSI. However, the client might (and likely does) have financial investments with other firms courtesy of his employer's 401k programs, whole life insurance policies, and other stocks, bonds, and funds. And that doesn't even consider substantial investments in nonfinancial instruments like his primary residence, vacation home, antiques, and collectibles.

Incenting clients to share their entire financial portfolio is complicated by how hard it is for a client to pull all that information together in one place. However, Mint.com has figured out how to aggregate financial spending from credit cards and bank checks. The inclusion of the client's expenditure data could be invaluable in building a client profile and developing specific, actionable financial recommendations.

Client Financial Goals: The final informational section of the dashboard contains the client's financial goals. There are likely only a small number of goals, and they probably don't change that often. However, it is difficult to develop meaningful client financial recommendations without up-to-date client financial goals. From a data collection perspective, this is probably the easiest data to capture, given that you have adequately addressed the client's privacy and security concerns (see Figure 4-14).

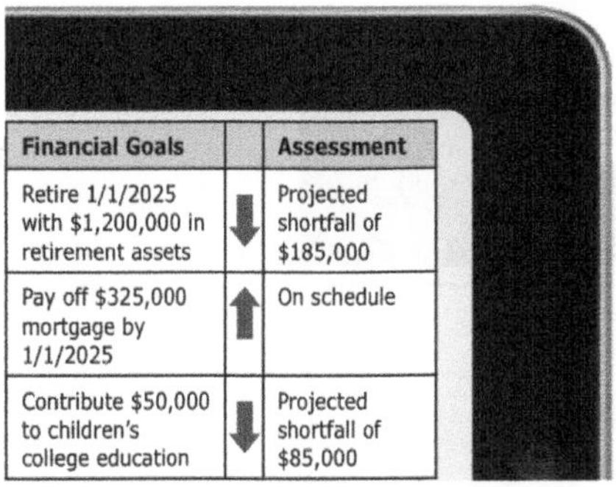

Financial Goals		Assessment
Retire 1/1/2025 with $1,200,000 in retirement assets	↓	Projected shortfall of $185,000
Pay off $325,000 mortgage by 1/1/2025	↑	On schedule
Contribute $50,000 to children's college education	↓	Projected shortfall of $85,000

Figure 4-14: Client financial goals

However, let's say that the client either won't share his financial goals or hasn't even thought through what his financial goals need to be. This is common when dealing with retirement planning, since many clients aren't clear or realistic about their retirement goals. In these situations, FSI could leverage the information that it has about "similar" clients to make retirement goal recommendations. If FSI has the client's current financial investments and current salary, FSI could make a pretty intelligent guess as to the client's retirement goals.

Recommendations Section of Financial Advisor Dashboard

Now let's get into the meat of the financial advisor dashboard. The client information sections of the dashboard were meant to provide an easy and efficient way to capture the client's key lifestyle, demographic, and financial data, as well as his financial goals. Now we can create predictive models to predict the likely results of different financial options and actions, and then create prescriptive models in order to deliver client-specific recommendations that help the client to reach his financial goals. This financial advisor dashboard covers four different areas for delivering client-specific financial recommendations:

- Financial contributions
- Spending analysis
- Asset allocation
- Other financial investments

Financial Contributions Recommendations

The first set of recommendations is focused on helping the client optimize financial contributions (see Figure 4-15). The types of client decisions that could be modeled include:

- Monthly investments and periodic increases and adjustments
- Life insurance coverage adjustments
- Onetime payments to jump-start lagging financial goals
- Reallocate monthly or periodic payments against different financial goals
- Change retirement, new car, and new home target dates

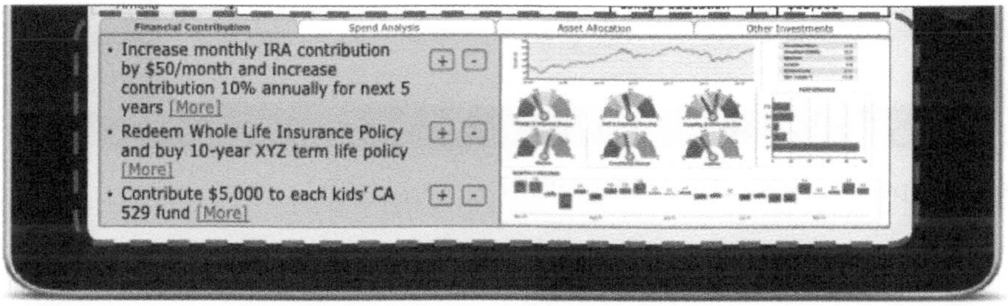

Figure 4-15: Financial contributions recommendations

We could employ data science to analyze the client's detailed financial data, compare that data with benchmarks across similar clients and develop client-specific analytic profiles. The financial advisor dashboard could provide a "what if" capability that allows the financial advisor to work with the client to test out different scenarios (e.g., changes to investment amounts, changes to financial goal target dates).

Spending Analysis Recommendations

The second set of recommendations is focused on helping the client optimize spending habits. This is where access to the client's credit card and banking statements (maybe via Mint.com and/or his checking accounts) could yield valuable insights to help the client minimize cash outflow and increase financial investments (see Figure 4-16). The types of spending decisions that would need to be modeled include:

- Consolidating expenditures of similar products and services
- Flagging expenditures that are abnormally high given the client's family situation, home location, etc.
- Integrating customer loyalty program information to find retailers who can provide best prices on food and household staples
- Increasing insurance deductibles to lower premiums
- Finding more cost-effective home, property, and auto insurance

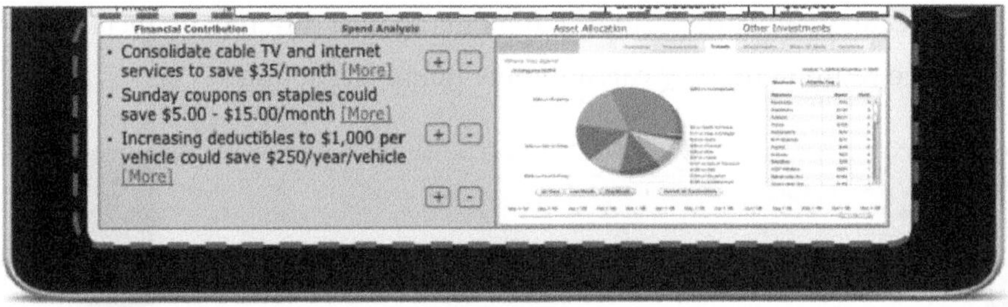

Figure 4-16: Spend analysis and recommendations

There are lots of opportunities to leverage external data sources and best practices across the FSI client base to find better deals in an attempt to reduce the client's discretionary spending. There are several retail, insurance, travel, hospitality, entertainment, cell phone, and other websites from which data could be gathered. This data could be used to create recommendations to reduce the client's spending and optimize the client's monthly budget, with the savings being used to increase financial contributions against the client's financial goals.

Asset Allocation Recommendations

The third set of recommendations is focused on helping clients optimize their asset allocation in light of their financial goals. By leveraging best practices across other clients, portfolios, and investment instruments, prescriptive analytics can be developed to make specific asset allocation recommendations that support asset allocation decisions such as (see Figure 4-17):

- Which stocks and bonds to sell or buy against specific financial goal portfolios
- Portfolio allocation decisions that properly balance the risk-return ratio of the client's portfolio in light of risk tolerance and financial goals
- Other financial instruments that can accelerate the client's progress against financial goals or reduce risk for those short-term financial goals

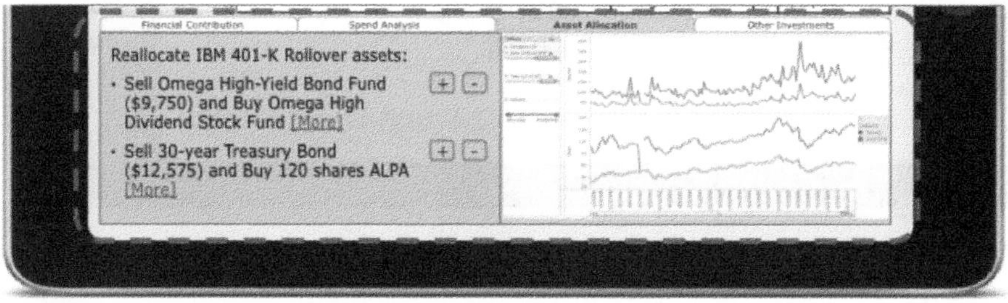

Figure 4-17: Asset allocation recommendations

There are many opportunities to leverage analytic best practices across FSI's client base to make investment recommendations that can improve performance given a client's desired risk level. To further protect the client's investment assets, an aggregated view of the marketplace could yield more timely insights into stocks and bonds that are suddenly hot or cold. This is also an area where real-time analytics can be leveraged to ensure that no sudden market movements expose the client to unnecessary asset allocation risks. The dashboard could also support an interactive "what if" collaboration directly with the client to glean even more data and insights about the client's investment preferences and tolerance for risk.

Other Investment Recommendations

The fourth set of recommendations is focused on other assets that clients need to consider as part of their overall financial strategy. Real estate (the client's home and any vacation homes) is probably the most obvious. This is an area where recommendations about other investment options can be delivered to help support client decisions regarding (see Figure 4-18):

- Identifying the ideal amount of insurance needed given home valuation changes
- Home improvement projects that yield the best ROI for particular house types, budgets, and locations over time
- Identifying the right time to buy or sell a home, and even making recommendations as to what price to bid for homes in select areas
- Best areas to look for secondary and/or vacation home investments
- Most cost-effective locations to live in after retirement

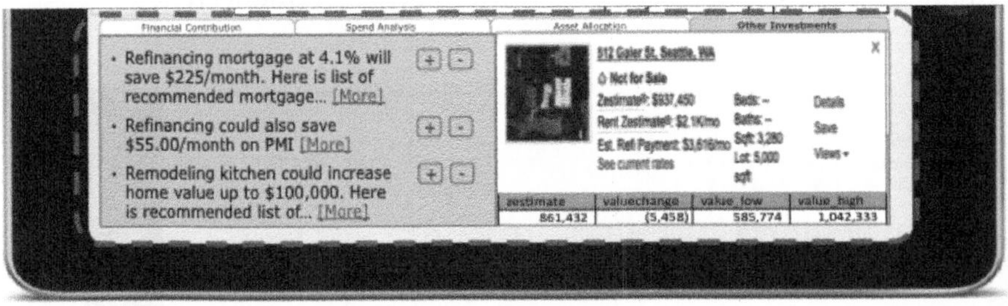

Figure 4-18: Other investment recommendations

There is a bevy of external data sources that can be leveraged to help facilitate analytics in this area. For example, Zillow and Realtor.com provide real estate valuations and monthly changes in real estate valuations that could be incorporated into the financial advisor dashboard. Cost of living metrics, which can be used to identify ideal retirement areas, can be found on many financial websites including data.gov.

Summary

Big data can power a more relevant and more actionable user experience. Instead of overwhelming business users with an endless array of charts, reports, and dashboards and forcing users to "slice and dice" their way to insights, we can instead leverage the wealth of available structured and unstructured data sources, in real-time, coupled with data science to uncover customer, product, and operational insights buried in the data. We can leverage those insights to create frontline employee, manager, and customer recommendations and then measure the effectiveness of those recommendations so that we are continuously refining our analytic models.

Big data can also have serious implications for B2B organizations that rely on brokers, agents, and advisors to reach their ultimate end consumer. While it may frustrate many B2B organizations that they lack that direct engagement with consumers, there are ways that B2B organizations can leverage new sources of data and analytics capabilities to not only improve the effectiveness of their brokers, agents, and advisors but also provide compelling reasons why the brokers, agents, advisors, and end consumers should directly share more data with the B2B organization to create a win-win-win for clients, advisors, and the B2B organization.

Homework Assignment

Use the following exercise to apply what you learned in this chapter.

Exercise #1: Select one of your organization's outward-facing dashboards, websites, or mobile apps. If not something from your organization, then select a website or dashboard that you use regularly. That might include something from your bank, credit card provider, cellular provider, or utility company. Grab a few screen captures of the dashboard or website.

Exercise #2: Think through how you as the user use this dashboard, website, or mobile to make decisions. Write down those decisions that you try to make from the website. For example, from your utility, you might want to make decisions about energy and water consumption, your waste/garbage plan, and maybe even which of the different appliance rebates you might want to consider.

Exercise #3: Next, add a recommendations panel that has suggestions for each of the decisions that you captured in Step 2. For our utility example, one recommendation might be "Only water 3 days a week from 6:00 a.m. to 7:00 a.m. to save approximately $12.50 per month on your monthly water bill." Or another recommendation might be "Replace your existing dryer with a more efficient model like the Samsung DV 457 to save $21.75 on your monthly energy bill."

Exercise #4: Finally, identify potential external data sources that might provide some interesting perspectives that could be used to guide your key decisions. For our utility example, you might want to consider integrating local solar energy costs (to determine if solar energy is a feasible energy option) or weather forecasts (to see if you can reduce lawn watering).

Part

II

Data Science

These three chapters introduce data science as a key business discipline that helps organizations "cross the analytics chasm" from the Business Monitoring to Business Insights and Business Optimization phases. These chapters will introduce the concept of data science and then broaden the discussion to cover what data science techniques to use in which business scenarios.

In This Part

CHAPTER

5

Differences Between Business Intelligence and Data Science

I was hired by a large Internet portal company in 2007 to head up efforts to develop its advertiser analytics. The objective of the advertiser analytics project was to help the Internet portal company's advertisers and agencies optimize their advertising spend across the Internet portal's ad network. The internal code name for the project was "Looking Glass" because we wanted to take the advertisers and agencies through an "Alice in Wonderland" type of experience in how we delivered actionable insights to help our key business stakeholders—Media Planners & Buyers and Campaign Managers—successfully optimize their advertising spend on the Internet portal's ad network. But in many ways, it was me that went through the looking glass.

Several months later (August 2008), I had the opportunity to keynote at The Data Warehouse Institute (TDWI) conference in San Diego. I taught a class at TDWI on how to build analytic applications, so I was both familiar with and a big fan of the TDWI conferences (and still am). However, in my keynote, I told the audience that everything that I had taught them about how to build analytic applications was wrong (see Figure 5-1).

Like with my own personal experience, many organizations and individuals are confused by the differences introduced by big data, especially the differences between Business Intelligence (BI) and data science. Big data is not big BI. Big data is a key enabler of a new discipline called data science that seeks to leverage new sources of structured and unstructured data, coupled with predictive and prescriptive analytics, to uncover new variables and metrics that are better predictors of performance. And while BI and data science share many of the same objectives (getting value out of data, dealing with dirty data, transforming and aligning data, helping support improved decision making), the questions, characteristics, processes, tools, and models couldn't be more different.

This chapter discusses the differences between BI and data science:

- The questions are different.
- The analytic characteristics are different.
- The analytic engagement processes are different.
- The data models are different.
- The business view is different.

Figure 5-1: Schmarzo TDWI keynote, August 2008

So let's start your journey through the "looking glass." I promise that the journey will be enlightening (but no hookah smoking)!

What Is Data Science?

Data science is a complicated new discipline that requires advanced skills and competencies in areas such as statistics, computer science, data mining, mathematics, and computer programming. As had been stated countless times, data scientists are the business "rock stars" of the 21st century.

Although what data scientists do can be quite complex, what they are trying to achieve is not. In fact, I find that the very best introductory book to data science is *Moneyball: The Art of Winning an Unfair Game* by Michael Lewis (W.W. Norton & Company, 2004). The book is about the Oakland A's General Manager Billy Beane's use of sabermetrics to help the small-market Oakland A's professional baseball team outperform competitors with significantly larger bankrolls. The book yields the most accurate description of data science:

> *Data science is about finding new variables and metrics that are better predictors of performance.*

That's it—nothing more—and yes, data science is that simple. But the power of that simple statement is game changing, as can be seen in Figure 5-2 and the success that Billy Beane and the Oakland A's have achieved by making player acquisitions and in-game decisions based on a different, more predictive set of metrics.

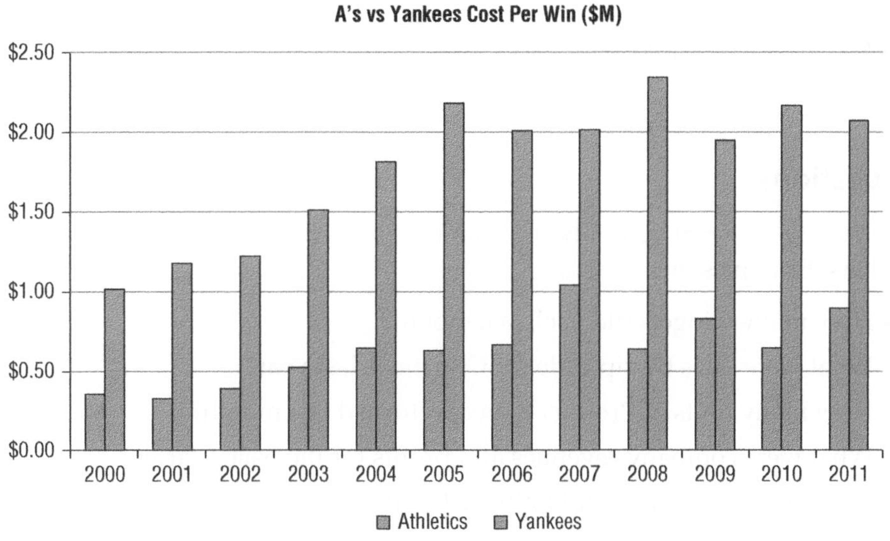

Figure 5-2: Oakland A's versus New York Yankees cost per win

The book also has another valuable lesson: good ideas can be copied. So organizations have to constantly be on the search for those new variables and metrics that are better predictors of performance—to find that next, more predictive "on-base percentage" metric.

BI Versus Data Science: The Questions Are Different

When clients ask me to explain the difference between a Business Intelligence analyst and a data scientist, I start by explaining that the two disciplines have different objectives and seek to answer different types of questions (see Figure 5-3).

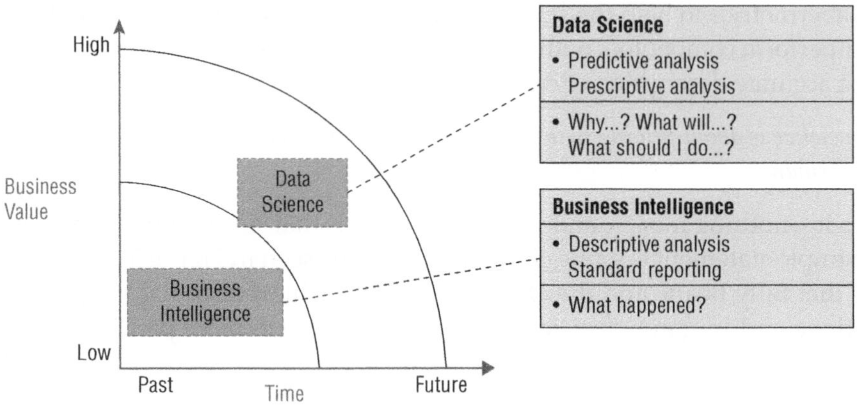

Image courtesy of EMC

Figure 5-3: Business Intelligence versus data science

BI Questions

BI focuses on descriptive analytics: that is, the "What happened?" types of questions. Examples include:

- How many widgets did I sell last month?
- What were sales by zip code for Christmas last year?
- How many units of Product X were returned last month?
- What were company revenues and profits for the past quarter?
- How many employees did I hire last year?

BI focuses on reporting on the current state of the business, or as is now commonly called Business Performance Management (BPM). BI provides retrospective reports to help business users to monitor the current state of the business and answer questions about historical business performance. These reports and questions are critical to the business, sometimes required for regulatory and compliance reasons.

BI can apply some rudimentary analytics (time series analysis, previous period comparisons, indices, shares, and benchmarks) to help business users to flag areas of under- and over-performance. But even these analytics are focused on monitoring what happened to the business.

Data Science Questions

On the other hand, data scientists are in search of variables and metrics that are better predictors of business performance. Consequently, data scientists focus on predictive analytics ("What is likely to happen?") and prescriptive analytics ("What should I do?") types of questions. For example:

- Predictive Questions (What is likely to happen?)
  - How many widgets will I sell next month?
  - What will sales by zip code be over this Christmas season?
  - How many units of Product X will be returned next month?
  - What are projected company revenues and profits for next quarter?
  - How many employees will I need to hire next year?
- Prescriptive Questions (What should I do?)
  - Order [5,000] Component Z to support widget sales for next month.
  - Hire [Y] new sales reps by these zip codes to handle projected Christmas sales.
  - Set aside [$125K] in financial reserve to cover Product X returns.
  - Sell the following product mix to achieve quarterly revenue and margin goals.
  - Increase hiring pipeline by 35 percent to achieve hiring goals.

To answer these predictive and prescriptive questions, data scientists build analytic models in an attempt to *quantify cause and effect*. Chapter 7 covers some of the analytic algorithms and techniques that data scientists might use to help them quantify cause and effect.

The Analyst Characteristics Are Different

Another area of difference between BI and data science is in the attitudinal characteristics and work approach of the people who fill those roles (see Table 5-1).

Table 5-1: BI Analyst Versus Data Scientist Characteristics

AREA	BI ANALYST	DATA SCIENTIST
Focus	Reports, KPIs, trends	Patterns, correlations, models
Process	Static, comparative	Exploratory, experimentation, visual
Data sources	Pre-planned, added slowly	On the fly, as needed
Transform	Up front, carefully planned	In-database, on demand, enrichment
Data quality	Single version of truth	"Good enough," probabilities
Data model	Schema on load	Schema on query
Analysis	Retrospective, descriptive	Predictive, prescriptive

Courtesy: EMC

The differences that jumped out most to me from Table 5-1 were the different perspectives on "data quality." For the BI analyst who is dealing with historical data, the data needs to be 100 percent accurate. BI and data warehouse organizations have invested heavily in data governance and master data management to ensure that the data in the data warehouse are 100 percent accurate.

On the other hand, the data scientist is trying to predict what is likely to happen in the future and, as a result, is dealing with probabilities, confidence levels, *F*-distributions, *t*-tests, and *p*-values. The future is never 100 percent accurate, so data scientists develop a sense of what is "good enough" in trying to predict what is likely to happen and recommend what actions to take. As Yogi Berra, the well-known New York Yankee catcher, was famously quoted, *"It's tough to make predictions, especially about the future."*

It takes a different attitude to be a data scientist, an attitude that accepts failure as a tool for learning. Data scientists learn to embrace failure as part of their agile, fail-fast approach in the search to uncover new metrics and variables that are better predictors of performance. A common approach that the data scientists embrace is modeled after the Cross Industry Standard Process for Data Mining (CRISP) model (see Figure 5-4).

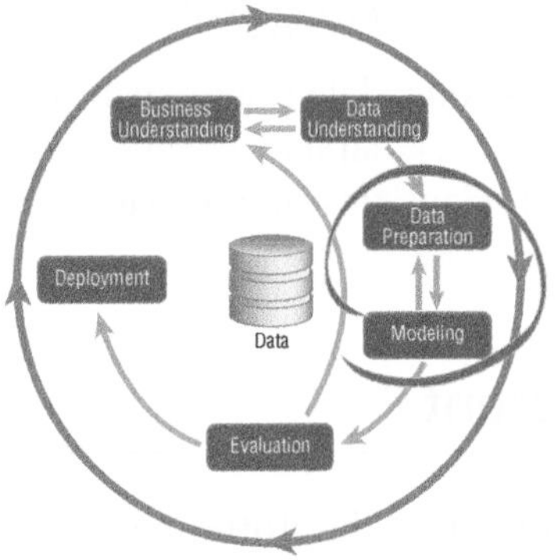

CRISP Stages

- Business Understanding
- Data Understanding
- Data Preparation
- Modeling
- Evaluation
- Deployment

Figure 5-4: CRISP: Cross Industry Standard Process for Data Mining

Data science takes a very similar approach: establish a business hypothesis or question; explore different combinations of data and analytics to build, test, and refine the analytic model; and wash, rinse, and repeat until the model proves that it can provide the required "analytic lift" while reaching a satisfactory goodness of fit. Finally the analytics are deployed or operationalized including possibly rewriting the analytics in a different language to speed the model execution (i.e., in-database analytics) and integrating the analytic models and results into the organization's operational and management systems.

The Analytic Approaches Are Different

Unfortunately, these explanations are insufficient to answer satisfactorily the question of what's different between Business Intelligence and data science. So let's examine closely the different engagement approaches (including goals, tools, and techniques) that the BI analyst and the data scientist use to do their jobs.

Business Intelligence Analyst Engagement Process

The BI analyst engagement process is a discipline that has been documented, taught and refined over three decades of building data warehouses and BI environments. Figure 5-5 provides a high-level view of the process that a typical BI analyst uses when engaging with the business users to build out the BI and supporting data warehouse environments.

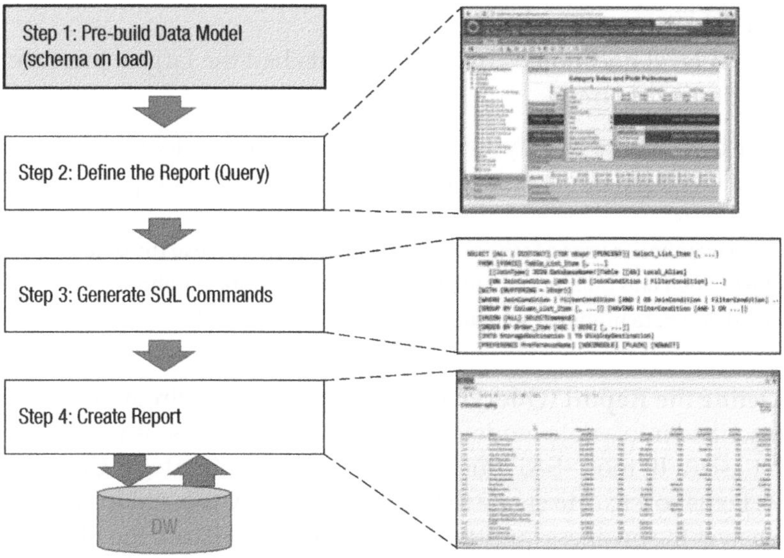

Figure 5-5: Business Intelligence engagement process

Step 1: Pre-build Data Model. The process starts by building the foundational data model. Whether you use a data warehouse or data mart or hub-and-spoke approach, whether you use a star, snowflake, normalized or dimensional schema, the BI analyst must go through a formal requirements gathering process with the business users to identify all (or at least the vast majority of) the questions that the business users want to answer. In this requirements gathering process, the BI analyst must identify the first-and second-level questions the business users want to address in order to build a robust and extensible data model. For example:

First-level question: How many patients did we treat last month?

- Second-level question: How did that compare to the previous month?
- Second-level question: What were the major DRG types treated?

First-level question: How many patients came through ER last night?

- Second-level question: How did that compare to the previous night?
- Second-level question: What were the top admission reasons?

First-level question: What percentage of beds was used at Hospital X last week?

- Second-level question: What is the trend of bed utilization over the past year?
- Second-level question: What departments had the largest increase in bed utilization?

The BI analyst then works closely with the data warehouse team to define and build the underlying data models that support these types of questions.

NOTE **The data warehouse uses a "schema on load" approach because the data schema must be defined and built prior to loading data into the data warehouse. Without an underlying data model or schema, the BI tools will not work.**

Step 2: Define the Report (Query). Once the analytic requirements have been transcribed into a data model, then step 2 of the process is where the BI analyst uses a BI tool—SAP Business Objects, MicroStrategy, Cognos, Qlikview, Pentaho, etc.—to create the SQL-based query to build the report and/or answer the business questions. The BI analyst will use the BI tool's graphical user interface (GUI) to generate the SQL query by selecting the measures and dimensions; selecting page, column, and page descriptors; specifying constraints, subtotals, and totals; creating special calculations (mean, moving average, rank, share of); and selecting sort criteria. The BI tool GUI hides much of the complexity of creating the SQL.

Step 3: Generate SQL Commands. Once the BI analyst or the business user has defined the desired report or query request, the BI tool automatically creates the necessary SQL commands (SQL statements). In some cases, the

BI analyst might modify the SQL commands generated by the BI tool to include unique SQL commands that may not be supported by the BI tool.

Step 4: Create Report. In step 4, the BI tool issues the SQL commands against the data warehouse and creates the corresponding report or dashboard widget. This is a highly iterative process, where the BI analyst will tweak the SQL (either using the GUI or hand-coding the SQL statement) to fine-tune the SQL request. The BI analysts can also specify graphical rendering options (bar charts, line charts, pie charts) until they get the exact report and/or graphic that they want (see Figure 5-6).

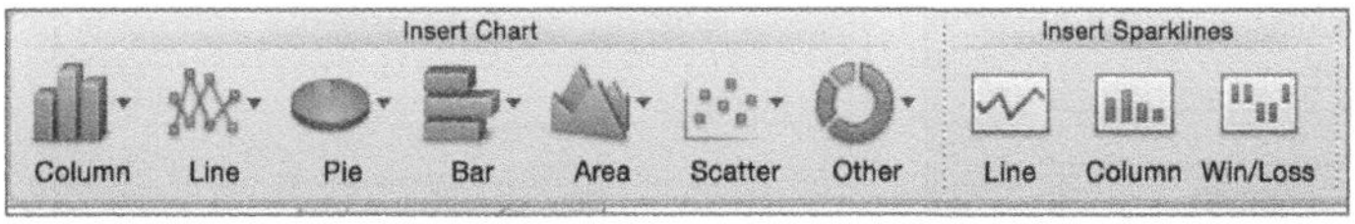

Figure 5-6: Typical BI tool graphic options

The BI tools are very powerful and relatively easy to use if the data model is configured properly. By the way, this is a good example of the power of schema on load. This traditional schema on load approach removes much of the underlying data complexity from the business users who can then use the BI tools graphical user interface to more easily query and explore the data (think self-service BI).

In summary, the BI approach relies on a pre-built data model (schema on load), which enables users to quickly and easily query the data—as long as the data that they want to query is already defined and loaded into the data warehouse. If the data is not in the data warehouse, then adding data to an existing warehouse can take months to make happen. Not only does modifying the data warehouse to include a new data source require a significant amount of time, but the process can be very costly, as data schemas have to be updated to include the new data source, new ETL processes have to be constructed to transform and normalize the data to fit into the updated data schemas, and existing reports and dashboards may have to be updated to include the new data.

The Data Scientist Engagement Process

The data science process is significantly different. In fact, there is very little from the BI analyst engagement process that can be reused in the data science engagement process (see Figure 5-7).

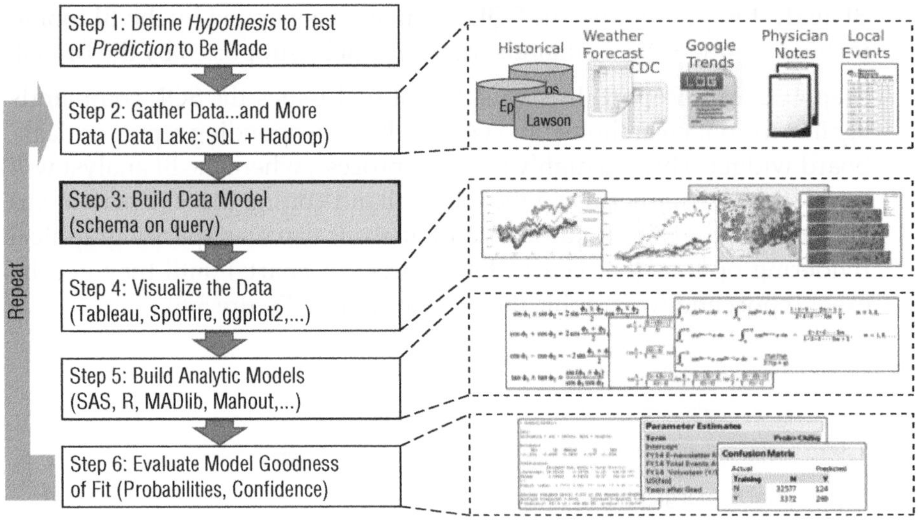

Figure 5-7: Data scientist engagement process

Step 1: Define Hypothesis to Test. Step 1 of the data science engagement process starts with the data scientists identifying the prediction they want to make or hypothesis that they want to test. This is a result of collaborating with the business subject matter expert to understand the key sources of business differentiation (e.g., how the organization delivers value) and then construct the associated hypotheses or predictions.

Step 2: Gather Data…and More Data. In step 2 of the data science engagement process, the data scientist gathers relevant or potentially interesting data from a multitude of sources—both internal and external to the organization—and pushes that data into the data lake or analytic sandbox. The data lake is a great foundational capability for this process, as the data scientists can acquire and ingest any data they want (as-is), test the data for its value given the hypothesis or prediction, and then decide whether to include that data in the analytic model. This is where an envisioning exercise can add considerable value in facilitating the collaboration between the business users and the data scientists to identify data sources that *may* help improve predictive results.

Step 3: Build Data Model. Step 3 is where the data scientists define and build the schema necessary to address the hypothesis being tested. The data scientists can't define the schema until they know the hypothesis that they are testing and understand what data sources they are going to use to build their analytic models.

NOTE **This *schema on query* process is notably different from the traditional data warehouse *schema on load* process. The data scientist doesn't spend months integrating all the different data sources together into a formal data model first. Instead, the data scientist will define the schema as needed based on the data that is being used in the analysis and the requirements of the analytic tool and/or algorithm. The data scientist will likely iterate through several different versions of the schema until finding a schema that supports the analytic model with a sufficient goodness of fit that accepts or rejects the hypothesis being tested.**

Step 4: Visualize the Data. Step 4 of the data science process leverages many of the outstanding data visualization tools available today to uncover relationships, correlations, and outliers in the data. The data scientists will use the data visualization tools to jump-start their analytic process by trying to identify correlations in the data worthy of investigation and outliers in the data that may need special treatment (e.g., log transformations). Data visualization tools like Tableau, Spotfire, DataRPM, and ggplot2 are great data visualization tools for exploring the data and identifying variables that the data scientists *might* want to test.

Step 5: Build Analytic Models. Step 5 is where the real data science work begins—where the data scientists use advanced analytic tools like SAS, SAS Miner, R, Mahout, MADlib, Alpine Miner, H2O, etc. to correlate different variables in an attempt to build a more accurate analytic models. The data scientists will explore different analytic techniques and algorithms to try to create the most predictive models. Again, think probabilities, confidence levels, *F*-distributions, *t*-tests, and *p*-values. Chapter 7 will cover some of the different analytic algorithms that the data scientists might use and in what context.

Step 6: Evaluate Model Goodness of Fit. In step 6, the data scientists ascertain the model's goodness of fit. The goodness of fit of a statistical model describes how well the model fits a set of observations (*F*-test, *p*-value, and *t*-statistic). A number of different analytic techniques will be used to determine the goodness of fit including Kolmogorov–Smirnov test, Pearson's chi-squared test, analysis of variance (ANOVA), and confusion (or error) matrix (see Figure 5-8).

The "goodness of fit" measures how well an analytic model fits a set of observations and measures the extent to which observed data match the values expected or predicted by the analytic model.

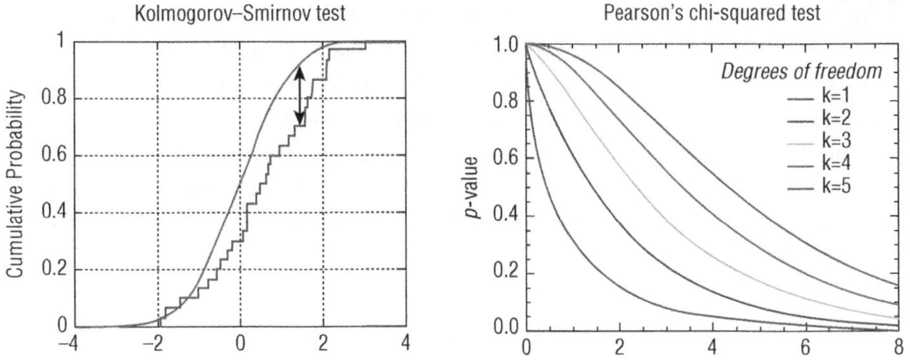

Source: Wikipedia

Figure 5-8: Measuring goodness of fit

The Data Models Are Different

The data models that are used in the data warehouse to support an organization's BI efforts are significantly different from the data models the data scientists prefer to use.

Data Modeling for BI

The world of BI (aka query, reporting, dashboards) requires a data modeling technique that allows business users to create their own reporting and queries. To support this need, Ralph Kimball pioneered dimensional modeling—or star schemas—while at Metaphor Computers back in the 1980s (see Figure 5-9).

The dimensional model was designed to accommodate the analysis needs of the business users, with two important design concepts:

- **Fact tables** (populated with metrics or measures) correspond to transactional systems such as orders, shipments, sales, returns, premiums, claims, accounts receivable, and accounts payable. Facts are typically numeric values that can be aggregated (e.g., averaged, counted, or summed).

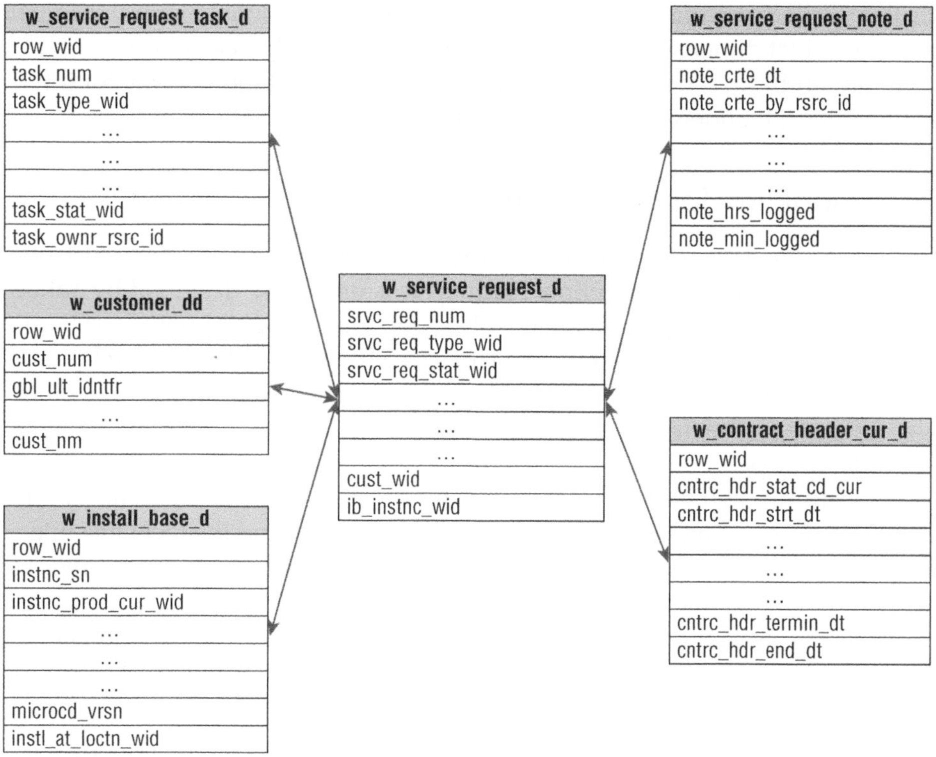

Figure 5-9: Dimensional model (star schema)

- **Dimension tables** (populated with attributes about that dimension) represent the "nouns" of that particular transactional system such as products, markets, stores, employees, customers, and different variations of time. Dimensions are groups of hierarchies and descriptors that describe the facts. It is these dimensional attributes that enable analytic exploration, attributes such as size, weight, location (street, city, state, zip), age, gender, tenure, etc.

Dimensional modeling is ideal for business users because it supports their natural question-and-answer exploration processes. Dimensional modeling supports BI concepts such as drill across (navigating across dimensions) and drill up/drill down (navigating up and down the dimensional hierarchies such as the product dimension hierarchy of product ➪ brand ➪ category).

Today, all BI tools use dimensional modeling as the standard way for interacting with the underlying data warehouse.

Data Modeling for Data Science

In the world of data science, Hadoop provides an opportunity to *think differently* about how we do data modeling. Hadoop was originally designed by Yahoo to deal with very long, flat web logs. Hadoop was designed with very large data blocks (Hadoop default block size is 64 MB to 128 MB versus relational database block sizes that are typically 32 Kb or less). To optimize this block size advantage, the data science team wants very long, flat records and long, flat data models.[1]

For example, some data scientists prefer to "flatten" a star schema by collapsing or integrating the dimensional tables that surround the fact table into a single, flat record in order to construct and execute more complex data queries without having to use joins (see Figure 5-10).

As an example in Figure 5-10, instead of three different star schemas with conformed or shared dimensions to link the different star schemas, the data science team wants three long, flat files with the following customer data:

- Customer demographics (age, gender, current and previous home addresses, value of current and previous home, history of marital status, kids and their ages and genders, current and previous income, etc.)
- Customer purchase history (annual purchases including items purchased, returns, prices paid, discounts, coupons, location, day of week, time of day, weather condition, temperatures)
- Customer social activities (entire history of social media posts, likes, shares, tweets, favorites, retweets, etc.)

[1] Apache Hadoop is an open-source software framework written in Java for distributed storage and distributed processing of very large data sets on computer clusters built from commodity hardware. All the modules in Hadoop are designed with a fundamental assumption that hardware failures (of individual machines or racks of machines) are commonplace and thus should be automatically handled in software by the framework. (Source: Wikipedia)

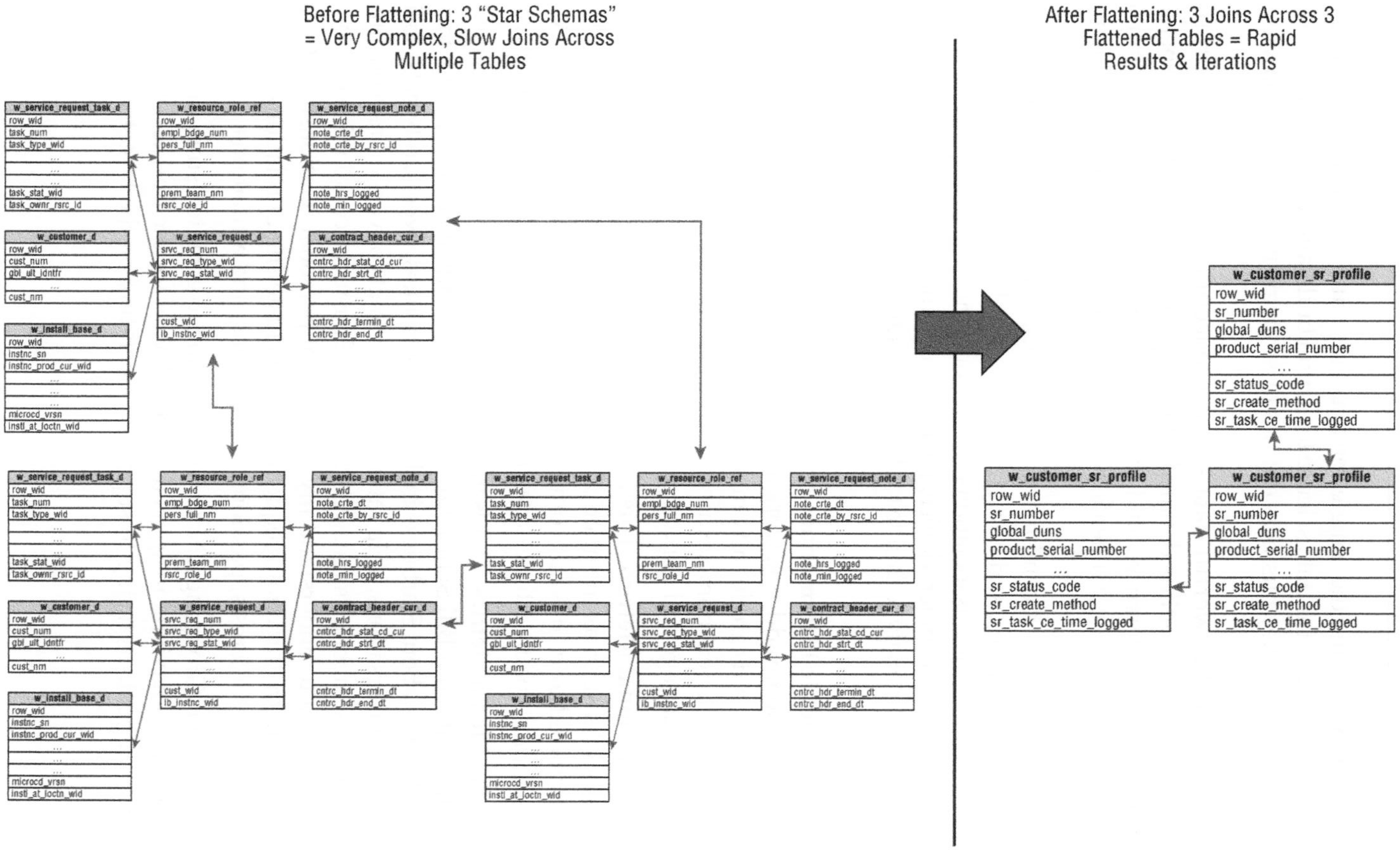

Figure 5-10: Using flat files to eliminate or reduce joins on Hadoop

The View of the Business Is Different

Instead of trying to build the "single version of the truth" or create a "360-degree view of the customer," the data science team will build analytic profiles on each of the organization's key business entities or strategic nouns at the individual entity level.

One of the most powerful data science concepts is the analytic profile. The data science team builds detailed analytic profiles that capture the behaviors, propensities, preferences, and tendencies of individual business entities (e.g., customers, merchants, students, patients, doctors, wind turbines, jet engines, ATMs).

An analytic profile is a combination of metrics, key performance indicators, scores, association rules, and analytic insights combined with the tendencies, behaviors, propensities, associations, affiliations, interests, and passions for an individual entity (customer, device, partner, machine).

For example, the analytic profile for Bill Schmarzo for Starbucks might include the following:

- **Demographic Information.** This is the basic information about me such as name, home address, work address, age, gender, marital status, length of time as gold card loyalty member, income level, value of home, length of time at current home, education level, number of dependents, age and make of car, age and gender of children, etc.
- **Transactional Metrics.** This is information about my transactions with Starbucks such as number of purchases, purchase amounts, product purchased and in what combinations, frequency of visits, recency of visits, most common time of day for visits, stores visited most frequently, etc.
- **Social Media Metrics.** This is information gathered about any social media comments that Bill Schmarzo might have made across different social media sites about Starbucks including posts, likes, tweets, retweets, social media conversations, Yelp ratings, blogs, e-mail conversations, consumer comments, mobile usage, web clicks, etc. Starbucks could mine the social media data to understand my network of personal relationships (number, strength, direction, sequencing, and clustering of relationships) and capture my interests, passions, associations, and affiliations.
- **Behavioral Groupings.** Now we're starting to get interesting, as we want to create behavioral insights that are relevant for the business initiatives that Starbucks is trying to support. Depending on the targeted business

initiative (customer retention, customer up-sell, customer advocacy, new store locations, channel sales, etc.), here is some behavioral information that Starbucks might want to capture about me: favorite drinks in rank order, favorite stores in rank order, most frequent time of day to visit a store, most frequent day of week to visit a store, recency of store visit, frequency of store visits in past week/month/quarter, how long do I stay at which stores ("pass thru" or "linger"), etc.

- **Classifications.** Now we want to create some "classifications" about Bill Schmarzo's life that might have impact on Starbucks's key business initiatives such as life stage classification (long marriage, kid in college, kid at home, weight/diet conscious, etc.), lifestyle classification (heavy traveler, heavy chai tea drinker, light exerciser, and so on), or product classification (morning coffee/oatmeal consumer, afternoon frap/cookie consumer, etc.).
- **Association Rules.** We might also want to capture some propensities about Bill's usage patterns that we can use to support Starbucks's key business initiatives, including propensity to buy oatmeal when he buys his venti chai latte when traveling in the morning, propensity to buy a cookie/pastry when traveling in the afternoon, propensity to buy product in the channel, etc.
- **Scores.** We also may want to create scores to support decision-making and process optimization. Scores that we might want to create (again, depending on Starbucks's key business initiatives) could include advocacy score (which measures my likelihood to recommend Starbucks and make positive comments for Starbucks on social media), loyalty score (which measures my likelihood to continue to visit Starbucks stores and buy Starbucks products versus competitors), product usage score (which is a measure of how much Starbucks product I consume—and revenue I generate—when I visit a Starbucks store), etc.

A profile could be made up of hundreds of metrics and scores that—when used in combination against a specific business initiative like customer retention, customer up-sell, new product introductions, or customer advocacy—can improve the predictive capabilities of the model (see Figure 5-11).

Some metrics and scores are more important than others, depending on the business initiative being addressed. For example, a financial services firm focused on customer acquisition, disposable income, retirement readiness, life stage, age, education level, and number of family members data may be the most important predictive metrics. However, for that same financial services firm focused on customer retention, metrics such as advocacy, customer satisfaction, attrition risk, social network associations, and select social media relationships may be the most important predictive metrics.

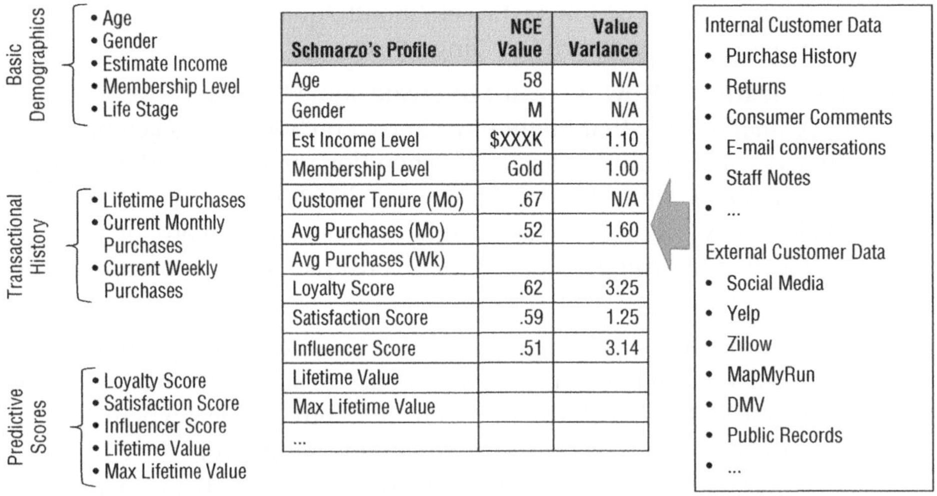

Figure 5-11: Sample customer analytic profile

For example, against a customer retention business initiative, an organization could compare a customer's most recent activities (e.g., purchases, mobile app usage, website visits, consumer comments, social posts) to the historical data, metrics, and scores that compose that customer's analytic profile in order to determine (score) his or her likelihood to attrite. If the customer's "Attrition Score" is above a certain level, then the organization could deliver a personalized "next best offer" in order to preempt customer attrition. The analysis process for the "Improve Customer Retention" business initiative is laid out in Figure 5-12.

The analysis process works like this:

Step 1: Establish a hypothesis that you want to test. In our customer retention example, our test hypothesis is that "Premium gold card members with greater than five days without a purchase or mobile app engagement have 25 to 30 percent higher probability of churn than similar customers."

Step 2: Identify and quantify the most important metrics or scores to predict a certain business outcome. In our example, the metrics and scores that we're going to use to test our customer attrition hypothesis includes

Customer Tenure (in months), Customer Satisfaction Score, Average Monthly Purchases, and Customer Loyalty Score. Notice that the metrics do not have the same weight (or confidence level). Some metrics and scores are more important than others in predicting performance given the test hypothesis.

Step 3: Employ the predictive metrics to build detailed profiles for each individual customer with respect to the hypothesis to be tested.

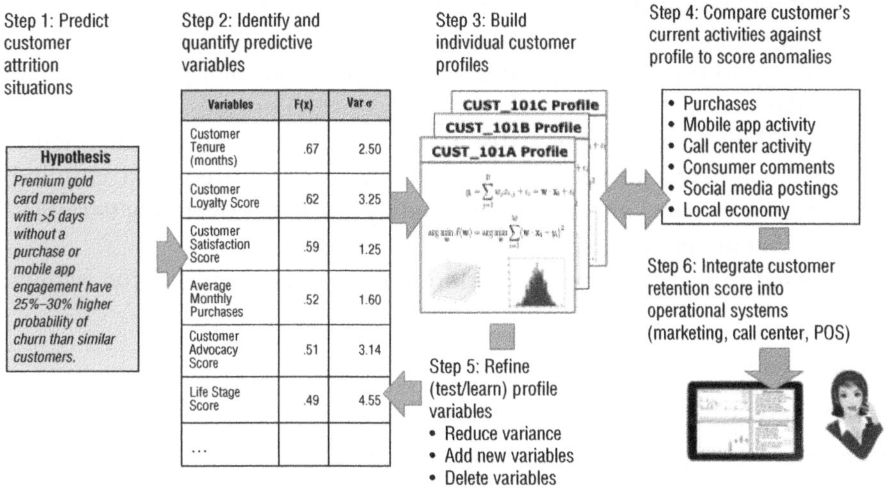

Figure 5-12: Improve customer retention example

Step 4: Compare an individual's recent activities and current state with his or her profile in order to flag unusual behaviors and actions that may be indicative of a customer retention problem. In our customer retention example, we might want to create a "Customer Attrition" score that quantifies the likelihood that particular customer is going to leave, and then create specific recommendations as to what actions or "next best offers" can be delivered to retain that customer.

Step 5: Continue to seek out new data sources and new metrics that may be better predictors of attrition. This is also the part of the data science process to continuously try to improve the accuracy and confidence levels of the metrics and scores using sensitivity analysis and simulations like the Monte Carlo experiments.

Step 6: Integrate the analytic insights, scores, and recommendations into the key operational systems (likely CRM, direct marketing, point of sales, and call center for the customer retention business initiative) in order to ensure that the insights uncovered by the analysis are actionable by frontline or customer-engaging employees.

Summary

Organizations are realizing that data science is very different from BI and that one does not replace the other. Both combine to provide the "dynamic duo" of analytics—one focused on monitoring the current state of the business and the other trying to predict what is likely to happen and then prescribe what actions to take.

Big data is a key enabler of a new discipline called data science. Data science seeks to leverage new sources of structured and unstructured data, coupled with advanced predictive and prescriptive analytics, to uncover new variables and metrics that are better predictors of performance.

As discussed in this chapter, BI is different from data science in the following ways:

- The questions are different.
- The analytic characteristics are different.
- The analytic engagement processes are different.
- The data models are different.
- The business view is different.

This chapter also introduced the very important data science concept called analytic profiles. Organizations are learning that more important than trying to create a 360-degree profile of the customer is identifying and quantifying those fewer but more important metrics that are better predictors of business or customer performance such as optimizing key business processes, influencing customer behaviors, and uncovering new monetization opportunities.

Hopefully your journey through the "looking glass" was as enlightening to you as it was to me!

Homework Assignment

Use the following exercises to apply what you learned in this chapter.

Exercise #1: Describe the key differences between BI and data science and what those differences mean to your organization.

Exercise #2: List sample descriptive (What happened?), predictive (What is likely to happen?), and prescriptive (What actions should I take?) questions that are relevant to the targeted business initiative that you identified in Chapter 2.

Exercise #3: For the targeted business initiative identified in Chapter 2, list some of the key metrics and variables that you might want to capture in order to support the predictive and prescriptive questions listed in Exercise #2.

CHAPTER

6

Data Science 101

There are many excellent books and courses focused on teaching people how to become a data scientist. Those books and courses provide detailed material and exercises that teach the key capabilities of data science such as statistical analysis, data mining, text mining, SQL programming, and other computing, mathematical, and analytic techniques. That is not the purpose of this chapter.

The purpose of Chapter 6 is to introduce some different analytic algorithms that business users should be aware of and to discuss when it might be most appropriate to use which types of algorithms. You do not need to be a data scientist to understand when and why to apply these analytic algorithms. A more detailed understanding of these different analytic algorithms will help the business users to collaborate with the data science team to uncover those variables and metrics that may be better predictors of business performance.

Data Science Case Study Setup

Data science is a complicated topic that certainly cannot be given justice in a single chapter. So to help grasp some of the data science concepts that are covered in Chapter 6, you are going to create a fictitious company against which you can apply the different analytic algorithms. Hopefully this will make the different data science concepts "come to life."

Our fictitious company, Fairy-Tale Theme Parks ("The Parks"), has multiple amusement parks across North America and wants to employ big data and data science in order to:

- Deliver a more positive and compelling guest experience in an increasingly competitive entertainment marketplace;
- Determine maximum potential guest lifetime value (MPGTV) to use as the basis for determining guest promotional spend and discounts and prioritizing Priority Access passes and in-park hotel rooms;
- Promote new technology-heavy 3D attractions (Terror Airline and Zombie Apocalypse) to ensure the successful adoption and long-term viability of those new rides that appeal to new guest segments;
- Ensure the success of new movie and TV characters in order to increase associated licensing revenues and ensure long-term character viability for new movie and TV sequels.

The Parks is deploying a mobile app called Fairy-Tale Chaperon that engages guests as they move through the park and helps guests enjoy the different attractions, entertainment, retail outlets, and restaurants. Fairy-Tale Chaperon will:

- Deliver Priority Access passes to different attractions and reward their most important guests with digital coupons, discounts, and "Fairy Dust" (money equivalent that can be spent only in the park).
- Promote social media posts to drive gamification and rewards around contests such as most social posts, most popular social posts, and most popular photos and videos.
- Track guest flow and in-park traffic patterns, tendencies, and propensities in order to determine which attractions to promote (to increase attraction traffic) and which attractions guests should avoid because of long wait times.
- Deliver real-time guest dining and entertainment recommendations based on guests' areas of interest and seat/table availability for select restaurants and entertainment.
- Reward guests who share their social media information that can be used to monitor guest real-time satisfaction and enjoyment via Facebook, Twitter, and Instagram. It also provides an opportunity to promote select photos in order to start viral marketing campaigns.

This chapter reviews a number of different analytic techniques. You are not expected to become an expert in these different analytic algorithms. However, the more you understand what these analytic algorithms can do, the better position you are in to collaborate with your data science team and suggest the art of the possible to your business leadership team.

Fundamental exploratory analytic algorithms that are covered in Chapter 6 are:

- Trend analysis
- Boxplots
- Geography (spatial) analysis
- Pairs plot
- Time series decomposition

More advanced analytic algorithms that are covered in this chapter are:

- Cluster analysis
- Normal curve equivalent (NCE) analysis
- Association analysis
- Graph analysis
- Text mining
- Sentiment analysis
- Traverse pattern analysis
- Decision tree classifier analysis
- Cohorts analysis

Throughout the chapter, you will contemplate how The Parks could leverage each of these different analytic techniques.

NOTE **Throughout this chapter I provide links to sites that can help you get comfortable with these different analytic algorithms. Many of the sites have exercises that use R.[1] I strongly recommend downloading R and RStudio now!**

NOTE **I commonly use Wikipedia to refine the definitions of many of these different analytic algorithms. Wikipedia is a great source for more details on each of these analytic algorithms.**

---

[1] R is a programming language and software environment for statistical computing and graphics. The R language is widely used among statisticians and data miners for developing statistical software and data analysis. R's popularity has increased substantially in recent years. (Source: Wikipedia)

Fundamental Exploratory Analytics

Let's start by covering some basic statistical analysis that was likely covered in your first statistics course (yes, I realize that you probably sold your stats book the minute the stats class was over). Trend analysis, boxplots, geographical analysis, pairs plot, and time series decomposition are examples of exploratory analytic algorithms that the data scientists use to get a "feel for the data." These exploratory analytic algorithms help the data science team to better understand the data content and gain a high-level understanding of relationships and patterns in the data.

Trend Analysis

Trend analysis is a fundamental visualization technique to spot patterns, trends, relationships, and outliers across a time series of data. One of the most basic yet very powerful exploratory analytics, trend analysis (applying different plotting techniques and graphic visualizations) can quickly uncover customer, operational, or product trends and events that tend to happen together or happen at some period of regularity (see Figure 6-1).

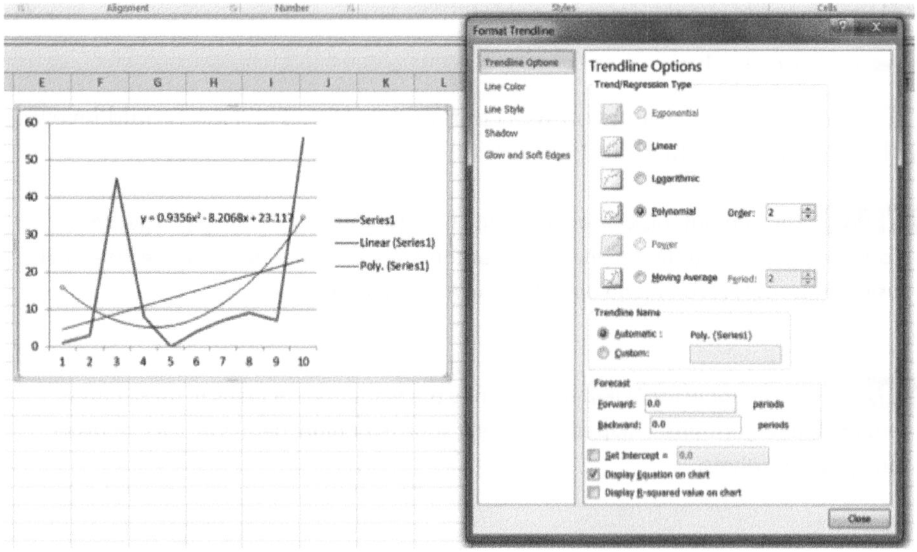

Figure 6-1: Basic trend analysis

In Figure 6-1, the data scientist manually tested a number of different trending options in order to identify the "best fit" trend line (in this example, using Microsoft Excel). Once the data scientist identifies the best trending option, the data scientist can automate the generation of the trend lines using R.

Next, the data scientist might want to dissect the trend line across a number of different business dimensions (e.g., products, geographies, sales territories, markets) in order to undercover patterns and trends at the next level of granularity. The data scientist can then write a program to juxtapose the detailed trend lines into the same chart so that it is easier to spot trends, patterns, relationships, and outliers buried in the granular data (see Figure 6-2).

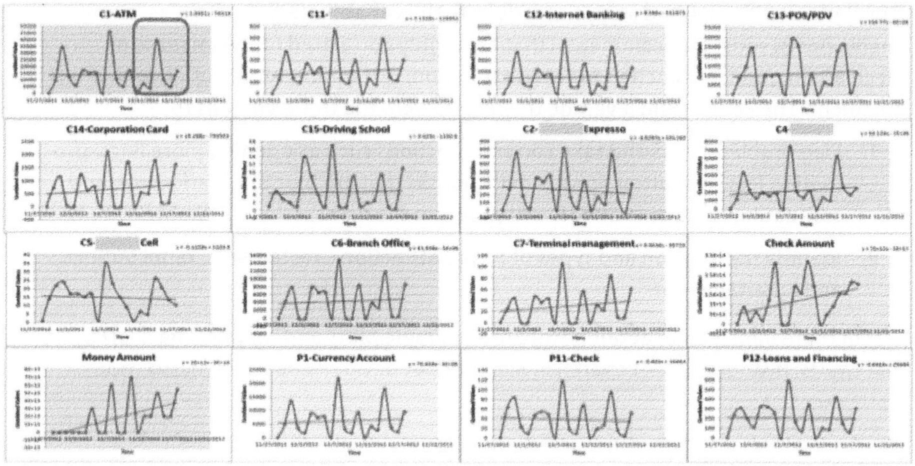

Figure 6-2: Compound trend analysis

Finally, trend analysis yields mathematical models for each of the trend lines. These mathematical models can be used to quantify reoccurring patterns or behaviors in the data. The most interesting insights from the trend lines can then be flagged for further investigation by the data science team (see Figure 6-3).

Type	Trend	Description
C1	y=2.0361x – 70319	C1-ATM
C11	y=3.1559x – 129991	C11-
C12	y=8.569x – 351973	C12-Internet Banking
C13	y=154.77x – 6E+06	C13-POS/PDV(usage of portable card reader)
C14	y=19.288x – 794994	C14-Corporation Card
C15	y=0.029x – 1190.9	C15-Driving School
C2	y=-4.6297x + 191240	C2- Expresso
C4	y=50.128x + 2E+06	C4-
C5	y=-0.1258x + 5203.8	C5- Cell
C6	y=61.958x + 3E+06	C6-Branch Office
C7	y=0.9636x + 39720	C7-Terminal management
Check Amount	y=7E+12x + 3E+17	Check Amount
Money Amount	y=2E+12x – 9E+16	Money Amount
P1	y=70.959x – 3E+06	P1-Currency Account
P11	y=-0.403x + 16663	P11-Check
P12	y=-0.6419x – 26684	P12-Loans and Financing
P14	y=152.51x – 6E+06	P14-Payments
P2	y=36.385x – 1E+06	P2-Savings Account
P22	y=-0.2699x + 11188	P22-Pension Account
P5	y=149.61x – 6E+06	P5-Debit Card
P6	y=1.7236x – 70460	P6-Credit Card
P7	y=-98.266x + 4E+06	P7-Salary Card
P9	y=-4.0006x + 168915	P9-Corporation Card
Unique Account	y=-211.32x + 9E+06	Unique Account
Volume	y=287.14x – 1E+07	Volume

- Branch, ATM, and Internet Service have positive growth. ***Branch office service could convert more into ATM and Internet Banking.***
- Branch, ATM, and Internet Service have positive growth. XYZ Express has negative growth. This may mean the ***XYZ Express users convert into XYZ Branches users.***
- Internet Banking and POS/PDV have positive growth. ***Move more customers to the web.***
- ATMs drive positive growth. ***More XYZ ATM potential users are in this area.***
- XYZ Cell has minor negative growth and BankCo has positive growth. ***This may mean XYZ Cell users may have called in for complaints or services.***

Figure 6-3: Trend line analysis

WARNING Some business users try to use trend analysis to predict future events through simple time series extrapolations. Extrapolating a time series trend to predict future behaviors and events is common but highly risky unless you operate within a 100 percent stable environment.

THE PARKS RAMIFICATIONS

The Parks could use trend analysis to identify the variables (e.g., wait times, social media posts, consumer comments) that are highly correlated to the increase or decrease in guest satisfaction for each attraction, restaurant, retail outlet, and entertainment. The Parks could leverage the results from the trend analysis to

1. Flag problem areas and take corrective actions such as opening more lines, promoting less busy attractions, moving kiosks that are blocking traffic flow, and resituating characters at different points in the parks;
2. Identify the location and types of future attractions, restaurants, retail outlets, and entertainment.

For more information about how to make simple plots and graphs (line charts, bar charts, histograms, dot charts) in R, check out `http://www.harding.edu/fmccown/r/`.

Boxplots

Boxplots are one of the more interesting and visually creative exploratory analytic algorithms. Boxplots quickly visualize variations in the base data and can be used to identify outliers in the data worthy of further investigation. A boxplot is a convenient way of graphically depicting groups of numerical data through their quartiles. Boxplots may also have lines extending vertically from the boxes (whiskers) indicating variability outside the upper and lower quartiles, hence the terms *box-and-whisker plot* and *box-and-whisker diagram* (see Figure 6-4).

One can quickly see the distribution of key data elements from the Boxplot in Figure 6-4. When you change the dimensions against which you are doing the boxplots, underlying patterns and relationships in the data start to surface.

THE PARKS RAMIFICATIONS

The Parks can employ boxplots to determine its most loyal guests for each of the park's attractions (e.g., Canyon Copter Ride, Monster Mansion, Space Adventure, Ghoulish Gulch). The Parks can use the results of the boxplot analysis to create guest current and maximum lifetime value scores against which to prioritize to whom to reward with Priority Access passes and other coupons and discounts.

For more information about creating boxplots in R, check out `http://www.r-bloggers.com/box-plot-with-r-tutorial/`.

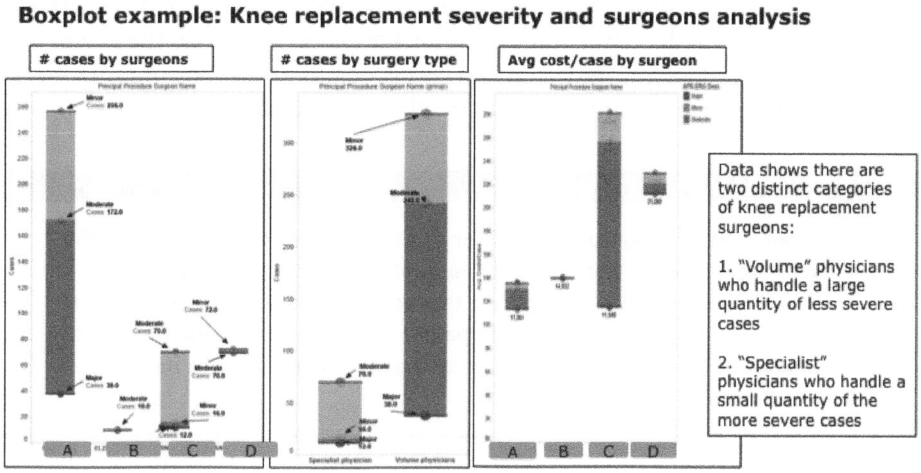
Boxplot example: Knee replacement severity and surgeons analysis
cases by surgeons
cases by surgery type
Avg cost/case by surgeon
Data shows there are two distinct categories of knee replacement surgeons:
1. "Volume" physicians who handle a large quantity of less severe cases
2. "Specialist" physicians who handle a small quantity of the more severe cases
A
B
C
D

Figure 6-4: Boxplot analysis

Geographical (Spatial) Analysis

Geographical or spatial analysis includes techniques for analyzing geographical activities and conditions using a business entity's topological, geometric, or geographic properties. For example, geographical analysis supports the integration of zip code and data.gov economic data with a client's internal data to provide insights about the success of the organization's geographical reach and market penetration (see Figure 6-5).

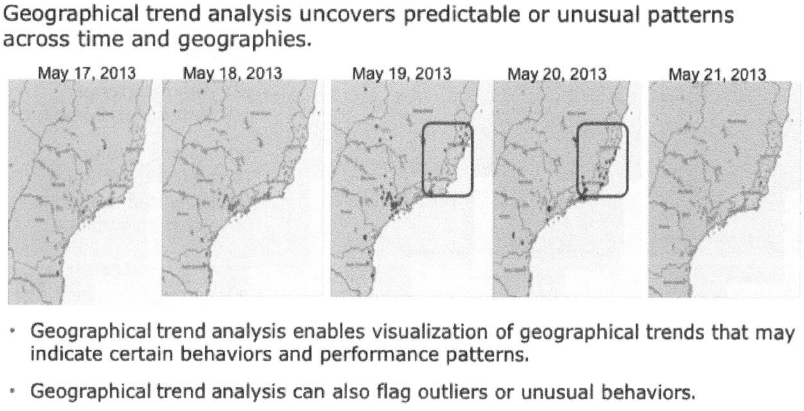
Geographical trend analysis uncovers predictable or unusual patterns across time and geographies.
May 17, 2013
May 18, 2013
May 19, 2013
May 20, 2013
May 21, 2013
• Geographical trend analysis enables visualization of geographical trends that may indicate certain behaviors and performance patterns.
• Geographical trend analysis can also flag outliers or unusual behaviors.

Figure 6-5: Geographical (spatial) trend analysis

In the example in Figure 6-5, geographical analysis is combined with trend analysis in order to identify changes in market patterns across the organization's key markets. Geographical analysis is especially useful for organizations looking to determine the success of their sales and marketing efforts.

THE PARKS RAMIFICATIONS

The Parks can conduct geographical trend analysis to spot any changes (at both the zip+4 and household levels) in the geo-demographics of guests over time and by seasonality and holidays. The Parks can use the results of this geographical plus seasonality analysis to create geo-specific campaigns and promotions with the objective of increasing attendance from under-penetrated geographical areas by day of week, holidays, and seasonality.

Pairs Plot

Pairs plot analysis may be my favorite analytics algorithm. Pairs plot analysis allows the data scientist to spot potential correlations using pairwise comparisons across multiple variables. Pairs plot analysis provides a deep view into the different variables that may be correlated and can form the basis for guiding the data science team in the identification of key variables or metrics to include in the development of predictive models (see Figure 6-6).

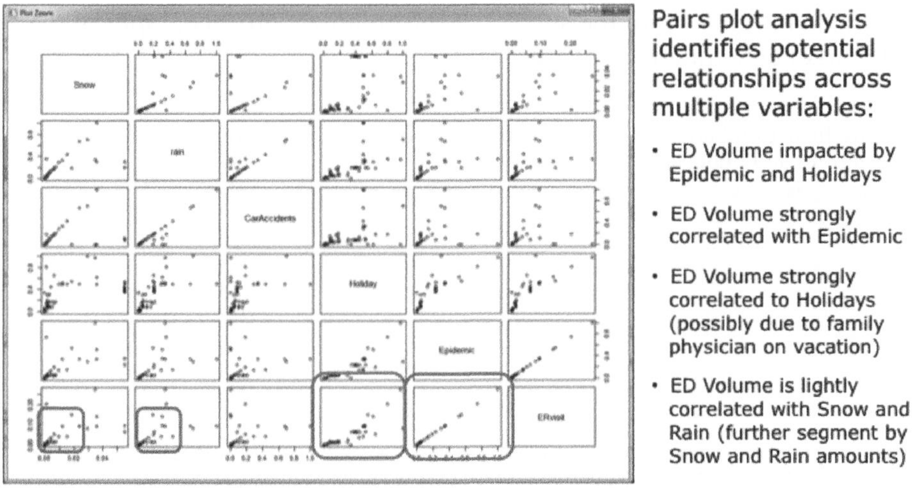
Pairs plot analysis identifies potential relationships across multiple variables:
• ED Volume impacted by Epidemic and Holidays
• ED Volume strongly correlated with Epidemic
• ED Volume strongly correlated to Holidays (possibly due to family physician on vacation)
• ED Volume is lightly correlated with Snow and Rain (further segment by Snow and Rain amounts)

Figure 6-6: Pairs plot analysis

Pairs plot analysis does lots of the grunt work of quickly pairing up different variables and dimensions so that one can quickly spot potential relationships in the data worthy of more detailed analysis (see the boxes in Figure 6-6).

> **THE PARKS RAMIFICATIONS**
>
> **The Parks can leverage pairs plot analysis to compare a multitude of variables to identify those variables that drive guests to particular attractions, entertainment, retail outlets, and restaurants. The Parks can use the results of the analysis to drive in-park promotional decisions and offers that direct guests to under-utilized attractions, entertainment, retail outlets, and restaurants.**
>
> **Additional paired plot options in R (e.g., pairs, splom, plotmatrix, ggcorplot, panelcor) can be found at** `http://www.r-bloggers.com/five-ways-to-visualize-your-pairwise-comparisons/`.

Time Series Decomposition

Time series decomposition expands on the basic trend analysis by decomposing the traditional trend analysis into three underlying components that can provide valuable customer, product, or operational performance insights. These trend analysis components are

- **Cyclical** component that describes repeated but non-periodic fluctuations,
- **Seasonal** component that reflects seasonality (seasonal variation),
- **Irregular** component (or "noise") that describes random, irregular influences and represents the residuals of the time series after the other components have been removed.

From the time series decomposition analysis, a business user can spot particular areas of interest in the decomposed trend data that may be worthy of further analysis (see Figure 6-7).

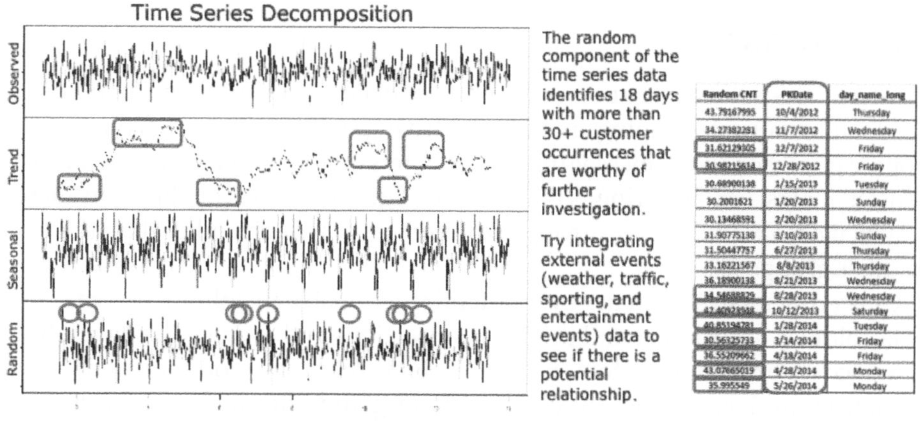
Time Series Decomposition
Observed
Trend
Seasonal
Random
The random component of the time series data identifies 18 days with more than 30+ customer occurrences that are worthy of further investigation.
Try integrating external events (weather, traffic, sporting, and entertainment events) data to see if there is a potential relationship.
Random CNT
PKDate
day_name_long
10/4/2012 Thursday
11/7/2012 Wednesday
12/7/2012 Friday
12/28/2012 Friday
1/15/2013 Tuesday
1/20/2013 Sunday
2/20/2013 Wednesday
3/10/2013 Sunday
6/27/2013 Thursday
8/8/2013 Thursday
8/21/2013 Wednesday
8/28/2013 Wednesday
10/12/2013 Saturday
1/28/2014 Tuesday
3/14/2014 Friday
4/18/2014 Friday
4/28/2014 Monday
5/26/2014 Monday

Figure 6-7: Time series decomposition analysis

For example in examining Figure 6-7, one can spot unusual occurrences in the areas of Seasonality and Trend (highlighted in the boxes) that may suggest the inclusion of additional data sources (such as weather or major sporting and entertainment events data) in an attempt to explain those unusual occurrences.

THE PARKS RAMIFICATIONS

The Parks can deploy time series decomposition analysis to identify and quantify the impact that seasonality and specific events are having on guest visits and associated spend. The Parks can use the results of the analysis to

1. **Create season-specific marketing campaigns and promotions to increase guest visits and associated spend,**
2. **Determine which events outside of the theme parks (concerts, professional sporting events, BCS football games) are worthy of promotional and sponsorship spend.**

For more information about time series decomposition in R, check out `http://www.r-bloggers.com/time-series-decomposition/`.

Analytic Algorithms and Models

The following analytic algorithms start to move the data scientist beyond the data exploration stage into the more predictive stages of the analysis process. These analytic algorithms by their nature are more actionable, allowing the data scientist to quantify cause and effect and provide the foundation to predict what is likely to happen and recommend specific actions to take.

Cluster Analysis

Cluster analysis is used to uncover insights about how customers and/or products cluster into natural groupings in order to drive specific actions or recommendations (e.g., personalized messaging, target marketing, maintenance scheduling). Cluster analysis or clustering is the exercise of grouping a set of objects in such a way that objects in the same group are more similar to each other than to those in other groups (clusters).

Clustering analysis can uncover potential actionable insights across massive data volumes of customer and product transactions and events. Cluster analysis can uncover groups of customers and products that share common behavioral tendencies and, consequently, and can be targeted with the same marketing treatments (see Figure 6-8).

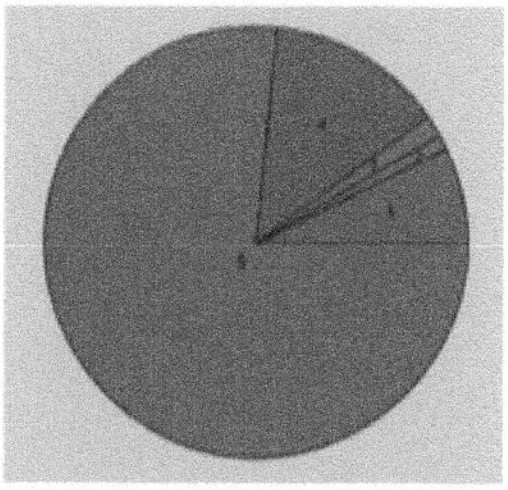

The most important clustering factors are slot_cnt, table_cnt, Wday, Hotel_nights, Hotel_rooms, and Diff_day that yielded 5 cluster:

- Group 1: Players focus on the very selected slot (avg = 2.4) and tables games (avg = 8.25).
- Group 2: Players focus primarily on the table games (avg = 24.4) with wilder choices. This is different from group 1 with table game focused.
- Group 3: Players focus primarily on the slot machines games with large variety (avg=51.47).
- Group 4: Players focus slot machine games (avg = 18.63).
- Group 5: Players tend to solely focus on specific slot machines (avg = 2.35) with higher hotel stays. It is very different from group 3 that also focuses on the slot machine).

cluster ID	Monday	Tuesday	Wednesday	Thursday	Friday	Saturday	Sunday	Total
1	165	203	194	205	320	365	311	1763
2	32	26	26	30	43	49	48	254
3	90	39	43	92	65	94	91	514
4	301	297	334	420	564	673	668	3257
5	2462	2527	2712	2897	2600	2748	2691	18637

cluster ID	Stat	Slot_cnt	Table_cnt	Diff_date_tck	Ticket_cnt	Hotel_nig		
1	Mean	2.468820862	8.247165533	0.126984127	0.009070295	0.2947		
	Variance	15.29851682	9.65753592	13.22493225	0.027144002	0.59030		
2	Mean	2.681102362	24.44094488	0	0	0.35826		
	Variance	27.74375214	59.97080701	0	0	0.69722		
3	Mean	51.74441687	0.461538462	0.004962779	0.004962779	0.379652605	0.379652605	0.406947891
	Variance	297.5588929	1.905855339	0.009925558	0.009925558	0.644062566	0.644062566	0.868807328
4	Mean	18.63616825	0.37703408	0.375498925	0.012588271	0.269266196	0.271108382	0.292293522
	Variance	40.70634502	1.144042429	34.11110713	0.035775148	0.543873939	0.569290939	0.698936292
5	Mean	2.352470891	0.426141546	0.189247196	0.009175296	0.673445297	0.675913505	0.695820143
	Variance	8.460378768	0.940630169	16.45726149	0.026048027	0.888204984	0.898181883	1.033086735

Figure 6-8: Cluster analysis

NOTE I can use a pie chart in Figure 6-8 because I was dealing with only a small number of clusters. Generally speaking, pie charts are not good for conveying information because a large number of pie segments obscures the data and makes it hard to uncover any underlying trends or relationships buried in the data.

THE PARKS RAMIFICATIONS

The Parks can leverage cluster analysis to create more actionable profiles of the park's most profitable guest clusters and highest potential guest clusters. The Parks can use the results of the analysis to quantify, prioritize, and focus guest acquisition and guest activation marketing efforts.

For more information about cluster analysis in R, check out `http://www.statmethods.net/advstats/cluster.html`.

Normal Curve Equivalent (NCE) Analysis

A technique first used in evaluating students' testing performance, normal curve equivalent (NCE), is a data transformation technique that approximately fits a normal distribution between 0 and 100 by normalizing a data set in preparation for percentile rank analysis. For example, an NCE data transformation is a way of standardizing scores received on a test into a 0–100 scale similar to a percentile rank but preserving the valuable equal-interval properties of a *z*-score (see Figure 6-9).

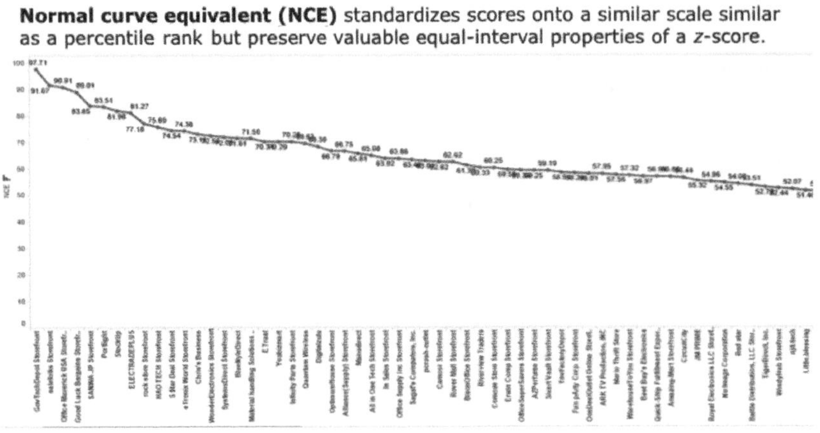
Normal curve equivalent (NCE) standardizes scores onto a similar scale similar as a percentile rank but preserve valuable equal-interval properties of a z-score.

Figure 6-9: Normal curve equivalent analysis

What I find most useful about the NCE data transformation is taking the NCE results and binning the results to look for natural groupings in the data. For example in Figure 6-10, you build on the NCE analysis to uncover price points (bins) across a wide range of high-margin, mid-margin, and low-margin product categories that might indicate the opportunity for pricing and/or promotional activities.

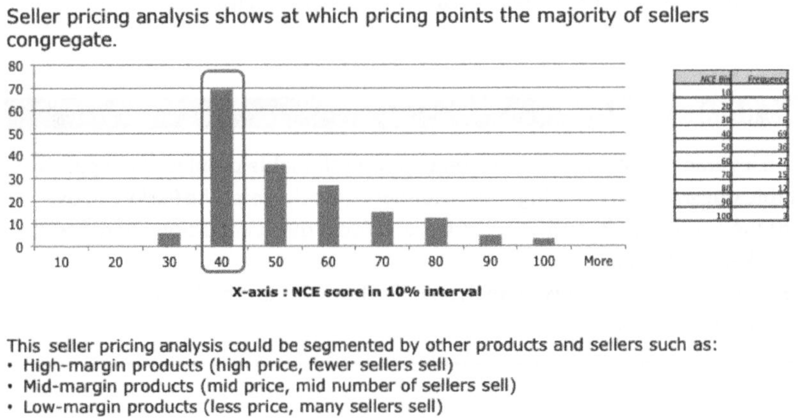
Seller pricing analysis shows at which pricing points the majority of sellers congregate.
80
70
60
50
40
30
20
10
0
10
20
30
40
50
60
70
80
90
100
More
X-axis : NCE score in 10% interval
This seller pricing analysis could be segmented by other products and sellers such as:
• High-margin products (high price, fewer sellers sell)
• Mid-margin products (mid price, mid number of sellers sell)
• Low-margin products (less price, many sellers sell)

Figure 6-10: Normal curve equivalent seller pricing analysis example

THE PARKS RAMIFICATIONS

The Parks can employ the NCE technique to understand price inflection points for packages of attractions and restaurants. The Parks can leverage the price inflection points to optimize pricing (e.g., create a package of attractions and restaurants by seasonality, holiday, day of week, etc.) and create new Priority Access packages.

For more information about how to use *z*-scores to normalize data using R, check out `http://www.r-bloggers.com/r-tutorial-series-centering-variables-and-generating-z-scores-with-the-scale-function/`. **For more insights into the NCE data transformation technique, see** `https://en.wikipedia.org/wiki/Normal_curve_equivalent`.

Association Analysis

Association analysis is a popular algorithm for discovering and quantifying relationships between variables in large databases. Association analysis shows customer or product events or activities that tend to happen together, which makes this type of analysis very actionable. For example, the association rule {buns, ketchup} → {burger} found in the point-of-sales data of a supermarket would indicate that if a customer buys buns and ketchup together, she is likely to also buy hamburger meat. Such information can be used as the basis for making pricing, product placement, promotion, and other marketing decisions.

Association analysis is the basis for market basket analysis (identifying products and/or services that sell in combination or sell with a predictable time lag) that is used in many industries including retail, telecommunications, insurance, digital marketing, credit cards, banking, hospitality, and gaming.

In Figure 6-11, the data science team examined the credit card transactions for one individual and uncovered several purchase occurrences that tended to happen together. For example, you can see a very strong relationship between Chipotle and Starbucks in the second line of Figure 6-11, as well as a number of purchase occurrences (e.g., Foot Locker + Best Buy) that tend to happen in combination.

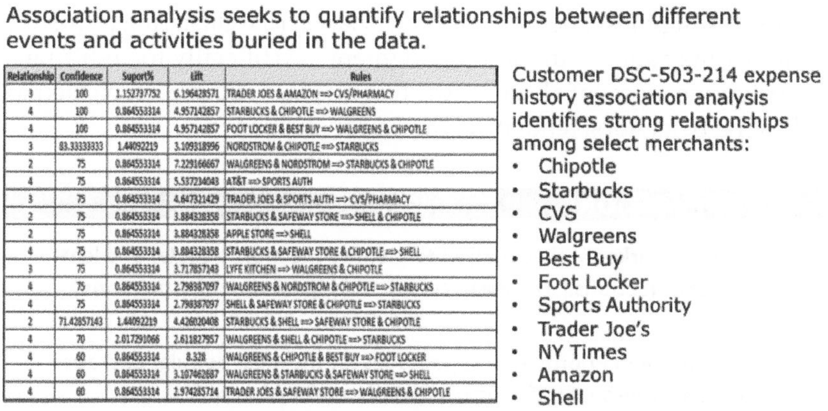
Association analysis seeks to quantify relationships between different events and activities buried in the data.

Relationship	Confidence	Suport%	Lift	Rules
3	100	1.152737752	6.196428571	TRADER JOES & AMAZON ==> CVS/PHARMACY
4	100	0.864553314	4.957142857	STARBUCKS & CHIPOTLE ==> WALGREENS
4	100	0.864553314	4.957142857	FOOT LOCKER & BEST BUY ==> WALGREENS & CHIPOTLE
3	83.33333333	1.44092219	3.109318996	NORDSTROM & CHIPOTLE ==> STARBUCKS
2	75	0.864553314	7.229166667	WALGREENS & NORDSTROM ==> STARBUCKS & CHIPOTLE
4	75	0.864553314	5.537234043	AT&T ==> SPORTS AUTH
3	75	0.864553314	4.647321429	TRADER JOES & SPORTS AUTH ==> CVS/PHARMACY
2	75	0.864553314	3.884328358	STARBUCKS & SAFEWAY STORE ==> SHELL & CHIPOTLE
2	75	0.864553314	3.884328358	APPLE STORE ==> SHELL
4	75	0.864553314	3.884328358	STARBUCKS & SAFEWAY STORE & CHIPOTLE ==> SHELL
3	75	0.864553314	3.717857143	LYFE KITCHEN ==> WALGREENS & CHIPOTLE
4	75	0.864553314	2.798387097	WALGREENS & NORDSTROM & CHIPOTLE ==> STARBUCKS
4	75	0.864553314	2.798387097	SHELL & SAFEWAY STORE & CHIPOTLE ==> STARBUCKS
2	71.42857143	1.44092219	4.426020408	STARBUCKS & SHELL ==> SAFEWAY STORE & CHIPOTLE
4	70	2.017291066	2.611827957	WALGREENS & SHELL & CHIPOTLE ==> STARBUCKS
4	60	0.864553314	8.328	WALGREENS & CHIPOTLE & BEST BUY ==> FOOT LOCKER
4	60	0.864553314	3.107462687	WALGREENS & STARBUCKS & SAFEWAY STORE ==> SHELL
4	60	0.864553314	2.974285714	TRADER JOES & SAFEWAY STORE ==> WALGREENS & CHIPOTLE

Customer DSC-503-214 expense history association analysis identifies strong relationships among select merchants:
• Chipotle
• Starbucks
• CVS
• Walgreens
• Best Buy
• Foot Locker
• Sports Authority
• Trader Joe's
• NY Times
• Amazon
• Shell

Figure 6-11: Association analysis

One very actionable data science technique is to cluster the resulting association rules into common groups or segments. For example, in Figure 6-12, the data science team clustered the resulting association rules across tens of millions of customers in order to create more accurate, relevant customer segments. In this process, the data science team

- Runs the association analysis across the tens of millions of customers to identify association rules with a high degree of confidence,
- Clusters the customers and their resulting association rules into common groupings or segments (e.g., Chipotle + Starbucks, Virgin America + Marriott),
- Uses these new segments as the basis for personalized messaging and direct marketing.

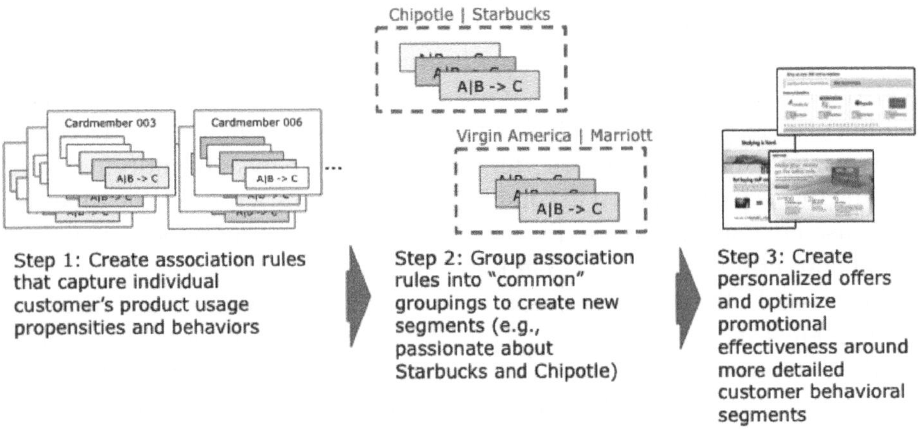
Chipotle | Starbucks
A|B -> C
Virgin America | Marriott
A|B -> C
Cardmember 003
A|B -> C
Cardmember 006
A|B -> C
Step 1: Create association rules that capture individual customer's product usage propensities and behaviors
Step 2: Group association rules into "common" groupings to create new segments (e.g., passionate about Starbucks and Chipotle)
Step 3: Create personalized offers and optimize promotional effectiveness around more detailed customer behavioral segments

Figure 6-12: Converting association rules into segments

One of the interesting consequences of this association rule clustering technique is that a customer may appear in multiple segments. Artificially force-fitting a customer into a single segment obscures the fine nuances about each particular customer's buying behaviors, tendencies, and propensities.

THE PARKS RAMIFICATIONS

The Parks can leverage market basket analysis to identify the most popular and least popular "packages of attractions." The Parks can use this "packages of attractions" data to

1. **Create new pricing and Priority Access packages for the most popular packages in order to optimize in-park traffic flow and reduce attraction wait times,**
2. **Create new pricing and Priority Access packages for the least popular "packages" in order to drive traffic to under-utilized attractions.**

For more information about association analysis in R, check out `http://www.rdatamining.com/examples/association-rules`.

Graph Analysis

Graph analysis is one of the more powerful analysis techniques made popular by social media analysis. Graph analysis can quickly highlight customer or machine (think Internet of Things) relationships obscured across millions if not billions of social and machine interactions.

Graph analysis uses mathematical structures to model pairwise relations between objects. A "graph" in this context is made up of "vertices" or "nodes" and lines called edges that connect them. Social network analysis (SNA) is an example of graph analysis. SNA is used to investigate social structures and relationships across social networks. SNA characterizes networked structures in terms of nodes (people or things within the network) and the ties or edges (relationships or interactions) that connect them (see Figure 6-13).

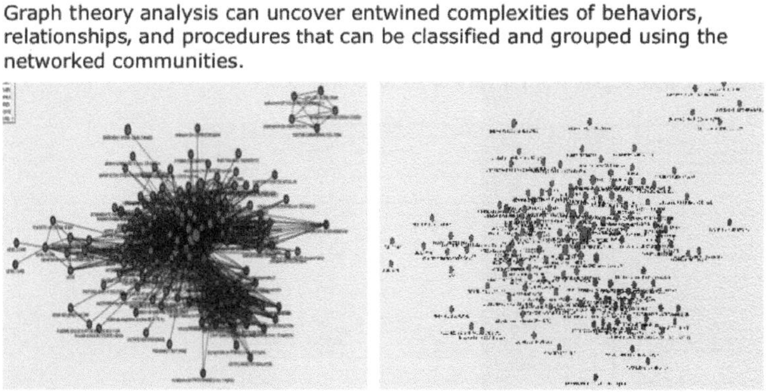

Graph theory analysis can uncover entwined complexities of behaviors, relationships, and procedures that can be classified and grouped using the networked communities.

Figure 6-13: Graph analysis

While graph analysis is most commonly used to identify clusters of "friends," uncover group influencers or advocates, and make friend recommendations on social media networks, graph analysis can also look at clustering and strength of relationships across diverse networks such as ATMs, routers, retail outlets, smart devices, websites, and product suppliers.

THE PARKS RAMIFICATIONS

The Parks can employ graph analysis to uncover strength of relationships among groups of guests (leaders, followers, influencers, cohorts). The Parks can leverage the graph analysis results to direct promotions (discounts, restaurant vouchers, travel vouchers) to group leaders in order to encourage these leaders to bring groups back to the parks more frequently.

For more information about social network analysis in R, check out `http://www.r-bloggers.com/an-example-of-social-network-analysis-with-r-using-package-igraph/`.

Text Mining

Text mining refers to the process of deriving usable information (metadata) from text files such as consumer comments, e-mail conversations, physician or technician notes, work orders, etc. Basically, text mining creates structured data out of unstructured data.

Text mining is a very powerful technique to show during an envisioning process, as many business stakeholders have struggled to understand how they can gain insights from the wealth of internal customer, product, and operational data. Text mining is not something that the data warehouse can do, so many business stakeholders have stopped thinking about how they can derive actionable insights from text data. Consequently, it is important to leverage envisioning exercises to help the business stakeholders to image the realm of what is possible with text data, especially when that text data is combined with the organization's operational and transactional data.

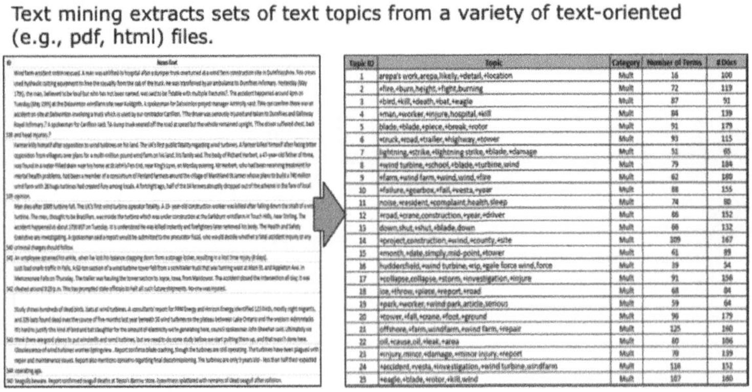
Text mining extracts sets of text topics from a variety of text-oriented (e.g., pdf, html) files.

Figure 6-14: Text mining analysis

For example, in Figure 6-14, the text mining tool has mined a history of news feeds about a particular product to uncover patterns and combinations of words that may indicate product performance and maintenance problems.

Typical text mining techniques and algorithms include text categorization, text clustering, concept/entity extraction, taxonomies production, sentiment analysis, document summarization, and entity relation modeling.

THE PARKS RAMIFICATIONS

The Parks can mine guest comments, social media posts, and e-mails to flag and rank areas of concern and problem situations. The Parks can leverage the text mining results to locate unsatisfied guests in order to drive personal (face-to-face) guest intervention efforts.

For more information about text mining analysis using R, check out `http://www.r-bloggers.com/text-mining-in-r-automatic-categorization-of-wikipedia-articles/`.

Sentiment Analysis

Sentiment analysis can provide a broad and general overview of your customers' sentiment toward your company and brands. Sentiment analysis can be a powerful way to glean insights about the customers' feelings about your company, products, and services out of the ever-growing body of social media sites (Facebook, LinkedIn, Twitter, Instagram, Yelp, Snapchat, Vine, etc.) (see Figure 6.15).

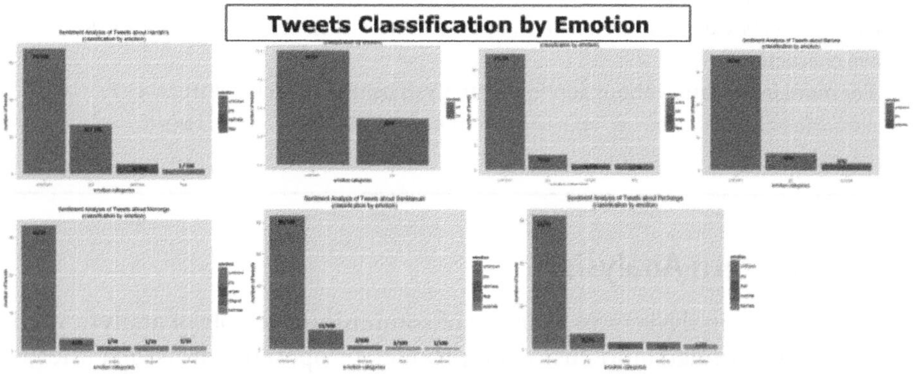

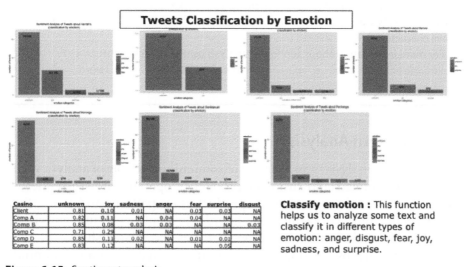

Casino	unknown	joy	sadness	anger	fear	surprise	disgust
Client	0.81	0.10	0.01	NA	0.03	0.03	NA
Comp A	0.82	0.11	NA	0.04	0.04	NA	NA
Comp B	0.85	0.08	0.03	0.03	NA	NA	0.03
Comp C	0.71	0.29	NA	NA	NA	NA	NA
Comp D	0.85	0.11	0.02	NA	0.01	0.01	NA
Comp E	0.83	0.12	NA	NA	NA	0.05	NA

Classify emotion : This function helps us to analyze some text and classify it in different types of emotion: anger, disgust, fear, joy, sadness, and surprise.

Figure 6-15: Sentiment analysis

In Figure 6-15, the data science team conducted competitive sentiment analysis by classifying the emotions (e.g., anger, disgust, fear, joy, sadness, surprise) of Twitter tweets about our client and its key competitors. Sentiment analysis can provide an early warning alert about potential customer or competitive problems (e.g., where your organization's performance and quality of service is considered lacking as compared to key competitors) and business opportunities (e.g., where key competitor's perceived performance and quality of service is suffering).

Unfortunately, it is sometimes difficult to get the social media data at the level of the individual, which is required to create more actionable insights and recommendations at the individual customer level. However, leading organizations are trying to incent their customers to "like" their social media sites or share their social media names in order to improve the collection of customer-identifiable data.

THE PARKS RAMIFICATIONS

The Parks can establish a sentiment score for each attraction and character and monitor social media sentiment for the attractions and characters in real-time. The Parks can leverage the real-time sentiment scores to take corrective actions (placate unhappy guests, open additional lines, open additional attractions, remove kiosks, move characters).

For more information about sentiment analysis using R, check out `https://sites.google.com/site/miningtwitter/questions/sentiment/sentiment`.

Traverse Pattern Analysis

Traverse pattern analysis is an example of combining a couple of analytic algorithms to better understand customer, product, or operational usage patterns. Traverse analysis links a customer or product usage patterns and association rules to a geographical or facility map in order to identify potential purchase, traffic, flow, fraud, theft, and other usage patterns and relationships.

The process starts by creating association rules from the customer's or product's usage data, and then maps those association rules to a geographical map (store, hospital, school, campus, sports arena, casino, airport) to identify potential performance, usage, staffing, inventory, logistics, traffic flow, etc. problems.

In Figure 6-16, the data science team created a series of association rules about slot and table play in a casino, and then used those association rules to identify potential foot flow problems and game location optimization opportunities. The data science team

- Created player performance association rules about what games the players tend to play in combination,

- Linked the game playing association rules to location ID, and then,
- Mapped rules and game performance data to a layout of the casino.

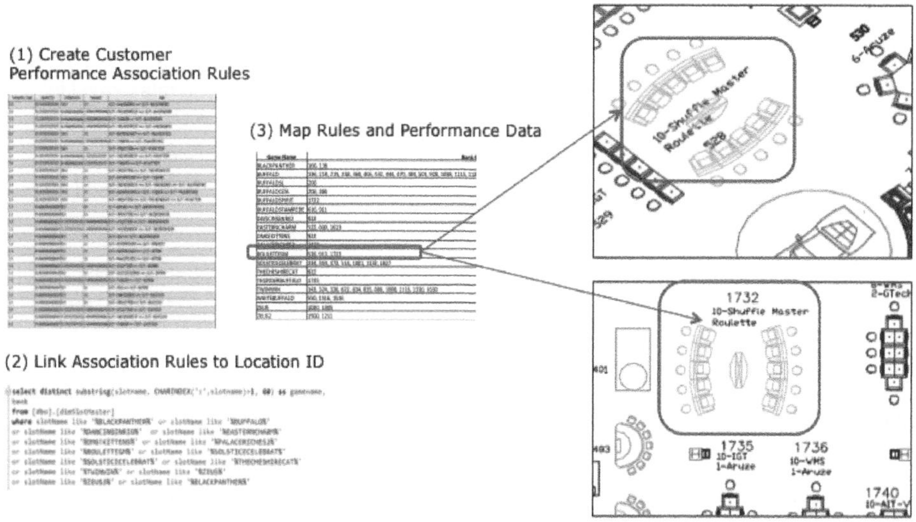

Figure 6-16: Traverse pattern analysis

The results of this analysis highlights areas of the casino that are sub-optimized when certain types of game players are in the casino and can lead to recommendations about the layout of the casino and the types of incentives to give players to change their game playing behaviors and tendencies.

THE PARKS RAMIFICATIONS

The Parks can employ traverse pattern analysis to understand park and guest flows with respect to attractions, entertainment, retail outlets, restaurants, characters, etc. The Parks can use the traverse pattern analysis results to

1. **Identify where to place characters and situate portable kiosks in order to increase revenues,**
2. **Determine what promotions to offer in order to drive traffic to idle attractions and restaurants.**

Decision Tree Classifier Analysis

Decision tree classifier analysis uses decision trees to identify groupings and clusters buried in the usage and performance data. Decision classifier analysis uses a decision tree as a predictive model that maps observations about an item to conclusions about the item's target value.

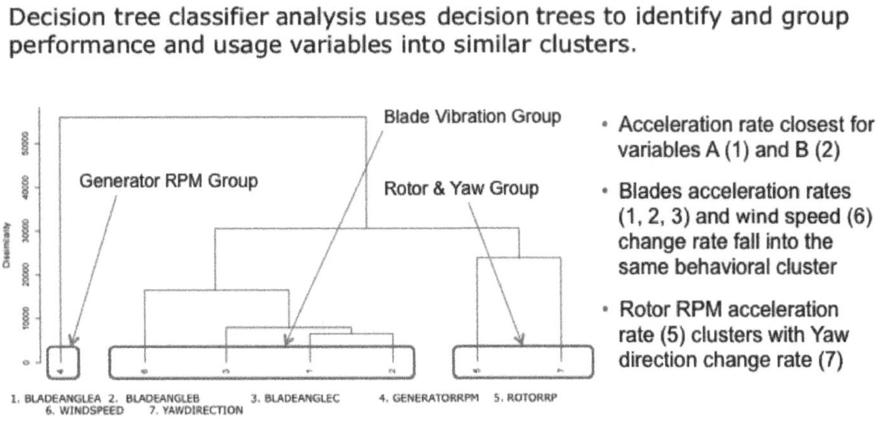
Decision tree classifier analysis uses decision trees to identify and group performance and usage variables into similar clusters.
Blade Vibration Group
Generator RPM Group
Rotor & Yaw Group
Acceleration rate closest for variables A (1) and B (2)
Blades acceleration rates (1, 2, 3) and wind speed (6) change rate fall into the same behavioral cluster
Rotor RPM acceleration rate (5) clusters with Yaw direction change rate (7)
1. BLADEANGLEA 2. BLADEANGLEB 3. BLADEANGLEC 4. GENERATORRPM 5. ROTORRP
6. WINDSPEED 7. YAWDIRECTION

Figure 6-17: Decision tree classifier analysis

In Figure 6-17, the data science team used the decision tree classifier analysis technique to identify and group performance and usage variables into similar clusters. The data science team uncovered product performance clusters that, when occurring in certain combinations, were indicative of potential product performance or maintenance problems.

THE PARKS RAMIFICATIONS

The Parks can use decision tree classifier analysis to quantify the variables that drive guest satisfaction and increase spend by guest clusters. The Parks can leverage the decision tree classifier analysis results to determine which variables to manipulate in order to drive guest satisfaction and associated guest spend.

For more information about building decision trees using R, check out "Tree-Based Models" at `http://www.statmethods.net/advstats/cart.html`.

Cohorts Analysis

Cohorts analysis is used to identify and quantify the impact that an individual or machines have on the larger group.

Cohorts analysis is commonly used by sports teams to ascertain the relative value of a player with respect to his or her influence on the success of the overall team. The National Basketball Association uses a real plus-minus (RPM) metric to measure a player's impact on the game, represented by difference between the team's total scoring and its opponent's. Table 6-1 shows top RPM players from the 2014–2015 NBA season.

Table 6-1: 2014–2015 Top NBA RPM Rankings

RANK	PLAYER	TEAM	MPG	RPM
1	Stephen Curry, PG	GS	32.7	9.34
2	LeBron James, SF	CLE	36.1	8.78
3	James Harden, SG	HOU	36.8	8.50
4	Anthony Davis, PF	NO	36.1	8.18
5	Kawhi Leonard, SF	SA	31.8	7.57
6	Russell Westbrook, PG	OKC	34.4	7.08
7	Chris Paul, PG	LAC	34.8	6.92
8	Draymond Green, SF	GS	31.5	6.80
9	DeMarcus Cousins, C	SAC	34.1	6.12
10	Khris Middleton, SG	MIL	30.1	6.06

Source: http://espn.go.com/nba/statistics/rpm/_/sort/RPM

This powerful technique (with slight variations due to the different nature of the variables and relationships) can be used to quantify the impact that a particular individual (student, teacher, player, nurse, athlete, technician) has on the larger group (see Figure 6-18).

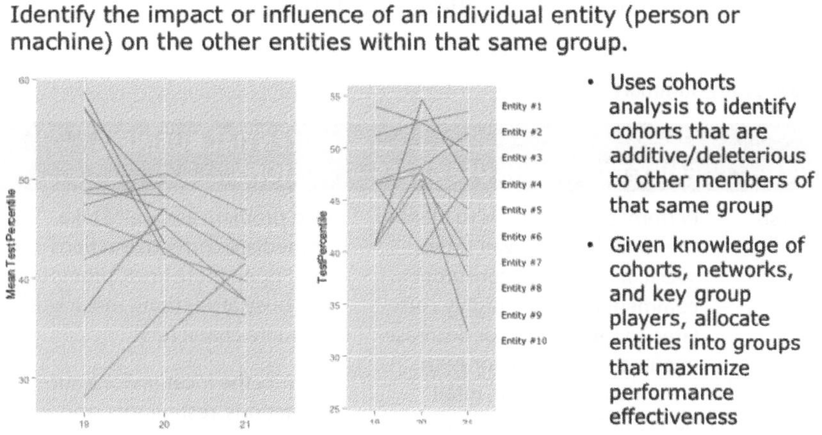
Identify the impact or influence of an individual entity (person or machine) on the other entities within that same group.
Mean Test Percentile
TestPercentile
Entity #1
Entity #2
Entity #3
Entity #4
Entity #5
Entity #6
Entity #7
Entity #8
Entity #9
Entity #10
• Uses cohorts analysis to identify cohorts that are additive/deleterious to other members of that same group
• Given knowledge of cohorts, networks, and key group players, allocate entities into groups that maximize performance effectiveness

Figure 6-18: Cohorts analysis

THE PARKS RAMIFICATIONS

The Parks can employ cohorts analysis to identify specific employees and characters that increase the overall park, attractions, characters, customer, and household satisfaction and spend levels. The Parks can use the results of the cohorts analysis to

1. **Decide how many and where to situate specific, popular characters;**
2. **Reward park associates that drive higher customer satisfaction scores.**

For more information about cohorts analysis in R, check out the article "Cohort Analysis with R – Retention Charts" at `http://analyzecore.com/2014/07/03/cohort-analysis-in-r-retention-charts/`.

Summary

The objective of Chapter 6 is to give you a taste for the different types of analytic algorithms a data science team can bring to bear on the business problems or opportunities that the organization is trying to address. This chapter better acquainted you with the different algorithms that the data science team can use to accelerate the business user and data science team collaboration process. While it is not the expectation of this book or chapter to turn business users into data scientists, it is my hope that Chapter 6 will set the foundation that helps business users and business leaders to *"think like a data scientist."*

This chapter introduced a wide variety of analytic algorithms that the data science team might use, depending on the problem being addressed and the types and varieties of data available. It also introduced a fictitious company (Fairy-Tale Theme Parks) against which you applied the different analytic techniques to see the potential business actions (see Table 6-2).

Table 6-2: Case Study Summary

ANALYTICS	FAIRY-TALE PARKS USE CASES	POTENTIAL BUSINESS ACTIONS
Trend analysis	Perform trend analysis to identify the variables (e.g., wait times, social media posts, consumer comments) that are highly correlated to the increase or decrease in guest satisfaction for each attraction, restaurant, retail outlet, and entertainment	Flag problem areas and take immediate corrective actions (e.g., open more lines, promote less busy attractions, move kiosks, resituate characters) Identify the location for future attractions, restaurants, and entertainment

ANALYTICS	FAIRY-TALE PARKS USE CASES	POTENTIAL BUSINESS ACTIONS
Boxplots	Leverage boxplots to determine most loyal guests for each of the park's attractions (e.g., Canyon Copter Ride, Monster Mansion, Space Adventure, Ghoulish Gulch)	Create guest current and maximum loyalty scores and use those scores to prioritize to whom to reward with Priority Access passes and other coupons and discounts
Geography (spatial) analysis	Conduct geographical trend analysis to spot any changes (zip+4 and household levels) in the geo-demographics of visitors over time and by seasonality and holidays	Create geo-specific marketing campaigns and promotions to increase attendance from under-penetrated geographical areas based on day of week, holidays, seasonality, and events (on-park and off-park events)
Pairs plot	Compare multiple variables to identify those variables that drive guests to which attractions, entertainment, and restaurants	Make in-park promotional decisions and offers that moves guests to under-utilized attractions, entertainment, retail outlets, and restaurants
Time series decomposition	Leverage time series decomposition analysis to quantify the impact that seasonality and events (in-park and off-park) has on guest visits and associated spend	Create season-specific marketing campaigns and promotions to increase number of guest visits and associated spend Determine which local events outside of the parks (concerts, professional sporting events, BCS football games) are worthy of promotional and sponsorship spend
Cluster analysis	Cluster guests to create more actionable profiles of The Parks's most profitable and highest potential guest clusters	Leverage cluster results to prioritize and focus guest acquisition and guest activation, cross-sell and up-sell marketing efforts
Normal curve equivalent (NCE) analysis	Leverage NCE analysis to understand the price inflection points for different packages of attractions and restaurants	Leverage the price inflection points to create packages of attractions and restaurants to optimize pricing (by season, day of week, etc.) and create new Priority Access packages
Association analysis	Leverage market basket analysis to identify most popular and least popular "baskets" of attractions	Leverage most common "baskets" to create new pricing and Priority Access packages in order to better control traffic and wait times Leverage least common "baskets" to create new pricing and Priority Access packages in order to drive traffic to under-utilized attractions

Continues

Table 6-2 (*continued*)

ANALYTICS	FAIRY-TALE PARKS USE CASES	POTENTIAL BUSINESS ACTIONS
Graph analysis	Leverage graph analysis to uncover direction and strength of relationships among groups of guests (leaders, followers, influencers, cohorts)	Send promotions (discounts, restaurant vouchers, travel vouchers) to group leaders in order to encourage leaders to bring their groups back to the parks more often
Text mining	Mine guest comments, social media posts, and e-mail threads to flag areas of concern and problem situations	Identify and locate unsatisfied guests in order to prioritize and focus personal (face-to-face) guest intervention efforts
Sentiment analysis	Establish a sentiment score for each attraction and character and monitor social media sentiment for the attractions and characters in real-time	Leverage real-time sentiment scores to take corrective actions (placate unhappy guests, open additional lines, open additional attractions, remove kiosks, move characters)
Traverse pattern analysis	Leverage traverse pattern analysis to understand park and guest flows with respect to attractions, entertainment, restaurants, retail outlets, characters, etc.	Identify where to place characters and situate portable kiosks in order to drive increased revenue Determine what promotions to offer in order to drive traffic to under-utilized attractions and restaurants
Decision tree classifier analysis	Use decision tree classifier analysis to quantify the variables that drive guest satisfaction	Leverage decision tree classifier analysis to determine which variables to manipulate in order to drive guest satisfaction and increase guest associated spend
Cohorts analysis	Identify specific employees and characters that tend to increase the overall park, attractions, characters, guest satisfaction, and spend levels	Leverage cohorts analysis to decide how many and where to situate characters Identify and reward park employees that drive higher guest satisfaction scores

I strongly recommend that you stay current with the different analytic techniques that your data science team is using. Take the time to better understand when to use which analytic techniques. Buy your data science team lots of Starbucks, Chipotle, and whiskey, and your team will continue to open your eyes to the business potential of data science.

Homework Assignment

Use the following exercises to apply what you learned in this chapter.

Exercise #1: Review each of the analytic algorithms covered in this chapter and write down one or two use cases where that particular analytic algorithm might be useful given your business situations.

Exercise #2: Revisit the key business initiative that you identified in Chapter 2. Write down two or three of the analytic algorithms covered in this chapter that you think might be appropriate to the decisions that you are trying to make in support of that key business initiative.

Exercise #3: Write down two or three bullet points about why you think those selected analytic algorithms might be most appropriate for your targeted business initiative.

CHAPTER

7

The Data Lake

There is a major industry change happening with respect to how organizations store, manage, and analyze data. Not since the introduction of the data warehouse in the late 1980s have we seen something with the potential to transform how organizations leverage data and analytics to power their key business initiatives and rewire their value creation processes. This new data and analytics architecture is called the data lake, and it has potential to be even more impactful than the data warehouse in transforming the way organizations integrate data and analytics into their business models. But as in all things related to big data, organizations must "think differently" with respect to how they design, deploy, and manage their data architecture.

Today's data warehouses are extremely expensive. As a result, most organizations limit how much data they store in their data warehouse, opting for 13 to 25 months of summarized data versus 15 to 25 years of detailed transactional and operational data. Unfortunately for data warehouses, it is in that detailed transactional, operational, sensor, wearable, social data and the growing body of internal and external unstructured data that actionable insights about your customers, products, campaigns, partners, and operations can be found.

For example, over the past 15 years, the US economy has gone through two full economic cycles where the economy was flying high, collapsed, and then recovered. By looking at each of their customer's product purchase patterns over those two economic cycles, organizations can predict how a customer is personally impacted by an economic downturn. A grocery chain, for instance, could monitor individual customer's shopping baskets and purchase patterns to uncover changes that may indicate changes in that customer's personal economic situation. From the detailed point-of-sales transactions, the grocer could see a change in an individual's purchase behaviors (i.e., moving from expensive to lower-cost products, using more coupons and discounts, increasing purchases of private label products, and so on), which might indicate a change in his or her financial situation. These insights could provide new monetization opportunities and better ways to serve that customer given his or her financial situation, such as a personalized promotion highlighting more economical items for that particular customer.

Introduction to the Data Lake

The data lake was born out of the "economics of big data" that allows organizations to store, manage, and analyze massive amounts of data at a cost that can be 20 to 50 times cheaper than at traditional data warehouse technologies. Because of the agile underlying Hadoop/HDFS architecture that typically supports the data lake, organizations can store structured data (relational tables, csv files), semi-structured data (web logs, sensor logs, beacon feeds), and unstructured data (text files, social media posts, photos, images, video) *as-is,* without the time-consuming and agility-limiting need to predefine a data schema prior to data load.

However, the real power of the data lake is to enable advanced analytics or data science on the detailed and complete history of data in an attempt to uncover new variables and metrics that are better predictors of business performance. The data lake can do the following:

- Eliminate data silos. Rather than having dozens of independently managed collections of data (e.g., data warehouses, data marts, spreadmarts), you can combine these sources into a single data lake for indexing, cataloging, and analytics. Consolidation of the data into a single data repository results in increased data use and sharing, while cutting costs through server and license reduction.
- Store, manage, protect, and analyze data by consolidating inefficient storage silos across the organization.
- Provide a simple, scalable, flexible, and efficient solution that works across block, file, or object workloads (i.e., a shared storage platform that natively supports both traditional and next generation workloads).
- Reduce the costs of IT infrastructure.
- Speed up time to insights.
- Improve operational flexibility.

- Enable robust data protection and security capabilities.
- Reduce data warehouse workloads by reducing the burden of analytics-intensive queries that would be best done in a special-purpose analytics sandbox environment.
- Free up data warehousing resources by off-loading Extract, Transform, and Load (ETL) processes from the data warehouse to the more cost-efficient, more powerful Hadoop-based data lake.

NOTE **It is typical that 40 to 60 percent of the data warehouse processing load is performing ETL work. Off-loading some of the ETL processes to the data lake can free up considerable data warehouse resources.**

- Unhandcuff the BI analysts and data science team from being reliant on the summarized and aggregated data in the data warehouse as the single source of data for their data analytics (and mitigate the unmanageable proliferation "spreadmarts"[1] that are being used by business analysts to work around the analytic limitations of the data warehouse).

The data lake solves a great many problems. However, it can also raise a lot of questions. In a paper titled "Beware the Data Lake Fallacy" (`http://www.gartner.com/newsroom/id/2809117`), Gartner raised cautions about the data lake, specifically around the assumption that all enterprise audiences are highly skilled at data manipulation and analysis. Gartner's point was that if a data lake focuses only on storing disparate data and ignores how or why data is used, governed, defined, and secured or how descriptive metadata is captured and maintained, the data lake risks turning into a data swamp. And without an adequate metadata strategy, every subsequent use of data means the analysts must start from scratch.

The ability of an organization to realize business value from big data relies on the organization's ability to easily and quickly:

- Identify the "right and/or best data"
- Define the analytics required to extract the value
- Bring the data into an analytics environment (sandbox) suited for advanced analytics or data science work
- Curate the data to a point where it is "suited" for analysis
- Stand up the required infrastructure to support the analytics in accordance with the desired performance and throughput requirements

[1] "Spreadmarts" are spreadsheets or desktop database management applications (Microsoft Access) that are created and maintained by business analysts outside the purview, support, and maintenance of the centralized information technology organization. Spreadmarts typically contain data that may have originated from the data warehouse but has been transformed and integrated with other data to support the business analysts' specific analysis needs.

- Execute the analytic models against the curated data to derive business value
- Deploy the analytics into the production infrastructure
- Deliver the analytic results in an actionable manner to the business

NOTE **Stating that the data lake is the "single repository for ALL your organization's data" does not mean that there are no other repositories of data across your organization. Your operational systems (such as SAP, Oracle Financials, PeopleSoft, and Siebel) will continue to store data for their own operational reporting needs, but the data from those data sources should eventually be loaded into the data lake. And your data warehouses, data marts, and Online Analytic Processing (OLAP) cubes will continue to store data for their own unique reporting and analysis needs, but the data for those repositories should be sourced from your data lake. In the end, the data lake is the "central" repository for ALL your organization's data.**

Characteristics of a Business-Ready Data Lake

The data lake is not an incremental enhancement to the data warehouse, and it is NOT data warehouse 2.0. The data lake enables entirely new capabilities that allow your organization to address data and analytic challenges that the data warehouse could not address.

There are five characteristics that differentiate a business-ready data lake from the data warehouse (see Figure 7-1):

Free up costly data warehouse and BI resources; enable your advanced analytics / data science environment
INGEST
STORE
ANALYZE
SURFACE
ACT
Capture data from wide range of traditional and new sources
Store all your data in one environment for cross-functional business analysis
Uncover new customer, product, and operational insights
Empower front-line employees; drive more profitable customer engagement
Integrate analytic insights into operational and management systems

Image courtesy of EMC

Figure 7-1: Characteristics of a data lake

- **Ingest.** Ability to rapidly ingest data from a wide range of internal and external data sources, including structured and unstructured data sources. The data lake can accomplish rapid data ingestion because it can load the data as-is; that is, the data lake does not require any data transformations or pre-building a data schema before loading the data.
- **Store.** A single or central repository for amassing ALL the organization's data including data from potentially interesting external sources. The data lake can store data even if the organization has not yet decided how it might use the data. As the Director of Analytics and Business Intelligence at Starbucks was quoted: "A full quarter of Starbucks transactions are made via its popular loyalty cards, and that results in "huge amounts" of data, but the company isn't sure what to do with [all that data] yet." The same goes for social media data, as Starbucks has a team who analyzes social data, but "We haven't figured out what exactly to do with it yet."[2]
- **Analyze.** Provides the foundation for the analytics environment (or analytics sandbox) where the data science team is free to explore and evaluate different internal and external data sources with the goal of uncovering new customer, product, and operational insights that can be used optimize key business processes and fuel new monetization opportunities.
- **Surface.** Supports the analytic model development and the extracting of the analytic results (e.g., scores, recommendations, next best offer, business rules) that are used to empower frontline employees' and business managers' decision making and influence customer behaviors and actions.
- **Act.** Enables the integration of the analytic results back into the organization's operational systems (call center, direct marketing, procurement, store operations, logistics) and management applications (reports, dashboards) that "closes the loop" with respect to optimizing data and analytics-based decision making across the organization.

Using the Data Lake to Cross the Analytics Chasm

I come from the data warehouse world, having gotten started in 1984 with Metaphor Computers. In fact, that was so long ago that we didn't even call it data warehousing, but instead called it "Decision Support" (which I'd argue is still a better name for what we are trying to do).

For most organizations, the data warehouses, and the Business Intelligence (BI) tools that run on top of the data warehouses, operate like a production environment with the following characteristics:

[2] http://adage.com/article/datadriven-marketing/starbucks-data-pours/240502/

- Ability to support the creation and delivery of operational and management reports and dashboards on a regularly scheduled basis (e.g., reports delivered end of day, end of week, end of quarter; dashboards updated every morning)
- Predictable compute and processing load to run the ETL routines, generate the management and operational reports, and update the management dashboards
- SLA-constrained in that there are not many extra processing cycles to get the ETL and report and dashboard generating jobs done within the 24-hour daily window
- Heavily governed (data governance, auditability, traceability, data lineage, metadata management) to ensure that the historical data being reported is 100 percent accurate
- Standardization of tools in order to better control BI and ETL tool acquisition, maintenance, training, and support costs

On the other hand, the analytics environment is dramatically different from the BI and data warehouse environment in its objectives, purpose, and operating characteristics (i.e., how it is used). The analytics environment is characterized as:

- An exploratory environment where the data analysts want to quickly ingest and analyze lots of data
- Unpredictable system load that is highly dependent on the analysts' daily work objectives, exploration needs, and ad hoc analytical requests
- Heavily experimentation oriented to give the data analysts the freedom to test new data sources, new algorithms, new data enrichment techniques, and new tools
- Loosely governed in that the data need not be managed under some governance umbrella until the data analysts first prove that there is some value in the data
- "Best tool for the job" with the data analysts using whatever data visualization, data exploration, and analytic modeling tools with which they felt most comfortable

As a data warehouse manager, I hated the analytics team. Why? Because whenever its members needed data, they always came to my data warehouse for the data because they were told that the data warehouse was the "single version of the truth." And the analytic team's data and query requests usually screwed up my production SLAs in the process (see Figure 7-2).

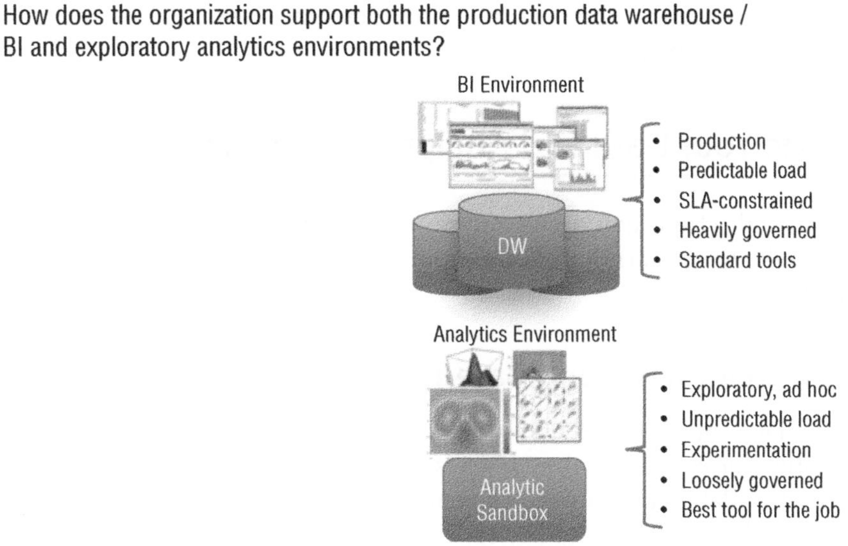

Figure 7-2: The analytics dilemma

The solution: put a Hadoop-based data store (data lake) in front of both the data warehouse and the analytics environments (see Figure 7-3).

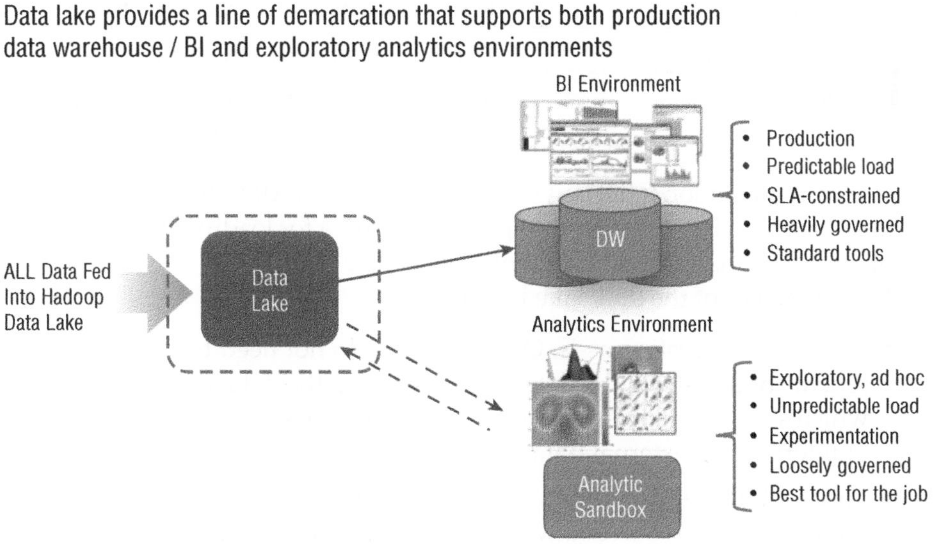

Figure 7-3: The data lake line of demarcation

The data lake provides a "line of demarcation" between the production requirements of the data warehouse and the ad hoc, exploratory nature of the analytics environment. In addition, the data lake provides other benefits that we will cover later in this chapter.

Modernize Your Data and Analytics Environment

There are several actions that organizations can take today to exploit the value of the data lake to modernize their existing data warehouse and analytics environments.

Action #1: Create a Hadoop-Based Data Lake

The Hadoop Distributed File Systems (HDFS) provides a powerful yet inexpensive foundation for your data lake. HDFS is a cost-effective large storage system with low-cost, scalable computing and analytical capabilities (e.g., MapReduce, YARN, Spark). Built on commodity hardware clusters, HDFS simplifies the acquisition and storage of diverse data sources (see Table 7-1).

Table 7-1: Data Lake Data Types

DATA TYPE	EXAMPLE
Structured data	Relational databases, data tables, csv files
Semi-structured data	Web logs, sensor feeds, XML, JSON
Unstructured data	Social media posts, text notes, consumer comments, images, videos, audio

Once in the Hadoop/HDFS system, MapReduce, YARN, Spark, and other Hadoop-based tools are available to prepare the data for loading into your data warehouse and analytic environments (see Figure 7-4).

The advantages of the data lake include:

- Rapid data ingestion as-is. Organizations do not need to pre-define the schema or transform the data prior to loading the data into the data lake, which simplifies and speeds the process of amassing data from a variety of internal and external data sources.
- Low-cost data and analytics environment built on commodity hardware servers and open source software that can be 20 to 50 times cheaper to store, manage, and analyze data than traditional data warehouse technologies.
- 100 percent linear compute scalability. When you need to double compute capacity, just double the number of nodes.

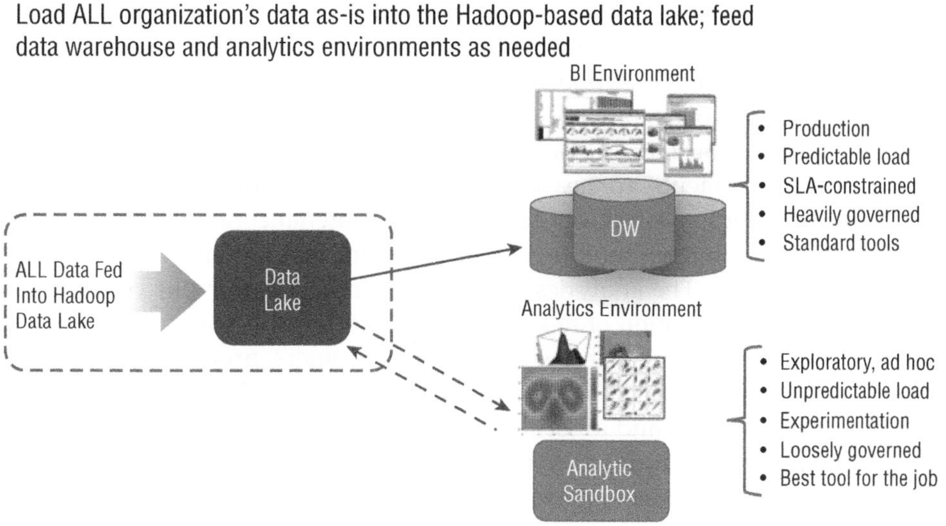

Figure 7-4: Create a Hadoop-based data lake

Action #2: Introduce the Analytics Sandbox

A data lake strategy supports the introduction of a separate analytics environment that off-loads the analytics being done today on your overly expensive data warehouse. This separate analytics environment provides the data science team an on-demand, fail-fast environment for quickly ingesting and analyzing a wide variety of data sources in an attempt to address immediate business opportunities independent of the data warehouse's production schedule and service level agreement (SLA) rules (see Figure 7-5).

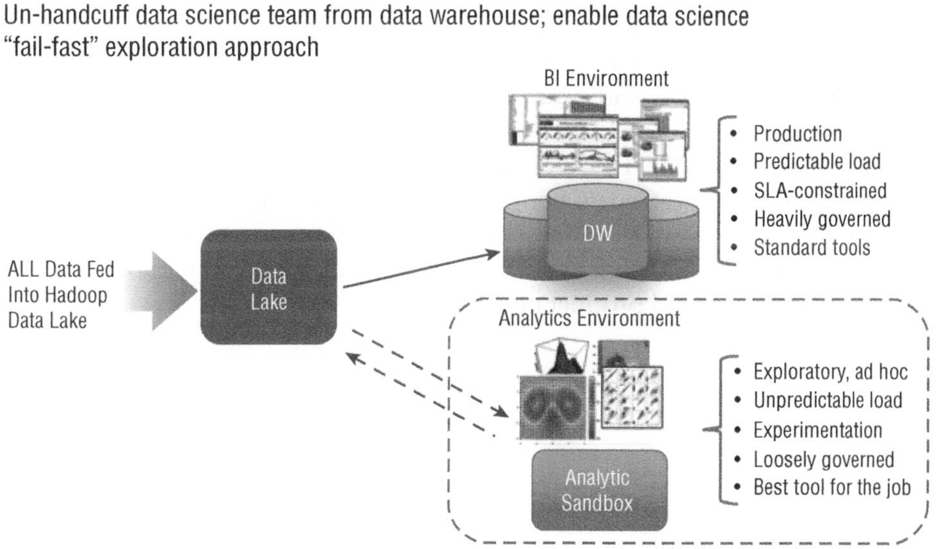

Figure 7-5: Create an analytic sandbox

The analytics environment in Figure 7-5 couldn't be more different from your data warehouse environment. Your data warehouse environment is a production environment that needs to support the regular (daily, weekly, monthly, quarterly, annual) production of operational and management reports and dashboards that are used to run the business. To do that, data warehouse environments have strict service level agreements, are heavily governed, and limit the number of BI and ETL tools in order to control tool acquisition, maintenance, and training costs.

An analytics environment, on the other hand, is much more ad hoc and on-demand driven. The analytics environment must support the continuous exploration and evaluation of new sources of internal and external data in an attempt to uncover actionable insights about customers, products, and operations. The analytics environment must support the data science team's need to test new analytic tools and algorithms and develop new data transformation and enrichment techniques in search of those variables and metrics that are better predictors of business performance.

Action #3: Off-Load ETL Processes from Data Warehouses

Doing the ETL processing within your existing data warehouse is a common practice today. However, if your data warehouse is already overloaded and it is very expensive to add more processing capacity, why do that batch-centric, data transformation heavy lifting in the expensive data warehouse environment? That's like having a high-powered, ultra-cool Tesla haul turnips around the farm.

Free up data warehouse resources and improve your ETL process effectiveness by off-loading the ETL processes off your expensive data warehouse platform. Instead, perform the ETL work in the data lake. This allows organizations to leverage the natively parallel Hadoop environment to bring to bear the appropriate number of compute capabilities at the appropriate times to get the job done more quickly and more cost-effectively (see Figure 7-6).

As we've discussed before, not only does using Hadoop for your ETL work make sense from a cost and processing effectiveness perspective, but it also gives organizations the capability to create new metrics that are often difficult to create using traditional ETL tools. For example, using Hadoop makes it much easier to create advanced customer purchase and product performance metrics around frequency (how often), recency (how recently), and sequencing (in what order) activities that could yield new insights that might be better predictors of customer behaviors and product performance.

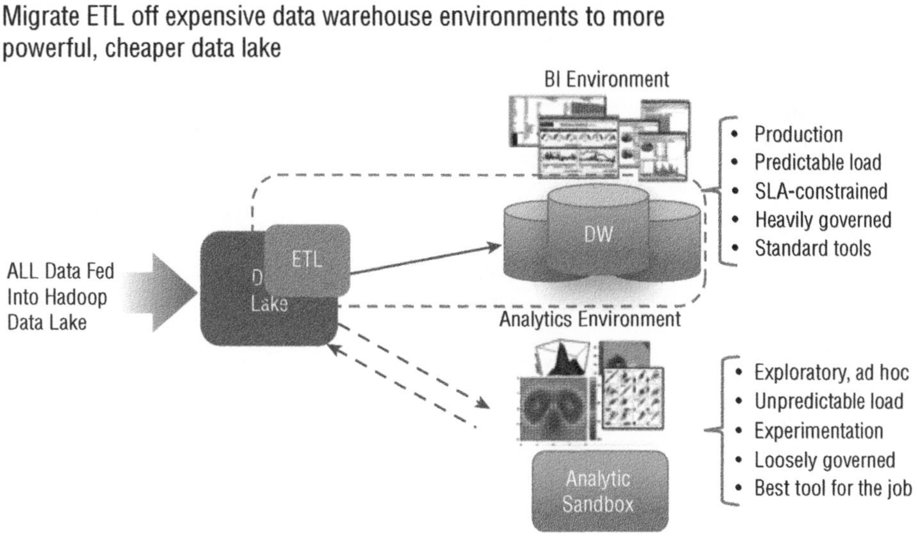

Figure 7-6: Move ETL to the data lake

Analytics Hub and Spoke Analytics Architecture

We have spent a considerable amount of this chapter describing the data lake; now let's discuss why your organization needs a data lake. The value and power of a data lake are often not fully realized until we get into our second or third analytic use case. That is because it is at that point where the organization needs the ability to self-provision an analytics environment (compute nodes, data, analytic tools, permissions, data masking) and share data across traditional line-of-business silos (one singular or centralized location for all the organization's data) in order to support the rapid exploration and discovery processes that the data science team uses to uncover variables and metrics that might be better predictors of business performance.

This is a "Hub and Spoke" analytics environment where the data lake is the "hub" that enables the data science teams to self-provision their own analytic sandboxes and facilitates the sharing of data, analytic tools, and analytic best practices across the different parts of the organization (see Figure 7-7).

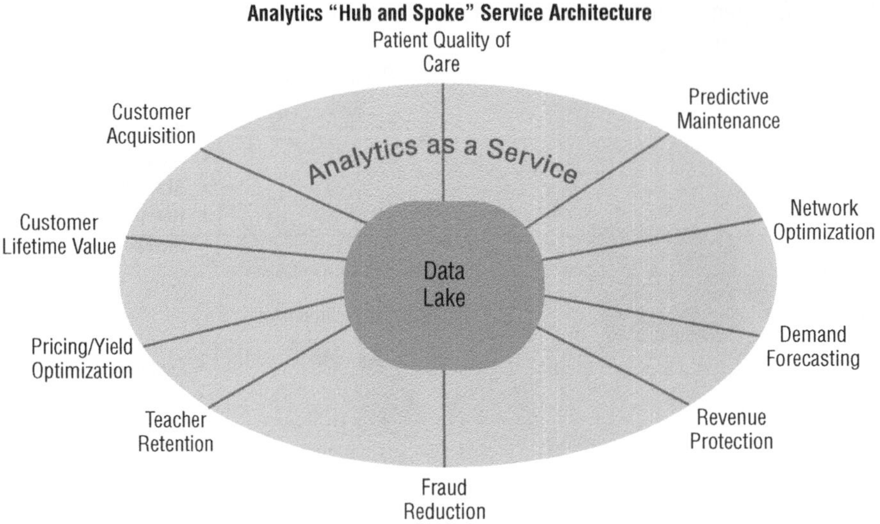

Figure 7-7: Hub and Spoke analytics architecture

The hub of the "Hub and Spoke" architecture is the data lake that provides:

- Centralized, singular, schema-less data store with raw (as-is) data and massaged data
- Mechanism for rapid ingestion of data with appropriate latency
- Ability to map data across sources and provide visibility and security to users
- Catalog to find and retrieve data
- Costing model of centralized service
- Ability to manage security, permissions, and data masking
- Supports self-provisioning of compute nodes, data, and analytic tools without IT intervention

The spokes of the "Hub and Spoke" analytics architecture are the analytic use cases or applications that help the organization to optimize key business processes, deliver a more compelling customer experience, and uncover new monetization opportunities. The "spokes" have the following characteristics:

- Ability to perform analytics (data science)
    - Analytics sandbox (HDFS, Hadoop, Spark, Hive, HBase)
    - Data engineering tools (Elastic Search, MapReduce, YARN, Pivotal HAWQ, SQL)
    - Analytical tools (SAS, R, Mahout, MADlib, H2O)
    - Visualization tools (Tableau, DataRPM, ggplot2)

- Ability to exploit analytics (application development)
    - Third platform application (mobile app development, website app development)
    - Analytics exposed as services to applications (APIs)
    - Integrate in-memory and/or in-database scoring and recommendations into business process and operational systems

The "Hub and Spoke" analytics architecture enables the data science team to develop the predictive and prescriptive analytics that are necessary to optimize key business processes, provide a differentiated customer engagement, and uncover new monetization opportunities.

Early Learnings

There is much we can learn from three decades dealing with the limitations of the data warehouse. There are several lessons that we can take away from our data warehousing experiences that we can apply today to ensure that we do not make the same mistakes in deploying a data lake strategy.

Lesson #1: The Name Is Not Important

Several decades ago, a battle raged between data warehouse advocates (associated with Bill Inmon and the Corporate Information Factory) and data mart advocates (associated with Ralph Kimball and star schemas) regarding nomenclature and terminology. Countless years were wasted at trade shows, at seminars, and in conference rooms across the world debating which approach was the "right" approach. As a reminder:

- **Data warehouse or enterprise data warehouse (EDW)** is a subject-oriented, nonvolatile, integrated, time variant collection of data in support of management's decisions. The enterprise data warehouse approach is often characterized as a top-down approach, more in alignment with the Online Transaction Processing (OLTP) systems from which the data was sourced. The data warehouse typically has an enterprise-wide perspective.
- **Data mart** is typically oriented to a specific business function, department, or line of business. This enables each department or line of business to use, manipulate, and develop the data any way it sees fit, without altering information inside other data marts or the enterprise data warehouse. Data marts use the concept of "conformed dimensions" to integrate data across business functions, replicating in many ways the same data that is captured in the enterprise data warehouse.

Interestingly, history has shown that both approaches worked! There were certainly terminology, architectural, and deployment differences between the two approaches, but the bottom line is that they both required the same key capabilities such as:

- Captures large amounts of historical data that could be used to analyze the performance of the key business entities (dimensions) and identify trends and patterns in the data
- Data governance procedures and policies to ensure that the data stored in the data warehouse and data marts were 100 percent accurate
- Master data management to ensure common definitions, terminology, and nomenclature across the lines of business
- Ability to join or integrate data from different data sources coming from different business functions
- End user query construction (using SQL and BI tools) that supported the generation of daily, weekly, monthly, and quarterly reports and dashboards and also supported the ad hoc slicing and dicing of the data—drill up, drill down, and drill across different data sources—to identify areas of over- and under-performance

The debate about whether it is a data lake or a data reservoir or an operational data store is neither useful nor constructive. Let's just pick a name and make it work—and data lake it is!

Lesson #2: It's Data Lake, Not Data Lakes

Having multiple data lakes replicates the same problems that were created with multiple data warehouses—disparate data siloes and data fiefdoms that don't facilitate sharing of the corporate data assets across the organization. Organizations need to have a *single* data lake from which they can source the data for their BI/data warehousing and analytic needs. The data lake may never become the "single version of the truth" for the organization, but then again, neither will the data warehouse. Instead, the data lake becomes the "single or central repository for all the organization's data" from which all the organization's reporting and analytic needs are sourced.

Unfortunately, some organizations are replicating the bad data warehouse practice by creating special-purpose data lakes—data lakes to address a specific business need. Resist that urge! Instead, source the data that is needed for that specific business need into a "analytic sandbox" where the data scientists and the business users can collaborate to find those data variables and analytic models that are better predictors of the business performance. Within the "analytic sandbox," the organization can bring together (ingest and integrate) the data that it wants to test, build the analytic models, test the model's goodness of fit, acquire new data, refine the analytic models, and retest the goodness of fit. Yep, the analytic sandbox *perfectly* supports the data science engagement process covered in Chapter 5, "Differences Between Business Intelligence and Data Science" (see Figure 7-8).

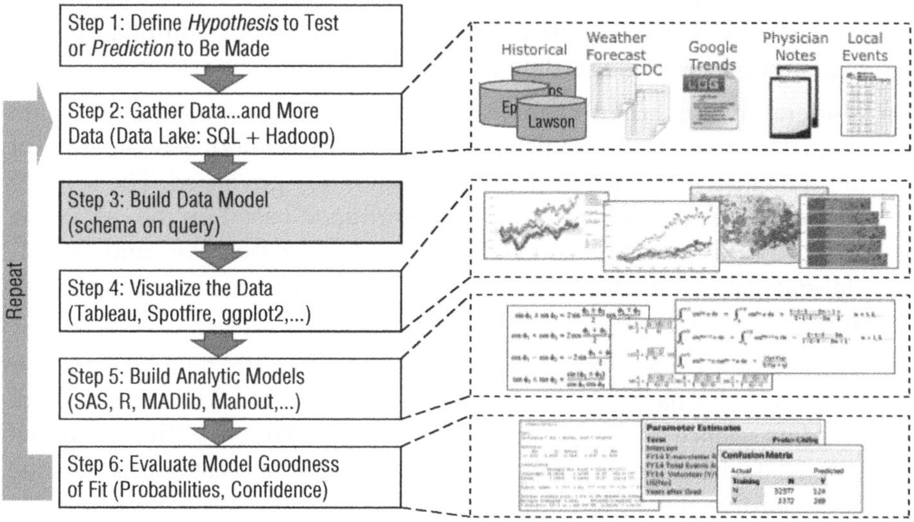

Figure 7-8: Data science engagement process

If organizations are trying to maintain multiple data lakes, then the organization risks the same results and management distrust that still exists today with many data warehouse implementations—executives arguing which numbers are correct because the data in the reports and dashboards is being sourced from different data warehouses and data marts. Let's nip this problem in the bud now! It's a single data lake.

Lesson #3: Data Governance Is a Life Cycle, Not a Project

I love (hate) the industry pundits who quickly jump on the "What about data governance?" issue when we talk about big data and the data lake. Well, what about it? Of course it is important, and of course smart organizations never forgot about it. As the volume of data grows in the data lake, governance becomes even more critical for answering the what, where, and who has access to data questions.

However, the data governance discussion takes on a new wrinkle when you contemplate data in the data warehouse versus data in the data lake. While data in the data warehouse strives for 100 percent governance, organizations are going to realize that there needs to be different "degrees" or levels of data governance in the data lake depending on how the data is being used, such as:

- **Highly Governed Data.** Data that will be sourced out of the data lake into the data warehouse needs to be highly governed. This includes operational and performance data, as well as data such as medical, financial, personally identifiable information, credit card info, account numbers, passwords, etc. Since this is the data that appears in management, compliance, and regulatory reporting, this data needs to be 100 percent governed.
- **Moderately Governed Data.** Data that is going to be used by the data science team to create predictive and prescriptive models in an attempt to predict performance needs to be moderately governed. The level of data governance will be ultimately determined based on the *cost* of the analytic models being wrong (think Type I "false positive" and Type II "false negative" modeling errors and the potential business impacts of those types of errors).
- **Ungoverned Data.** Data that is just being held in the data lake and for which no value has yet been attributed to that data would be ungoverned. The data science team is free to acquire and experiment with this ungoverned data. However, once there is some level of value established for the data (i.e., data is used to power a financial client "Retirement Readiness" score), then the data needs to move into the moderately governed data classification.

In the big data world, the goal for the smart organization should be "just-enough data governance." Why waste management cycles governing data when that data might not even be useful to the organization? But once the value of that data has been ascertained in how that data is going to be used to optimize key business processes and uncover new monetization opportunities, then the appropriate level of data governance (highly governed, moderately governed, ungoverned) can be applied to that specific data source.

Lesson #4: Data Lake Sits Before Your Data Warehouse, Not After It

Several traditional data warehouse vendors are trying to convince their customers that the data lake should sit after the data warehouse; that is, the data lake should be populated from the data warehouse versus populating the data warehouse from the data lake. Sorry, but that's a self-serving proposition from vendors who are already seeing the economic impact on their revenues and profits with respect to the power of the data lake to reshape how organizations store, manage, analyze, and value data.

The problem with this "Data Warehouse First" argument is that many of the data lake benefits (rapid data ingest, capturing data as-is with no need to prebuild a data schema, support for unstructured data sources, no loss of data fidelity due to data transformations, single repository for all the organization's internal and external data) are lost if the data first needs to go through the data warehouse.

I am sure that the "Data Warehouse First" message initially resonates with organizations that have spent years building out their data warehouse capabilities. But data warehouse teams are beginning to understand the benefits of loading the data first into the data lake, including freeing up data warehouse resources from doing the ETL work and supporting the advanced analytic modeling that cannot easily be done within the data warehouse.

What Does the Future Hold?

The cost, processing, and agility advantages of Hadoop/HDFS would make it appear that it is only a matter of time before Hadoop/HDFS replaces the Relational Data Base Management Systems (RDBMS) as the data warehouse platform of choice. The Hadoop/HDFS cost, processing and agility advantages over the expensive commercial and proprietary RDBMS products will soon become too much for organizations to ignore.

Today there is much inertia for organizations to move off the RDBMS data warehouse platform. Organizations not only have invested years and even decades of effort to build their data warehouse environment on these RDBMS platforms but also have created a multitude of BI reports and dashboards on these RDBMS-based data warehouses that act as a giant anchor in dissuading organizations from contemplating transitioning to a Hadoop/HDFS data warehouse platform.

But the times they are a changin'. The development and rapid adoption of open source "SQL on Hadoop" products like Pivotal HAWQ (now part of the Open Data Platform initiative), Cloudera Impala, and Hortonworks Stinger are enabling the legions of SQL-trained developers to develop SQL-based reports and dashboards on Hadoop.

Plus the development of new software products like AtScale (that acts as a layer between Hadoop/HDFS and an organization's existing BI tools) and Xplain.io[3] (that automates the rewriting of RDBMS SQL to work on Hadoop) will accelerate the inevitability of the transition of the data warehouse platform to Hadoop/HDFS (see Figure 7-9).

[3] Acquired by Cloudera.

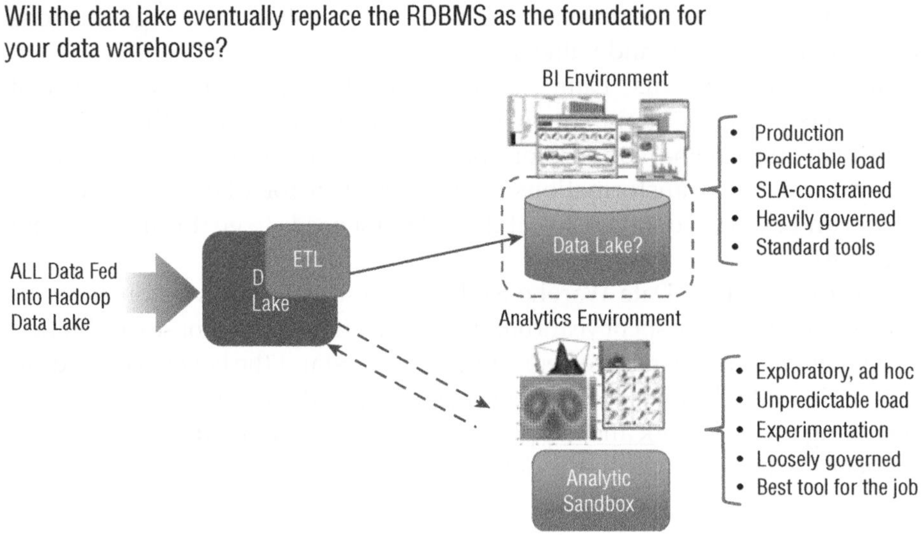

Figure 7-9: What does the future hold?

For many organizations, data warehouse decisions are fraught with personal biases. And years and decades of data warehouse and BI development, personnel training, and tool acquisition will make any transition off the RDBMS data warehouse platform to a Hadoop data warehouse platform more of a religious debate than a financial or technology decision. But soon, the economics of big data, plus the continued development of new tools to support the data warehouse on Hadoop, will be too compelling to ignore. And I want to be there when that day comes!

Summary

These are certainly marvelous times to be in the data business. The data lake leverages new big data technology innovations to enable organizations to extend and enhance their existing data warehouse and ETL investments while empowering business analysts and data scientists to explore new data sources and data enrichment techniques to tease out new actionable insights about their customers, products, and operations.

Figure 7-10 shows EMC's pre-engineered Federation Business Data Lake. It is one of the industry's most complete, well-thought-out data lake architectures, as it lays out the key components and services necessary (including data governance, cataloging, data ingest, indexing, and searching) as organizations move to an enterprise-ready data lake—or as I like to call it, data lake 2.0.

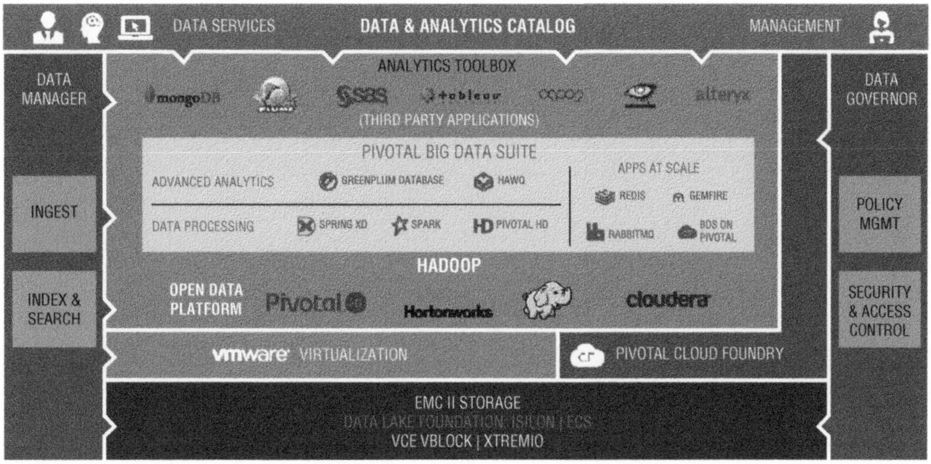

Figure 7-10: EMC Federation Business Data Lake

The industry is only at the early stages of the data lake era. There is much still to be written about how the data lake will dramatically change the ways that organizations store, manage, analyze, and value data. Heck, maybe I will need to write a third book after all. Watch this space!

Homework Assignment

Use the following exercises to apply what you learned in this chapter.

Exercise #1: List the benefits that the data lake could bring to your organization's existing data warehousing environment.

Exercise #2: List the benefits that the data lake brings to your organization's business analysts and data scientists.

Exercise #3: List the issues that are preventing your organization from moving its data warehouse environment from an RDBMS-based platform to a Hadoop-based platform.

Exercise #4: For each of the issues listed in Exercise #3, capture what your organization would need to see happen (e.g., tools, training, references, management support) in order to address that issue.

Part

III

Data Science for Business Stakeholders

In This Part

CHAPTER

8

Thinking Like a Data Scientist

One of the most frequent questions I get is: "How do I become a data scientist?" Wow, tough question. There are many outstanding books and university courses that outline the different skills, capabilities, and technologies that a data scientist is going to need to learn and eventually master. I've read several of these books and am impressed with the depth of the content.

Most of these books spend the vast majority of their time covering topics such statistics, data mining, text mining, and data visualization techniques. Yes, these are very important data science skills, but they are not nearly sufficient to make our data science teams effective. And it is not practical, or even beneficial, to try to turn your entire workforce into data scientists. Nevertheless, it is realistic to teach the business stakeholders to "think like a data scientist" in order for the business stakeholders to understand the types of business opportunities that can be driven by applying predictive and prescriptive analytics to new sources of customer, product, and operational data and to help the data science team to uncover those variables and metrics that are better predictors of performance.

The potential of thinking like a data scientist first hit me when I was the Vice President of Advertiser Analytics at a large Internet portal company. I was chartered with building the analytics to help our advertisers and agencies improve the performance of their marketing spend across the Internet portal's ad network. When I joined the company, I knew very little about the digital marketing world. So I spent the first three months on the road shadowing the company's top advertisers and their respective advertising agencies to better understand their analytic expectations and requirements.

After about three weeks on the road, I thought the project was going to be a disaster. Every one of the analytic teams at the advertisers and ad agencies with whom we met just wanted more data in a timelier manner. We were already giving these analyst teams most of data that we had, but yet they did not seem to be able to leverage this data to improve their performance across our ad network.

That is when one of my team members had one of those light bulb moments—we were talking to the wrong people. It wasn't the analysts within these advertisers and ad agencies who were making the digital marketing execution decisions, but it was the media planners and buyers (who were making the decision to which ad networks to allocate the marketing or campaign spend prior to campaign launch) and the campaign managers (who were trying to make in-flight campaign adjustments using retrospective, after-the-fact, descriptive reporting).

So we switched the entire focus of our product development efforts to focus on these key business stakeholders and to capture the decisions that they had to make and the questions that they had to answer in support of their digital marketing campaigns. And that's when the fundamentals behind the "thinking like a data scientist" process were born.

This chapter will introduce a framework, techniques, and hands-on exercises to help business stakeholders "think like a data scientist." The "thinking like a data scientist" framework will help the business stakeholders to collaborate with data scientists to uncover those variables and metrics that can improve business performance and drive business and financial value.

Data science teams need help from the business users—or subject matter experts (SME)—to understand the decisions the business is trying to make, the hypotheses that the business wants to test, and the predictions that the business needs to make. The eight-step "thinking like a data scientist" framework covers:

Step 1: Identify Key Business Initiative

Step 2: Develop Business Stakeholder Personas

Step 3: Identify Strategic Nouns

Step 4: Capture Business Decisions

Step 5: Brainstorm Business Questions

Step 6: Leverage "By" Analysis

Step 7: Create Actionable Scores

Step 8: Putting Analytics into Action

In essence, to improve the overall effectiveness of our data science teams, we need to teach the business users to think like a data scientist. As an outcome from this eight-step process, the business stakeholders and the data scientists should be better prepared to uncover those variables and metrics that are better predictors of performance.

The Process of Thinking Like a Data Scientist

The basic goal of data science is to *uncover new variables or metrics that are better predictors of* performance. But "performance" of what? That is, upon what should the data science team focus its analytic exploration and modeling development efforts? It should be no surprise that the starting point for our "thinking like a data scientist" process starts by understanding the organization's key business initiatives.

Step 1: Identify Key Business Initiative

Would you expect anything different from me than starting with what's important to the business? So, how can you spot a key business initiative? As was covered in Chapter 3, "The Big Data Strategy Document," a key business initiative is characterized as:

- Critical to the immediate-term performance of the organization
- Documented (communicated either internally or publicly)
- Cross-functional (involves more than one business function)
- Owned and championed by a senior business executive
- Has a measurable financial goal
- Has a well-defined delivery time frame (9 to 12 months)
- Undertaken to deliver significant, compelling, and/or differentiated financial or competitive advantage

It is critical to the success of your big data efforts to target business initiatives that are focused on the next 9 to 12 months. Any business initiatives longer than 12 months lack the sense of urgency to motivate the organization and risks becoming a "science experiment" project with all sorts of new and sometimes random requirements being thrown into the mix.

CROSS-REFERENCE **See Chapter 3, "The Big Data Strategy Document," to review ideas on how to leverage publicly available information (e.g., annual reports, analyst calls, executive speeches, company blogs, SeekingAlpha.com) in order to uncover an organization's key business initiatives.**

For purposes of this exercise, we are going to pretend that our client is Foot Locker and that our target business initiative is *"improve merchandising effectiveness"* as highlighted in Foot Locker's 2010 annual report (see Figure 8-1).

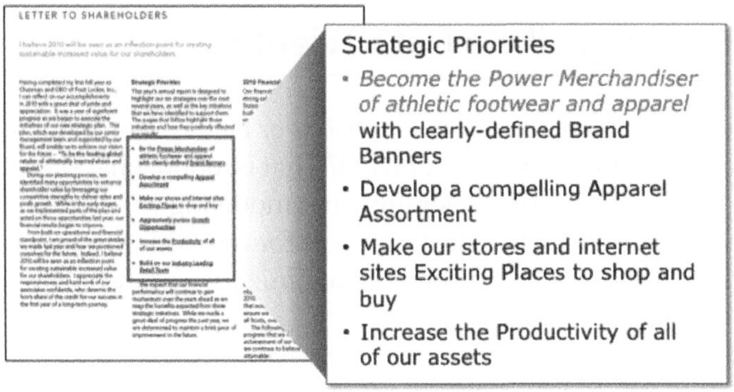

Foot Locker's 2010 Annual Report

Figure 8-1: Foot Locker's key business initiatives

Merchandising is defined as the planning and promotion of sales by presenting a product to the right market at the proper time, by carrying out organized, skillful advertising, using attractive displays, etc.[1] Figure 8-2 shows some examples of different merchandising approaches at a Foot Locker retail store.

Figure 8-2: Examples of Foot Locker's in-store merchandising

Step 2: Develop Business Stakeholder Personas

The next step in the "thinking like a data scientist" process is to identify the key business stakeholders who either impact or are impacted by the targeted

[1] http://dictionary.reference.com/browse/merchandising

business initiative (e.g., sales, marketing, finance, store operations, logistics, inventory, manufacturing). There are typically three to five different business stakeholders who are impacted by a given business initiative. We want to develop a *persona* for each of these business stakeholders to understand better their work environment and job characteristics. Understanding the work environment and job characteristics of the business stakeholders helps to start identifying the decisions and questions that these stakeholders must address with respect to the targeted business initiative.

A persona is a one- to two-page "day in the life" description that makes the key business stakeholders "come to life" for the data science and user experience (UEX) development teams. Personas are useful in understanding the goals, tasks, key decisions, key questions, and pain points of the key business stakeholders. The persona helps the data science team to start to identify the most appropriate data sources and analytic techniques to support the decisions that the business users are trying to make and the questions that they are trying to answer. Personas should be created for each type of business stakeholder affected by the targeted business initiative.

For the Foot Locker *"improve merchandising effectiveness"* business initiative, the business stakeholders for whom we would want to build personas could include:

- **Customers,** who contemplate visiting a store, visit the store, and make purchase decisions while they are in the store. Customers can come to the store under many scenarios (e.g., buy something for themselves, buy something for someone else like a son or daughter, browse to see what might be interesting, or browse for products that they then buy online). In each of these scenarios, the customer considers many factors (function, price, value, urgency, aesthetics, social perceptions, etc.) before making a purchase decision.
- **Store managers,** who are in charge of the general operations of a store. Store managers are responsible for meeting the store's sales and budget goals. To accomplish that goal, store managers make decisions to create schedules, ensure the store is stocked, create and maintain budgets, and coordinate in-store merchandising and marketing programs.
- **Merchandise managers,** who oversee the selection, acquisition, promotion, and sale of products in a retail setting. Merchandise managers typically sit at the corporate headquarters and study market trends and customer demographics in order to make decisions about how to best price, stock, display, and promote products.
- **Buyers,** who are responsible for sourcing new products and analyzing existing product sales. Buyers, who also typically sit at corporate, need to research, plan, analyze, and choose the types, quality, and prices of the products that they need to source. These buying decisions will be based

on consumer demands, industry trends, budget, and the company's overall business strategy.

A persona for the store manager could look like Figure 8-3.

Overview: Typically 3 to 5 years of industry experience. Started as store associate. Many have college degrees, but many don't.

Quote: "I'm a sports junkie, so working here only seemed natural"

Key Decisions	Key Business Questions	Pain points
Inventory Management	• What's the likely impact of corporate programs on sales and inventory? • What's the inventory status for soon-to-be-obsolete products? • What products are sitting on shelves and in the backroom too long?	Doesn't get guidance on the impact of corporate marketing and merchandising programs on his store
Markdown Management	• What are the best staff incentives to move over-stock and obsolete products? • What's the best merchandising options to move over-stock and obsolete products?	Identifying products that should be marked down as hit and miss
In-store Merchandising	• What merchandising and markdowns are best given the product I need to move? • Which products should I feature together to drive basket revenues and margins? • Which products get front-of-door feature?	Measuring in-store merchandising effectiveness is tedious and doesn't yield insights for next time

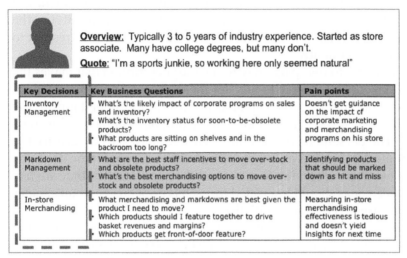

Figure 8-3: Foot Locker's store manager persona

Icon source: theamm.org

I highlighted in Figure 8-3 some of the key decisions that the store manager needs to make in support of the *"improve merchandising effectiveness"* business initiative.

Step 3: Identify Strategic Nouns

Strategic nouns are the key business entities around which the targeted business initiative is focused. It is around these key business entities that we are trying to understand and quantify their behaviors, tendencies, propensities, patterns, interests, passions, affiliations, and associations in order to predict likely actions and prescribe actionable recommendations. These strategic nouns are critical to our data scientist thinking process because these are the entities around which we will ultimately build individual *analytic profiles* and the supporting predictive and prescriptive models. Examples of strategic nouns include customers, patients, students, employees, stores, products, medications, trucks, wind turbines, etc.

For the Foot Locker *"improve merchandising effectiveness"* business initiative, the strategic nouns or key business entities on which we will focus are (see Figure 8-4):

- Customers
- Products

- Marketing campaigns
- Stores

Figure 8-4: Foot Locker's strategic nouns or key business entities

Step 4: Capture Business Decisions

The next part of the "thinking like a data scientist" process is to capture the decisions that the business stakeholders need to make about the strategic nouns in support of the targeted business initiative. We started to capture some of the key decisions as we built out the business stakeholder personas. However, we want to expand the efforts by brainstorming with each of the different stakeholders the decisions they need to make about each strategic noun in support of the targeted business initiative.

Capturing and validating these decisions is critical to the "thinking like a data scientist" process. Leading organizations like Uber and Netflix are disruptive because they build a business model that seeks to simplify their targeted personas' key decisions. For Uber, one of the decisions that it addresses is "How do I easily get from where I am to where I want to be?" For Netflix, one of the decisions that it addresses is "What content [movie, TV show] can I easily watch tonight?"

For our Foot Locker example, here are some *customer* promotional decisions that the business stakeholders need to make in support of the *"improve merchandising effectiveness"* business initiative:

- Select customers to whom to send promotional offers.
- Determine which types of promotional offers to send to those targeted customers.
- Determine when to send those promotional offers.

Here are some *product* promotional decisions that the business stakeholders need to make in support of the *"improve merchandising effectiveness"* business initiative:

- Decide which products or combinations of products to promote.
- Decide which types of in-store merchandising to employ.
- Choose the best places within the stores to display promoted products.
- Choose the best in-store promotions for reducing outdated inventory.

The capture and validation of the key business decisions are critical because these decisions:

- Drive the development of the analytic (predictive and prescriptive) models by the data science team to support these decisions
- Support the determination of the user experience/user presentation requirements, that is, where and how do the analytic insights (recommendations, scores, rules) get presented to the business stakeholders in a way that is actionable

Step 5: Brainstorm Business Questions

Probably the hardest part of the "thinking like a data scientist" exercise is to brainstorm the questions the business stakeholders need to answer to support the decisions that support the targeted business initiative. As you can see from Figure 8-5, the questions form the foundation for the entire "thinking like a data scientist" process.

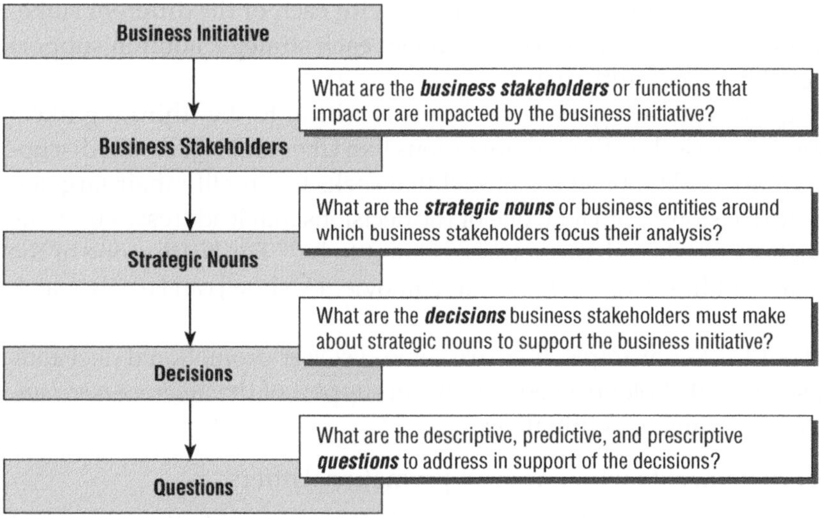

Figure 8-5: Thinking like a data scientist decomposition process

I am confident when I say that I have never met business users who did not already know the questions that they are trying to answer. However, the biggest challenge is not to capture the questions that they are trying to answer but to get the business users to expand their line of thinking to contemplate the questions *that they have given up trying to answer.*

The reason why this may be the hardest part of the process is that it requires the business stakeholders to think differently about the types of questions that they can ask. We want the business stakeholders to expand their thinking about the business questions to include:

- Predictive analytics: *Predicting* what is likely to happen
- Prescriptive analytics: *Recommending* what to do next

A key part of the "thinking like a data scientist" process is getting the business stakeholders to transition from descriptive analytics (using Business Intelligence tools to report on what happened) to predictive analytics (to predict what is likely to happen) to prescriptive analytics (to recommend what to do).

As discussed in Chapter 5, "Differences Between Business Intelligence and Data Science," we need the business stakeholders to transition their thinking to contemplate these predictive questions and prescriptive statements. See Table 8-1 for an example of the evolution from descriptive to predictive to prescriptive analytics.

Table 8-1: Evolution of Foot Locker's Business Questions

WHAT HAPPENED? (DESCRIPTIVE ANALYTICS)	WHAT WILL HAPPEN? (PREDICTIVE ANALYTICS)	WHAT SHOULD I DO? (PRESCRIPTIVE ANALYTICS)
How many Nike Hyperdunks did I sell last month?	How many Nike Hyperdunks will I sell next month?	Order [50] Nike Hyperdunks to support next month's sales projections.
What were apparel sales by zip code for Christmas last year?	What will be apparel sales by zip code over this Christmas season?	Hire [3] temporary reps for Store 12234 to handle projected Christmas sales.
How many of Jordan AJ Futures were returned last month?	How many of Jordan AJ Futures will be returned next month?	Set aside [$125K] in financial reserve to cover Jordan AJ Futures returns.

Continues

Table 8-1 *(continued)*

WHAT HAPPENED? (DESCRIPTIVE ANALYTICS)	WHAT WILL HAPPEN? (PREDICTIVE ANALYTICS)	WHAT SHOULD I DO? (PRESCRIPTIVE ANALYTICS)
What were company revenues and profits for the past quarter?	What are projected company revenues and profits for next quarter?	Mark down [LeBron Foundation apparel] by 20 percent to reduce inventory before new product releases.
How many employees did I hire last year?	How many employees will I need to hire next year?	Increase hiring pipeline by 35 percent to achieve hiring goals.

Continuing our Foot Locker *"improve merchandising effectiveness"* example, we want the business stakeholders to brainstorm the questions that support the *customer* promotional decisions from the perspectives of descriptive, predictive, and prescriptive analytics. Here are some examples of these different types of *customer* promotional questions:

Descriptive Analytics (Understanding what happened)

- What customers are most receptive to what types of merchandising campaigns?
- What are the characteristics of customers (e.g., age, gender, customer tenure, life stage, favorite sports) who are most responsive to merchandising offers?
- Are there certain times of year where certain customers are more responsive to merchandising offers?

Predictive Analytics (Predicting what will happen)

- Which customers are most likely to visit the store for a back-to-school promotion?
- Which customers are most likely to respond to the new Michael Jordan basketball shoe?
- Which customers are most likely to respond to a 50 percent off in-store markdown on Nike apparel?
- Which customers are likely to respond to an offer of a free pair of Jordan Elite socks when they buy new shoes?

Prescriptive Analytics (Recommending what to do next)

- E-mail Bill Schmarzo a 50 percent discount coupon for two pairs of Nike Elite socks when he buys his new pair of Air Jordans.
- Text Max Schmarzo that he will receive a triple-point bonus when he buys Nike apparel this coming weekend.
- Mail Alec Schmarzo a $20 cash coupon good only if he visits the store within the next 14 days.

For our Foot Locker *"improve merchandising effectiveness"* example, we want to brainstorm the questions that support our *product* promotional decisions. Here are some examples of the different types of *product* promotional questions that support the *"improve merchandising effectiveness"* business initiative:

Descriptive Analytics (Understanding what happened)

- What are the top selling products and product categories?
- What products are most responsive to in-store merchandising campaigns?
- How many basketball shoes did I sell during last year's high school and youth basketball seasons?
- Which products are hot movers that I might want to feature at the front of the store?
- Which products are slow movers that I might need an in-store merchandising campaign to move?
- Which products sell best at which times of the year/sports season?

Predictive Analytics (Predicting what will happen)

- Which shoes and apparel are most likely to sell with a back-to-school promotional event?
- Which basketball shoes and what sizes am I likely to need to stock given the upcoming high school and youth basketball seasons?
- What is the likely market basket revenue and margin from a Buy One Get One Free (BOGOF) event?

Prescriptive Analytics (Recommending what to do next)

- With the upcoming high school basketball season, promote Air Jordans and Nike Elite socks in the same display at the front of the store.
- Given the end of the football season, provide in-store BOGOF promotion of football apparel.
- Reduce prices 50 percent on the inventory of baseball cleats in anticipation of incoming new baseball equipment.

CROSS-REFERENCE Because of the depth of the topics, step 6, "leverage 'By' analysis to uncover new metrics and variables that might be better predictors of performance," and step 7, "create actionable scores that the business stakeholders can use to support the targeted business initiative," are covered in Chapters 9 and 10, respectively.

Step 8: Putting Analytics into Action

This is the part of the "thinking like a data scientist" process when the highly specialized data science work happens (using some of the analytic techniques covered in Chapter 6). The data science team will test, refine, and validate that we have identified the right metrics, variables, and scores. The data science team can then recommend to the business stakeholders how the analytics will support the decisions that support the targeted business initiative.

For example, it is not sufficient to know that there is an increase in head injuries, lacerations, and broken bones for hospitals near a National Football League (NFL) football stadium after an NFL game. One has to know (from the data science work) that there is a 27 percent increase if one is to make prescriptive recommendations about additional emergency room nurses, physicians, and supplies.

After the data science team has done its magic to validate the metrics, variables, and scores that are better predictors of business performance, then the next step in the "thinking like a data scientist" process is "putting the analytics into action" with respect to what analytics-driven scores or recommendations to deliver to the business stakeholders. We spent a considerable amount of time in Chapter 4, "The Importance of the User Experience," detailing how critical the user experience is to the ultimate success of the organization's big data initiatives. Remember: If you can't present the analytic results in a way that is actionable, then why even bother.

You can facilitate the development of a compelling and actionable user experience by starting with a simple "recommendations worksheet." The recommendations worksheet links the decisions that our business stakeholders need to make to the predictive and prescriptive analytics that the data science team is going to build. The recommendations worksheet starts with the decisions captured in step 4, and then identifies the potential recommendations that could be delivered to the business stakeholders in support of those decisions. Finally, the worksheet captures the potential scores (and the supporting variables and metrics) that can be used to power the recommendations.

In summary,

Decisions → Recommendations → Scores (Supporting Metrics)

See Figure 8-6 for a simple template that we can use to guide the recommendations process.

Business Initiative: ______________________		
Persona: ____________________		
Decisions	Potential Recommendations	Potential Scores / Metrics

Figure 8-6: Recommendations worksheet template

Let's see the recommendations worksheet in action. For our Foot Locker *"improve merchandising effectiveness"* business initiative, the resulting recommendations worksheet could look like Figure 8-7.

Business Initiative: *Improve Merchandising Effectiveness*		
Persona: Store Manager		
Decisions	Potential Recommendations	Potential Scores / Metrics
Optimize product markdowns	• When to start markdowns? • Initial product markdowns (% or dollar amounts)? • When to accelerate markdown timing? • How much to accelerate markdown pricing (% or dollar amounts)?	**Merchandise Markdown Score** • Product inventory (on-hand + on-order) • Product actual sales vs. forecast sales • Product actual sales trends • Replacement product forecasts • Product price sensitivities • Market basket percentage • Current sports season • Local economic conditions
Improve In-store merchandising effectiveness	• What products to feature in-window, store-entrance, and end-caps? • What products to feature together? • When to change featured products?	**Hot Product Score** • Product forecasted sales • Historical brand basket percentage • Endorser sentiment score • Consumer comments • Store employee notes • Reviews (Amazon, RunRepeat)
...		

Figure 8-7: Foot Locker's recommendations worksheet

The last step (and possibly the most fun step) is the creation of the user experience mock-up that validates that we are building the right analytics and have a thorough understanding of where and how to deliver the analytic results, scores, and recommendations (e.g., management dashboards, reports, call center, procurement, sales, marketing, finance, etc.). See Figure 8-8 for an example of the store manager actionable dashboard.

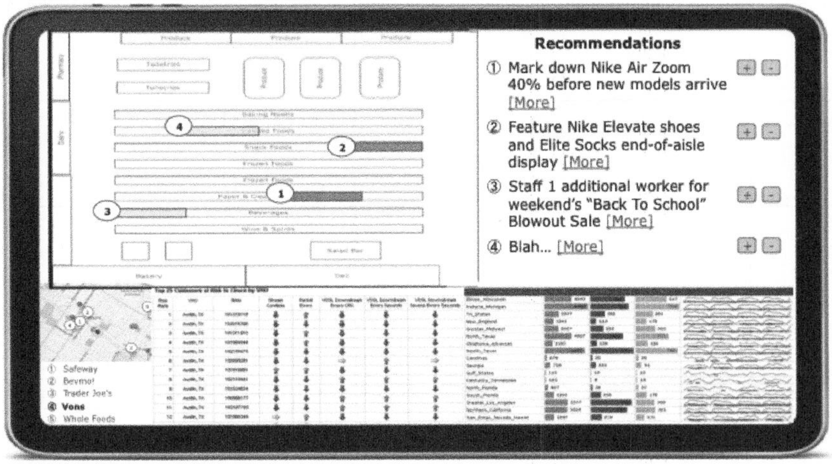

Figure 8-8: Foot Locker's store manager actionable dashboard

During the envisioning and requirements gathering and validation processes, do not worry about the quality of the mock-up. Using PowerPoint and a few standard dashboard images can go a long way in fueling the creative thinking of the targeted business stakeholders. Heck, most of my mock-ups look like they were drawn with a crayon!

Summary

Data scientists are critical to the ability to integrate data and analytics into the organization's business models. But an important challenge is to get your business users to "think like a data scientist" when contemplating data sources and metrics that might be better predictors of business performance. Having a business organization that can "think like a data scientist" will drive better collaboration with your data science team and ultimately lead to better predictive and prescriptive results and increased value to the business.

We introduced the "thinking like a data scientist" eight-step process that includes:

Step 1: Identify Key Business Initiative

Step 2: Develop Business Stakeholder Persona

Step 3: Identify Strategic Nouns

Step 4: Capture Business Decisions

Step 5: Brainstorm Business Questions

Step 6: Leverage "By" Analysis

Step 7: Create Actionable Scores

Step 8: Putting Analytics into Action

We used a Foot Locker example to help drive home the concepts and techniques in the eight-step "thinking like a data scientist" process. As a result, not only do the business stakeholders better understand how the data science process works, but the business stakeholders also understand what they can do to help the data science process deliver new value to the organization by helping to uncover new data sources, metrics, variables, and scores.

CROSS-REFERENCE **As noted earlier in this chapter, steps 6 and 7 are covered in Chapters 9 and 10, respectively.**

Homework Assignment

Use the following exercises to apply what you learned in this chapter.

Exercise #1: Start with the key business initiative that you identified in Chapter 2. Write down the key business stakeholders who either impact or are impacted by the targeted business initiative. Capture organizational roles versus individual names at this point.

Exercise #2: Develop a one-page persona for one of the key business stakeholders identified in Exercise #1. Use the persona template that we discussed in this chapter.

Exercise #3: Write down the key business entities (or strategic nouns) for the targeted business initiative. These can be both humans (e.g., customers, students, patients, technicians, engineers, etc.) and things (e.g., jet engines, trucks, ATMs, test suites, curriculums, stores, competitors).

Exercise #4: Brainstorm the *business decisions* that the *business stakeholders* need to make about the *business entities* in support of the targeted *business initiative*.

Exercise #5: Brainstorm the business questions that the business stakeholders might want to ask and answer with respect to each of the decisions listed in Exercise #4. Be sure to contemplate (1) descriptive questions, (2) predictive questions, and (3) prescriptive statements. I repeated the decomposition process slide in Figure 8-9 for reference.

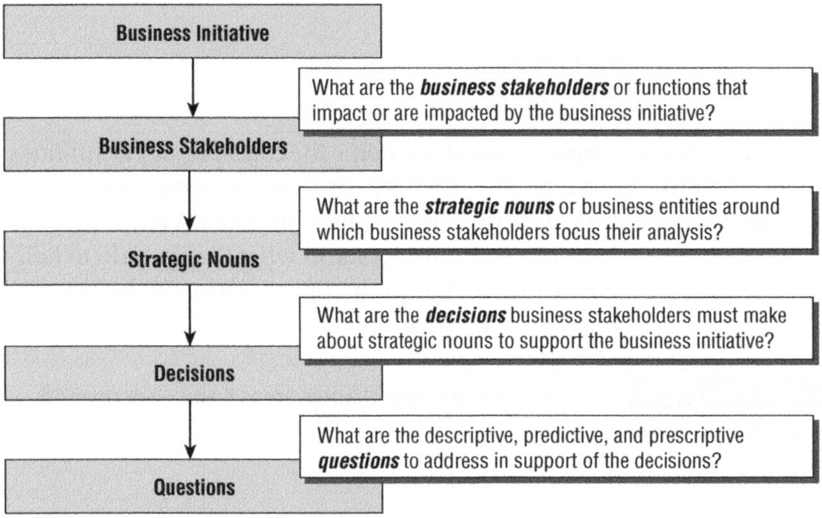

Figure 8-9: Thinking like a data scientist decomposition process

CHAPTER

9

"By" Analysis Technique

Chapter 8, "Thinking Like a Data Scientist," briefly introduced the "By" analysis as a technique around which the business subject matter experts (SMEs) and the data science team could collaborate to uncover new variables and metrics that might be better predictors of business performance. "By" analysis is a technique that was historically used during the data warehouse requirements gathering processes to ensure that the data warehouse schema was robust enough to support the full range of Business Intelligence queries and reports that business users might request. Data science builds on the "By" analysis to create a collaborative technique to drive alignment between the business users and the data scientists to identify and brainstorm variables and metrics that might be better predictors of business performance. The "By" analysis technique re-enforces the importance of the "thinking like a data scientist" process.

Remember the data science definition from *Moneyball: The Art of Winning an Unfair Game* covered in Chapter 5:

> *Data science is about finding new variables and metrics that are better predictors of performance.*

The "By" analysis technique supports this data science objective by powering the partnership between the business users and the data scientists to leverage new sources of customer, product, operational, market, and competitive data, coupled with advanced analytics, to uncover metrics and variables that may be better predictors of business performance.

Continuing with the baseball analogy, Major League Baseball (MLB) teams such as the Boston Red Sox are continually exploring and testing new sources of data and new analytics in hopes of uncovering new variables and metrics that are better predictors of player performance; that is, they are trying to find that next more predictive "on-base percentage" (see Figure 9-1).

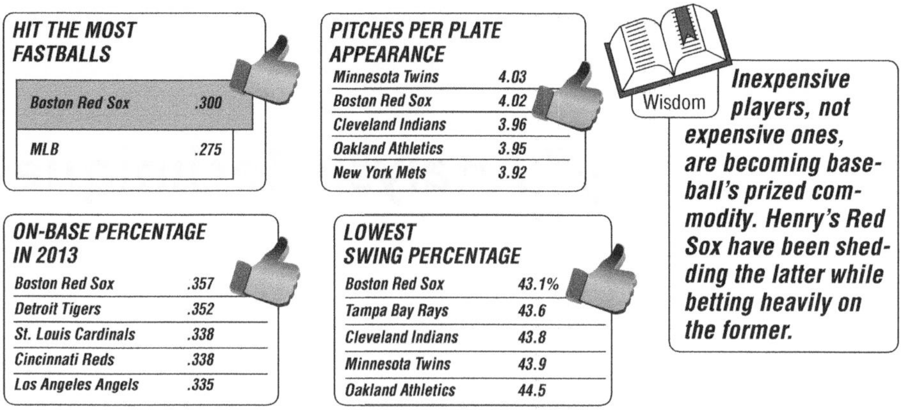

Figure 9-1: Identifying metrics that may be better predictors of performance

Ultimately, these new variables and metrics will be used to determine a player's financial value in achieving the team's business objectives. Identifying these metrics and variables is no guarantee that they will be better predictors of performance (as seen from the Red Sox's most recent performance), but it gives the data science teams a starting point for their data science exploration and "fail-fast" analytic processes.

"By" Analysis Introduction

The "By" analysis technique exploits a business user's natural "question and answer" enquiry process to identify new data sources, dimensional characteristics, variables, and metrics that could be leveraged by the data science team in building the predictive and prescriptive analytic models to help predict business performance. The "By" analysis leverages a business stakeholder's natural curiosity to brainstorm new:

- Metrics, measures, and key performance indicators
- Dimensions (e.g., *strategic nouns*) and the attributes and characteristics associated with those dimensions or strategic nouns
- Areas for potential analytics exploration

The "By" analysis technique leverages the normal business stakeholder question and query exploration process; it fuels the natural inquisitive human nature to seek out new variables and metrics that may be better predictors of business performance.

The "By" analysis uses a simple *"I want to [verb] [metric] by [dimensional attribute]"* format to capture the business stakeholder brainstorming process and reveal new data and analytic areas of exploration. The "By" analysis format looks like this:

- "I want to"
- [Verb] such as see, know, report, compare, trend, plot, predict, score, etc.
- [Metric] such as sales, margin, profits, social media posts, comments, physician notes, vibration levels, sensor codes, etc.
- "By"
- [Dimension or dimensional attribute] such as city, state, zip code, date, time, seasonality, product category, remodel date, store manager demographics, etc.

Here is an example of a "By" analysis statement:

> *I want to [report] [online sales and product margin]* by… *[product category, website, keyword search term, referring website, display ad, day part, day of week, customer behavioral category, customer re-targeting category].*

The above "By" analysis sentence breaks down as such:

- The verb is [report],
- The metric is [online sales and product margin], and
- The dimensional attributes and characteristics are [product category, website, keyword search term, referring website, display ad, day part, day of week, customer behavioral category, customer re-targeting category].

The data science team is responsible for quantifying which variables or combinations of variables are better predictors of performance. Consequently, you want to give the data science team as many variables as is practical to consider. For example, in one project the business stakeholders (teachers, in this case) wanted to know the impact that a change in the value of a house might have on a student's classroom performance. So the data science team grabbed some Zillow data to see if there was any correlation (there wasn't).

Here are some additional "By" analysis statements:

- I want to [trend] [hospital admissions] by… [disease category, zip code, patient demographics, hospital size, area demographics, and day of week].

- I want to [compare] [current versus previous maintenance issues] by... [turbine, turbine manufacturer, date installed, last maintenance date, maintenance person, and weather conditions].
- I want to [predict] [student performance] by... [age, gender, family size, child number within family, family income, previous test scores, current homework scores, and parent's education level].

I hope that you can see that these types of sentences are very easy to create. Also, the "By" analysis technique is perfect for a facilitated brainstorming session where the goal is to fuel the group innovative thinking process to identify additional variables and metrics that might be better predictors of business performance. And remember, as you go through any brainstorming process, **all** ideas are worthy of consideration, and the brainstorming process should not filter the suggestions and thereby inadvertently throttle the creative thinking process.

The dimensional attributes and characteristics that follow the "by" phrase are the gold in the data science exploration process. The wide and diverse variety of dimension and dimensional attributes uncovered by the "By" analysis are critical to guiding the data science team's analytic exploration and modeling process. The "By" analysis can suggest additional variables and metrics that the data science team may want to explore in creating the prescriptive actions, scores, and recommendations that are used to support the targeted business initiative.

"By" Analysis Exercise

Continuing with the sports theme, let's introduce an exercise that allows you to put the "By" analysis to work. Pretend that you are the head coach for the National Basketball Association's (NBA's) Golden State Warriors and have to play the Cleveland Cavaliers in the 2015 NBA Championship Finals. Your job as the head coach of the Golden State Warriors is to craft a defensive plan and game strategy that maximizes your chances (or probability) of winning the game by minimizing the shooting and offensive effectiveness of Cleveland's superstar, LeBron James.

Let's start the analysis process by gaining some fundamental insights regarding the "hot spots" for shooters across the NBA; that is, where the locations or "spots" are on the court where shooters are most efficient as measured by "points per shot" (see Figure 9-2).

NOTE **The "points per shot" metric takes into account (normalizes) the value of a two-point shot versus the value of a three-point shot. The chart in Figure 9-2 shows that, generally speaking, three-point shooting is more effective than two-point shooting except near the rim (dunks result in a pretty high shooting percentage).**

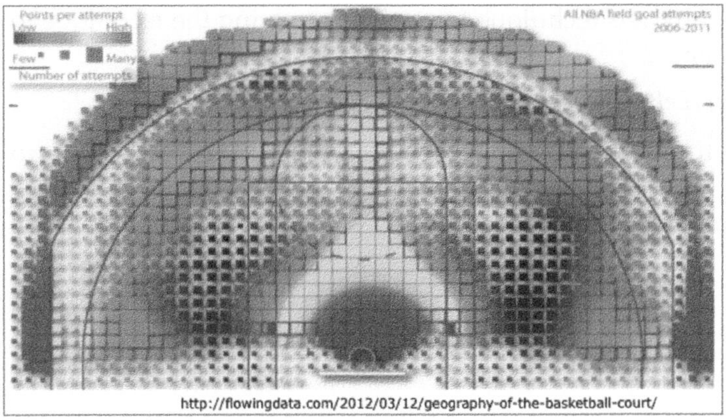

Figure 9-2: NBA shooting effectiveness

Let's drill down into our analysis process by understanding LeBron James's specific shooting tendencies and performance. The shooting hot spot chart in Figure 9-3 provides a good starting point in the development of our defensive strategy against LeBron James. Figure 9-3 shows LeBron James's shooting percentages from different spots on the court. This chart helps us to start to contemplate the key decision: *"Where do we want to direct or force LeBron James to go while on the court in order to mitigate his offensive prowess?"*

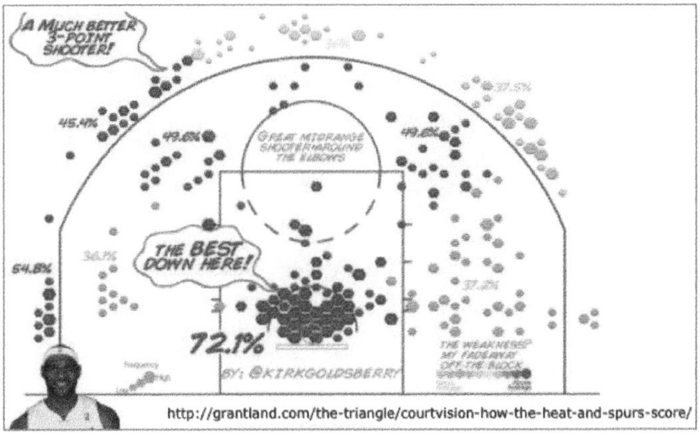

Figure 9-3: LeBron James's shooting effectiveness

While the chart in Figure 9-3 is interesting in highlighting areas *in general* where LeBron's shooting percentages are better or worse, to be actionable you need to get more detailed insights. To create more actionable insights, we need to understand *"what detailed data or insights do I need in order to create specific, actionable recommendations to mitigate LeBron James's shooting effectiveness?"* This is the perfect time to employ the "By" analysis technique.

Let's put the "By" analysis technique to work by applying the technique to the following statement:

I want to [know] [LeBron James's shooting percentage] by…

Take a moment to jot down some variables or metrics that come to mind following the "by" phrase (e.g., "I want to know LeBron James's shooting percentage by… opponent").

- ____________________
- ____________________
- ____________________
- ____________________

Below are some variables and metrics that I came up with using the "By" analysis technique:

- At home versus on the road
- Number of days of rest
- Shot area
- Opposing team
- Defender
- Game location
- Game location elevation
- Game time weather
- Game time temperature
- Game time humidity
- Time (hours) since last game
- Average time of ball possession
- Time left in game
- Total minutes played in game
- Number of shots attempted
- Number of shots made
- Location of shots attempted
- Location of shots made
- Volume of boos
- Number of fouls
- Number of assists

- Playing a former team
- Time of day
- Record of opponent
- Feelings toward opponent
- Performance in last game
- Number of negative Twitter comments
- Stadium temperature
- Stadium humidity
- Number of fans in attendance
- Number of LeBron jerseys in attendance

Here's the interesting point: people who have never been an NBA basketball coach and even people who may have never even played basketball can come up with some of the more interesting dimensions and dimensional attributes in trying to identify variables and metrics that may be better predictors of LeBron James's shooting tendencies and performance.

Building on some of the suggestions that came out of the LeBron James "By" analysis technique, let's triage LeBron James's shooting percentages for the 2014–2015 regular season by a couple of dimensions identified in the brainstorming session: [Home versus Road] and [Number of Days Rest]. Table 9-1 shows LeBron James's shooting percentages.

Table 9-1: LeBron James's Shooting Percentages

2014–2015	OVERALL SHOOTING PERCENTAGE	OVERALL SHOOTING INDEX	3-POINT SHOOTING PERCENTAGE	3-POINT SHOOTING INDEX
Regular season	48.8	100.0	35.4	100.0
Home	47.3	96.9	35.6	100.6
Road	50.2	102.9	35.3	99.7
0 days rest	49.8	102.0	38.0	107.3
1 day rest	46.3	94.9	32.3	91.2
2 days rest	51.3	105.1	37.3	105.4
3 days rest	52.7	108.0	42.9	121.2
4 days rest	57.1	117.0	60.0	169.5
6+ days rest	48.5	99.4	30.8	87.0

Source: `http://stats.nba.com/player/#!/2544/stats/`

You're now starting to get some interesting insights. Remember, insights are only observations buried in the data that look unusual when compared to an individual's standard performance. Just from the simple analysis in Table 9-1, you can start uncovering some insights about LeBron's shooting tendencies that the data science team might want to explore further. For example:

- LeBron shoots significantly worse when he's had just one day of rest (8.8 percent worse from three-point range).
- If you give LeBron four days of rest, watch out! His shooting percentages improve overall and improve dramatically for three-point shooting (69.5 percent better three-point shooting with four days of rest).

As discussed in Chapter 2, "Big Data Business Model Maturity Index," once you start uncovering insights buried across the wide variety and depth of data, you need the business subject matter experts to assess the value of these insights against the S.A.M. criteria:

- Is the insight of **Strategic** value to what you are trying to accomplish?
- Is the insight **Actionable** (i.e., is the insight at a level upon which I can act on that insight)?
- Is the insight of **Material** value (i.e., is the value of the insight greater than the cost to act on that insight)?

Once an "insight" has passed the S.A.M. criteria, you want the data science team to build the analytic models that quantify cause and effect, assess goodness of fit, and create the prescriptive actions or recommendations that provide guidance to the frontline employees (LeBron James's defenders in this example) and managers (Golden State Warriors coaching staff) in the achievement of their business initiative of minimizing LeBron James's shooting and offensive performance effectiveness.

Foot Locker Use Case "By" Analysis

Continuing the Foot Locker use case that was started in Chapter 8, "Thinking Like a Data Scientist," we want to apply the "By" analysis to uncover new variables and metrics that might be better predictors of performance for the "improve merchandising effectiveness" business initiative.

Chapter 8 captured the descriptive, predictive, and prescriptive questions that supported the Foot Locker "improve merchandising effectiveness" business initiative. As a reminder, below are some of the customer promotional questions that were captured:

Descriptive Analytics (Understanding what happened)

- What customers are most receptive to what types of merchandising campaigns?
- Are there certain times of year where certain customers are more responsive to merchandising offers?

Predictive Analytics (Predicting what will happen)

- Which customers are most likely to visit the store for a back-to-school promotion?
- Which customers are most likely to respond to the new Michael Jordan basketball shoe?

Prescriptive Analytics (Recommending what to do next)

- E-mail Bill Schmarzo a 50 percent discount coupon when he buys two pairs of Nike Elite socks when he buys his new pair of Air Jordans.
- Text Max Schmarzo triple-point bonus when he buys Nike apparel this coming weekend.
- Mail Alec Schmarzo a $20 cash coupon good only if he visits the store within the next 14 days.

Let's put the "By" analysis technique to work against the following question:

> *"What customers are most receptive to Foot Locker's merchandising campaigns by…?"*

Again, take a moment to jot down some variables or metrics that come to mind following the "by" phrase. I'll wait for you to jot down your ideas (again, one variable or metric per line).

- ______________________
- ______________________
- ______________________
- ______________________

The following is a list of some of the variables and metrics that I came up with when I applied the "By" analysis technique to the Foot Locker's customer question: *"What customers are most receptive to Foot Locker's merchandising campaigns by…?"*

- Age
- Gender
- Marital status
- Number of children
- Length of marriage
- Income level
- Education level
- VIP loyalty card member
- VIP member length of time
- VIP rewards expired (%)
- VIP rewards expired ($)
- Own or rent residence
- Tenure in current home
- Value of current home
- Favorite sports
- Favorite sports teams
- High school sports interest
- College sports interest
- Active athlete
- Type of athletic activity
- Exercise minutes per week
- Number of days per week exercised
- ...

For purposes of completeness, you would want to perform the "By" analysis exercise for a couple of additional customer questions in order to capture a robust set of variables and metrics that could be used to predict the performance of the "improve merchandising effectiveness" business initiative.

Continuing the Foot Locker example that started in Chapter 8, below are the product promotional questions that were captured:

Descriptive Analytics (Understanding what happened)

- What products are most successful with what merchandising campaigns?
- How many basketball shoes did I sell during last year's high school and youth basketball seasons?
- Which products are slow movers that I might need an in-store merchandising campaign to move?

Predictive Analytics (Predicting what will happen)

- Which shoes and apparel are most likely to sell with a back-to-school promotional event?
- What is the likely market basket revenue and margin from a Buy One Get One Free (BOGOF) event?

Prescriptive Analytics (Recommending what to do next)

- With the upcoming high school basketball season, promote Air Jordans and Nike Elite socks in the same display at the front of the store.
- Given the end of the football season, provide in-store BOGOF promotion of football apparel.

- Reduce prices 50 percent on the inventory of baseball cleats in anticipation of incoming new baseball equipment.

In the following list, the "By" analysis technique is applied to the Foot Locker's **product** question: *"What products are most successful with what merchandising campaigns by...?"*

- Product category
- Product size
- Product style
- Product color
- Product form
- Product type
- Brand
- Primary sport
- Retail price
- Product release date
- Product discontinue date
- Brand age
- Athlete endorser
- Athlete endorser Q score[1]
- Athlete endorser sentiment
- Last TV advertisement date
- Brand social sentiment
- Product Yelp rating
- ...

Very important note about the "By" analysis technique: the variables and metrics uncovered from the "By" analysis technique are only limited by the creative thinking of the business users; that is, the people who live these decisions and questions daily.

Hopefully you can see that the number and variety of variables and metrics uncovered using the "By" analysis technique can be quite bountiful, and the more variables and metrics, the better from a data science perspective.

Summary

The "By" analysis technique is a powerful tool in not only helping to understand the key metrics and dimensions of the business but also yielding insights into areas of the business ripe for data science analysis. The "By" analysis technique fuels the creative discovery of new variables and metrics by leveraging the natural question and answer exploration of the business users. The "By" analysis technique uses a simple sentence format:

- "I want to"
- [Verb] such as see, know, report, compare, trend, plot, predict, score, etc.
- [Metric] such as sales, margin, profits, social media posts, comments, physician notes, vibration levels, sensor codes, etc.

[1] Q score is a measure of the familiarity and appeal of a brand, celebrity, company, or entertainment product.

- "By"
- [Dimension or dimensional attribute] such as city, state, zip code, date, time, seasonality, product category, remodel date, store manager demographics, etc.

Finally, and maybe most important, the "By" analysis is a technique that can drive the collaboration between the business users and the data scientists to uncover new variables and metrics that can guide the data scientists' analytics exploration and model development process. The "By" analysis technique reenforces the importance of the "thinking like a data scientist" process.

In Chapter 10, we will cover how to combine these variables and metrics to develop actionable scores that can be used to address the business decisions that support the "improve merchandising effectiveness" business initiative.

Homework Assignment

Use the following exercises to apply what you learned in this chapter.

Exercise #1: Pick one of the questions for one of your key business entities or strategic nouns that you came up with in Chapter 8 and apply the "By" analysis technique. If possible, get a small group of co-workers together and brainstorm the "By" analysis as a group to uncover even more potential variables and metrics. Fuel the creative process with coffee and donuts—lots of donuts—if necessary.

Exercise #2: Pick a different question for the same key business entity and apply the "By" analysis technique to see what additional variables and metrics you uncover. Again, do not worry at this point if the data is available. Now is not the time to filter the creative thinking outcomes. You will have time to evaluate the value and implementation feasibility of each of the potential variables and data sources later in the process.

CHAPTER

10

Score Development Technique

In New Zealand, people are taking a "thinking like a data scientist" approach to optimizing social worker spending and casework prioritization. A related *BusinessWeek* article titled "A Moneyball Approach to Helping Troubled Kids" (May 11, 2015) highlights the role that *scores* play in identifying and prioritizing problem areas and deciding what corrective actions to take. Here are a couple of excerpts from the article:

> *Using data from welfare, education, employment, and the housing agencies and the courts, the government identified the most expensive welfare beneficiaries – kids who have at least one close adult relative who's previously been reported to child safety authorities, been to prison, and spent substantial time on welfare. "There are million-dollar [cost] kids in those families," Minister of Finance Bill English says. "By the time they are 10, their likelihood of incarceration is 70 percent. You've got to do something about that."*
>
> *...one idea is to rate families, giving them a number [score] that could be used to identify who's most at risk in the same way that lenders rely on credit scores to determine creditworthiness. "The way we may use it, it's going to be like it's a FICO score," says Jennie Feria, Head of Los Angeles' Department of Children and Family Service. The information, she says, could be used both to prioritize cases and to figure out who needs extra services.*

In wrapping up the "thinking like a data scientist" process that began in Chapter 8 and continued in Chapter 9, this chapter focuses on the role of scores in supporting an organization's key business decisions. As exhibited in the preceding New Zealand welfare example, scores are a very effective data science concept in aggregating a wide variety of variables and metrics in order to come up with a yardstick or guide that can be used to support key business and operational decisions.

Scores are very important concepts in the world of data science. Many times, the results of the data science efforts will be presented as scores that can help to guide frontline employees' and managers' decision making in support of the targeted business initiative.

The power of a score is that it is relatively easy to understand from a business stakeholder perspective. It focuses the data science efforts on identifying and exploring new metrics and variables to include in a score that might be a better predictor of business performance or an individual's behaviors.

The purpose of the score technique is to look for groupings of metrics and variables that can be combined to create an actionable score that you can use to support your key **business decisions**. These scores are critical components of the "thinking like a data scientist" process because they can guide the decisions your frontline employees are trying to make and/or predict the likelihood of a customer's actions, outcomes, or behaviors.

Definition of a Score

Let's start by defining *score*:

- A score is a dynamic rating or grade standardized to aid in comparisons, performance tracking, and decision making.
- A score can help predict the likelihood of certain actions or outcomes.
- A score is an actionable, analytic-based measure that supports the decisions your organization is trying to make and guides the outcomes the organization is trying to predict.

A common example of a score is the *intelligence quotient* or IQ. An IQ is derived from several standardized tests in order to create a single number that assesses an individual's intelligence. The IQ is standardized at 100 with a standard deviation of 15, which means that 68 percent of the population is within 1 standard deviation of the 100 standard (between 85 and 115). This standardization makes the IQ easier to compare different students, candidates, or applicants and support key hiring, promotion, and college application decisions.

The true beauty of a score is its ability to convert a wide range of variables and metrics—all weighted, valued, and correlated differently depending on what is being measured—into a single number that can be used to guide decision making. And the true power of the score is the ability to start simple, and then constantly fine-tune and expand the score with new metrics, variables, and the relationships that might yield better predictors of business performance or an individual's behaviors.

FICO Score Example

Many organizations have built their business models on the development of scores that help organizations to make better decisions. For example, Traackr and Apinions are companies that assign scores to influencers on social media to help identify who organizations should target from a media perspective. FICO may be the best example of an organization that has built its business around the development of a score.[1] The FICO score is used to predict the likelihood of a borrower to repay a loan. Fair, Isaac, and Company first introduced the FICO score in 1989. Most readers are probably familiar with the FICO score (and you have probably seen your own FICO score several times), which combines multiple variables and metrics about a loan applicant's financial, credit, and payment history to create a singular score that lenders use to predict a borrower's ability to repay a loan (see Figure 10-1).

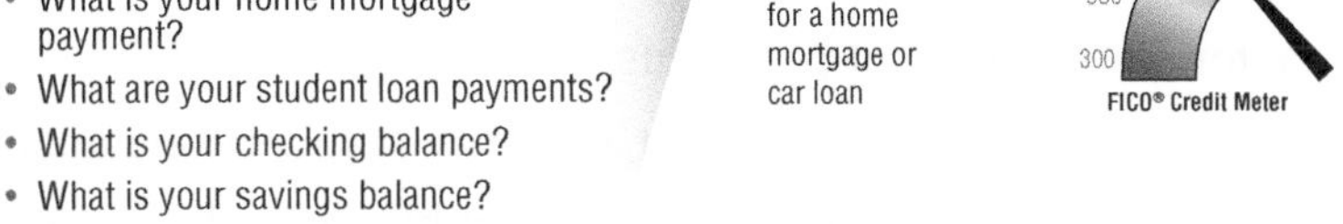

DESCRIPTIVE ANALYTICS
• What are your credit card balances?
• What is your credit card payment history?
• How long have you had the credit cards?
• What is your credit utilization?
• How many car loans do you have?
• What is your home mortgage payment?
• What are your student loan payments?
• What is your checking balance?
• What is your savings balance?
PREDICTIVE ANALYTICS
FICO score is used by lenders to predict your ability to repay a loan:
• Your credit worthiness in applying for credit or a loan
• The interest rate and loan terms that you receive for a home mortgage or car loan
300
580
670
740
800
850
FICO® Credit Meter

Figure 10-1: FICO score considerations

An individual's FICO score can range between 300 and 850. A FICO score above 650 indicates that the individual has a very good credit history, while people with scores below 620 will often find it substantially more difficult to obtain financing at a favorable rate (see Figure 10-2).[2]

---

1 FICO is a software company based in San Jose, California, and founded by Bill Fair and Earl Isaac in 1956. Its FICO score, a measure of consumer credit risk, has become the standard for measuring a consumer's ability to repay a loan in the United States.

2 http://tightwadtravelers.com/check-fico-credit-score-free

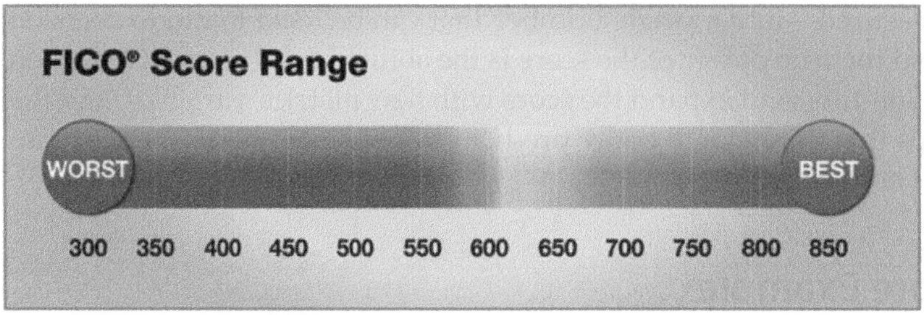

Figure 10-2: FICO score decision range

The FICO score amalgamates a wide range of consumer financial, credit, and payment metrics in order to generate the single score for a specific individual. The powerful concept behind the FICO score is that it combines this wide range of consumer financial, credit, and payment metrics into a single, predictive score that predicts an individual's likelihood to repay a loan.

To dive deeper into the FICO score example, we see the data elements that are used in the calculation of an individual's FICO score include payment history, credit utilization, length of credit history, new credit applications, and credit mix.[3]

Payment History. Thirty-five percent of the FICO credit score is based on a borrower's payment history, making the repayment of past debt the most important factor in calculating credit scores. According to FICO, past long-term behavior is used to forecast future long-term behavior. This is a measure of how do you handle credit; think credit "behavioral analytics." This particular category encompasses the following metrics and variables:

- Payment information on various types of accounts, including credit cards, retail accounts, installment loans, and mortgages
- The appearance of any adverse public records, such as bankruptcies, judgments, suits, and liens, as well as collection notices and delinquencies
- Length of time for any delinquent payments
- Amount of money still owed on delinquent accounts or collection items
- Length of time since any delinquencies, adverse public records, or collection notices
- Number of past-due items listed on a credit report
- Number of accounts being paid as agreed

[3] FICO's five factors: The components of a FICO credit score (`http://www.creditcards.com/credit-card-news/help/5-parts-components-fico-credit-score-6000.php`).

Credit Utilization. Thirty percent of the FICO credit score is based on a borrower's credit utilization; that is, the percentage of available credit that has been borrowed by that individual. The credit utilization calculation is composed of six variables:

- The amount of debt still owed to lenders
- The number of accounts with debt outstanding
- The amount of debt owed on individual accounts
- The types of loans
- The percentage of credit lines in use on revolving accounts, like credit cards
- The percentage of debt still owed on installment loans, like mortgages

Length of Credit History. Fifteen percent of the FICO credit score is based on the length of time each account has been open and the length of time since the account's most recent activity. FICO breaks down "length of credit history" into three variables:

- Length of time the accounts have been open
- Length of time specific account types have been open
- Length of time since those accounts were used

New Credit Applications. Ten percent of the FICO credit score is based on borrowers' new credit applications. Within the new credit application category, FICO considers the following variables:

- Number of accounts that have been opened in the past 6 to 12 months, as well as the proportion of accounts that are new, by account type
- Number of recent credit inquiries
- Length of time since the opening of any new accounts, by account type
- Length of time since any credit inquiries
- The re-appearance on a credit report of positive credit information for an account that had earlier payment problems

Credit Mix. Ten percent of the FICO credit score is based on repaying the variety of debt, which is a measure of the borrower's ability to handle a wide range of credit including:

- Installment loans including auto loans, student loans, and furniture purchases
- Mortgage loans

- Bank credit cards
- Retail credit cards
- Gas station credit cards
- Unpaid loans taken on by collection agencies or debt buyers
- Rental data

The point of showing all the details behind the FICO score calculation is to reinforce the basic concept (and power) of a score—that a score can take into consideration a wide range of descriptive variables and metrics to create a **single predictive number** that can be used to support an organization's key decisions or, in the case of the FICO score, used by lenders to predict a loan applicant's likelihood to repay a loan. That's a very powerful concept. Scores are a critical concept in getting your business stakeholders to contemplate how they might want to integrate different variables and measures to create actionable, predictive scores to support their key business decisions.

Other Industry Score Examples

Different types of scores can be created to support decision making across a wide variety of industries. In fact, the ability to create actionable scores is only limited by the creative thinking of the business stakeholders; hence, the importance of getting business stakeholders to "think like a data scientist."

For example, here are some scores to consider for the financial services industry:

- **Retirement Readiness Score.** This would be a score that measures how ready each client is for retirement. This score could include variables such as age, current annual income, current annual expenses, net worth, value of primary home, value of secondary homes, desired retirement age, desired retirement location (Iowa is a lot cheaper than Palo Alto!), number of dependent children, number of dependent parents, desired retirement lifestyle, and so forth.
- **Job Security Score.** This score would measure the security of each individual's job. This score could include variables such as industry, job type, employer(s), job level/title, job experience, age, education level, skill sets, industry publications and presentations, Klout scores, and so on.
- **Home Value Stability Score.** This score would measure the stability of the value of a particular house. This score could consider variables such as current value, supply/demand ratio of area, house sales history, value of house compared to comparable houses, tax assessment compared to comparable houses, whether it's a primary residence or rental residence, local price-to-rent ratio, local housing value trends (maybe pulled from Zillow), distance from a high school or junior high school, quality rating of that high school or junior high school, distance from shopping, and others.

Interestingly, combining the **home value stability** score with the FICO score would have provided a more holistic assessment of banks' housing market exposure prior to the 2007 financial market meltdown. The FICO score was insufficient when trying to determine the level of housing market risk as financial organizations were writing mortgage loans. Coupling the FICO score with a **home value stability** score could have provided invaluable insights as banks decided (made decisions) as to whom to make home mortgage loans and in which housing markets (e.g., deciding which housing markets were "over-valued").

The key point in this mortgage market collapse example is that it is important to consider how multiple scores can provide different perspectives on the decision that is being evaluated. Using different scores can provide a more holistic assessment of the true conditions around which to make these key business decisions.

Table 10-1 shows additional scores from a variety of industries.

Table 10-1: Potential Scores for Other Industries

FINANCIAL SERVICES	CREDIT CARDS	MANUFACTURING	GAMING/ HOSPITALITY
FICO	Attrition Risk	Equipment Maintenance	Player/Customer Lifetime Value
Retirement Readiness	Fraud Risk	Supplier Reliability	Gaming Preferences
Investment Risk	Product Preferences	Supplier Quality	
EDUCATION	**HEALTH CARE**	**UTILITIES**	**PRO SPORTS**
Graduation Readiness	Wellness Condition	Energy Efficiency	Fatigue Factor
Cohorts Influence	Stress Risk	Conservation Effectiveness	Motivation Factor

The purpose of the score technique is to look for groupings of common or similar variables and metrics that can be meshed together to create a score that can guide your decision making. These scores are a critical component of the "thinking like a data scientist" process. Scores can provide invaluable support for the decisions that you are trying to make or what actions or outcomes you are trying to predict with respect to your targeted business initiative.

LeBron James Exercise Continued

Let's continue the LeBron James example that you started in Chapter 9. The exercise asked you to play the role as the head coach for the National Basketball Association's (NBA's) Golden State Warriors in preparing to play the Cleveland Cavaliers in the 2015 NBA Championship Finals. Your job as the head coach of the Golden State Warriors is to craft a defensive plan and game strategy that maximizes your chances (or probability) of winning the series by minimizing the shooting and offensive effectiveness of Cleveland's superstar, LeBron James.

We used the "By" analysis technique in Chapter 9 to tease out a variety of variables and metrics that **might** be predictors of LeBron James's shooting prowess. Below is the list of the variables that came out of that "By" analysis process.

I want to [know] [LeBron James's shooting percentage] by…

- At home versus on the road
- Number of days rest
- Shot area
- Opposing team
- Defender
- Game location
- Game location elevation
- Game time weather
- Game time temperature
- Game time humidity
- Time (hours) since last game
- Average time of ball possession
- Time left in game
- Total minutes played in game
- Number of shots attempted
- Number of shots made
- Location of shots attempted
- Location of shots made
- Volume of boos
- Number of fouls
- Number of assists
- Playing a former team
- Time of day
- Record of opponent
- Feelings toward opponent
- Performance in last game
- Number of negative Twitter comments
- Stadium temperature
- Stadium humidity
- Number of fans in attendance
- Number of LeBron jerseys in attendance

Next we want to understand the decisions that the Golden State Warriors coaching staff needs to make in crafting a defensive strategy against LeBron James. Chapter 8 introduced the recommendations worksheet as a tool to link the key business decisions to the recommendations and the supporting scores (see Figure 10-3).

In the "mitigate LeBron James's offensive effectiveness" business initiative, some of the key decisions that the Golden State Warriors coaching staff need to make are:

- Who is going to guard LeBron?

- What is the best individual defensive strategy against LeBron?
- What is the best team defensive strategy against LeBron?

Business Initiative: ____________		
Persona: ____________		
Decisions	Potential Recommendations	Potential Scores / Metrics

Figure 10-3: Recommendations worksheet

Next, you want to identify the recommendations you could deliver in support of those key decisions. For example, for the "Who is going to guard LeBron James?" decision, you might want to make the following recommendations:

- Which defender?
- Which defender at which times of the game?
- Which defender in which game situations?

Figure 10-4 shows the updated recommendations worksheet.

Business Initiative: *Mitigate LeBron James's offensive effectiveness*		
Persona: Golden State Coaching Staff		
Decisions	Potential Recommendations	Potential Scores / Metrics
Who is going to guard LeBron James?	• Which defender? • Which defender at which times of the game? • Which defender in which game situations?	
What is the best individual defensive approach?	• Do we deny LeBron the ball? • Do we deny the 3-point jumper? • Do we deny the 2-point jumper? • Do we deny the drive into the lane?	
What is the best team defensive approach?	• When do we guard LeBron straight up? • When do we double-team LeBron? • When do we hedge? • When do we help?	

Figure 10-4: Updated recommendations worksheet

Now you want to review the variables and metrics that came out of the "By" analysis and look for common groupings. For example, the following variables and metrics that came out of the "By" analysis relate to how "**Fatigued**" LeBron might be at any point in the game:

- Hours since last game
- How many games played in the season
- Average number of minutes played per game
- Minutes played in the current game
- Minutes handling the ball in the current game
- Number of shots taken in the current game
- Time remaining in the current game
- Away or home game

This fatigue score could be used to measure how tired or exhausted LeBron is at any point in the game. The fatigue score is created from a combination of historical metrics (number of games played in the season so far, average number of minutes played) combined with real-time, in-game metrics (minutes played in the game, number of shots taken in the game, minutes handling the ball in the game). Updating LeBron's fatigue score throughout the game (since many of the supporting metrics change during the game) can lead to in-game recommendations such as defenders, individual defensive strategy, and team defensive strategy.

A "**Motivation**" score could be created out of the following variables and metrics:

- In-game performance
- Record of opponent
- Defender guarding him
- Volume of boos
- Playing against a former team
- Number of LeBron jerseys in the stands

The motivation score would be a measure of how "motivated" LeBron is for this particular game, and how hard he is willing to push himself when he gets tired to get the win. The motivation score, when combined with the fatigue score, can lead to in-game recommendations about defenders, individual defensive strategy, and team defensive strategy. Figure 10-5 shows the final version of the recommendation worksheet.

It is interesting how the combination of multiple minor metrics has the potential to yield a much more actionable and predictive score. This process of uncovering and grouping metrics and variables into higher-level scores is highly iterative with lots of trial and error as the data science team tries to validate which combinations of metrics and variables are actually better predictors of performance.

<table>
<tr><th colspan="3">Business Initiative: Mitigate LeBron James's offensive effectiveness</th></tr>
<tr><td colspan="3">Persona: <u>Golden State Coaching Staff</u></td></tr>
<tr><th>Decisions</th><th>Potential Recommendations</th><th>Potential Scores / Metrics</th></tr>
<tr><td>Who is going to guard LeBron James?</td><td>• Which defender?
• Which defender at which times of the game?
• Which defender in which game situations?</td><td rowspan="3">Fatigue Score
• Hours since last game
• How many games played in the season
• Average number of minutes played per game
• Minutes played in the current game
• Minutes handling the ball in the current game
• Number of shots taken in the current game
• Time remaining in the current game
• Away or home game

Motivation Score
• In-game performance
• Record of opponent
• Defender guarding him
• Volume of boos
• Playing against a former team
• Number of LeBron jerseys in the stands</td></tr>
<tr><td>What is the best individual defensive approach?</td><td>• Do we deny LeBron the ball?
• Do we deny the 3-point jumper?
• Do we deny the 2-point jumper?
• Do we deny the drive into the lane?</td></tr>
<tr><td>What is the best team defensive approach?</td><td>• When do we guard LeBron straight up?
• When do we double-team LeBron?
• When do we hedge?
• When do we help?</td></tr>
</table>

Figure 10-5: Completed recommendations worksheet

Foot Locker Example Continued

Throughout Chapters 8 and 9, you applied "thinking like a data scientist" techniques and concepts in an exercise based on Foot Locker. You will now complete the Foot Locker exercise by pulling everything together to identify and create actionable scores that help Foot Locker "improve merchandising effectiveness."

In Chapter 9 we conducted the "By" analysis for Foot Locker's "improve merchandising effectiveness." The results of the "By" analysis for one customer question is shown in the following list:

- Age
- Gender
- Marital status
- Number of children
- Length of marriage
- Income level
- Education level
- VIP loyalty card member
- VIP member length of time
- VIP rewards expired (%)
- VIP rewards expired ($)
- Own or rent residence
- Tenure in current home
- Value of current home
- Favorite sports
- Favorite sports teams
- High school sports interest
- College sports interest
- Active athlete
- Type of athletic activity
- Exercise minutes per week
- Number of days per week exercised

Glancing over the different metrics and variables that came out of that "By" analysis, you want to look for common groupings. For example:

- You could group metrics and variables such as "VIP member," "Length of time (tenure) as a VIP member," "Frequency of use of VIP card," "Frequency of redeeming reward points," and "Percentage of expired rewards" into a "**Customer Loyalty**" score.
- You could group metrics and variables such as "Favorite sports," "Favorite sports teams," "High school sports team supporter," "College sports team supporter," and "Amount of team branded apparel purchased" into a "**Sports Passion**" score.
- Finally, you could group metrics and variables such as "Active athlete," "Type of athletic activity," "Frequency of athletic activity," "Average weekly amount of athletic activity," and "Wears health monitor" into an "**Athletic Activity**" score.

Figure 10-6 shows the results of the grouping of metrics and variables into actionable scores about Foot Locker's customers. You would want to do a similar exercise for Foot Locker's other key business entities such as products and stores.

Improve Merchandising Effectiveness: ***Customer*** *Questions*

What customers are most receptive to Foot Locker's merchandising campaigns *by* ...

- Age
- Gender
- Marital status
- Number of children
- Length of marriage
- Income level
- Education level
- VIP loyalty card member
- VIP member length of time
- VIP rewards expired (%)
- VIP rewards expired ($)
- Own or rent residence
- Tenure in current home
- Value of current home
- Favorite sports
- Favorite sports teams
- High school sports interest
- College sports interest
- Active athlete
- Type of athletic activity
- Exercise minutes per week
- Number of days per week exercised
- ...

Figure 10-6: Potential Foot Locker customer scores

Finally, let's pull everything together into a recommendations worksheet that highlights how you might use the Foot Locker customer scores to help guide your merchandising decisions (see Figure 10-7).

The brainstorming of the different metrics and variables using the "By" analysis technique and the subsequent grouping of the resulting metrics and variables into common scores is probably the most enjoyable part of the "thinking like a data scientist" process. You are free to apply your creative juices to brainstorm data sources and metrics that *might* be used as part of your score. Again, no idea is a bad idea. Let the data science team decide via its analytic modeling which data sources and metrics are the best predictors of business performance.

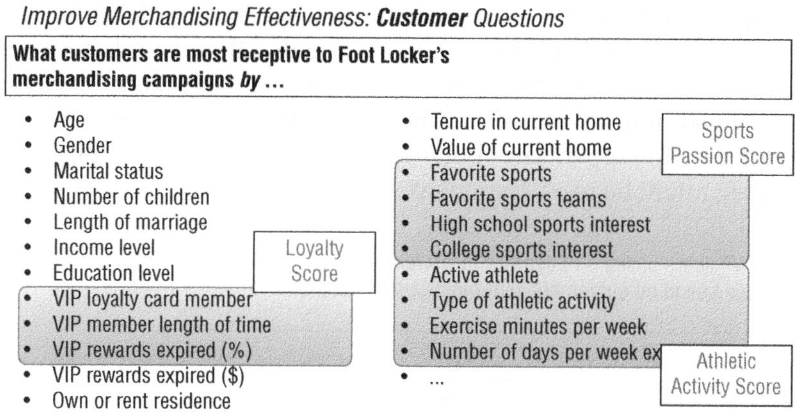

Figure 10-7: Foot Locker recommendations worksheet

But how do you put these scores or analytics into action? How does an organization like Foot Locker leverage these scores to improve its customer engagement and merchandising decisions?

One example might be how the Foot Locker marketing stakeholders use the scores to prioritize their customer offers and promotions. For example, today most organizations determine the customer lifetime value (CLTV) based on the previous 12 to 18 months of sales (see Figure 10-8).

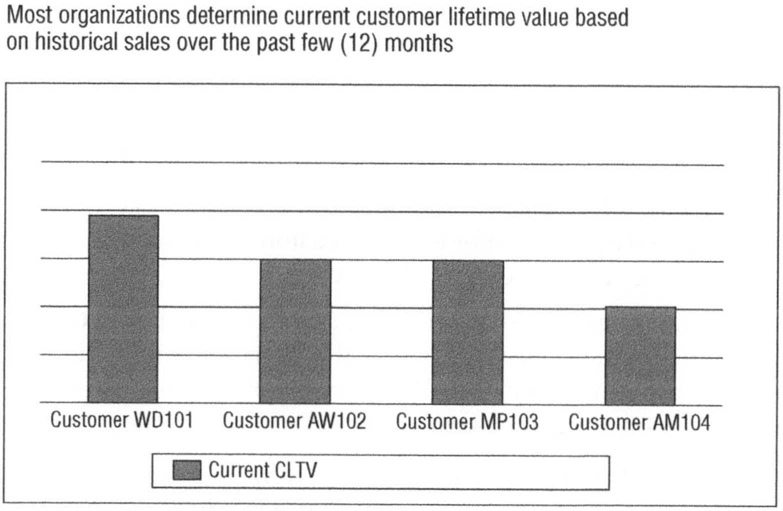

*CLTV = customer lifetime value

Figure 10-8: CLTV based on sales

The goal of the CLTV score is to help marketing and store personnel to determine the "value" of a customer that can subsequently be used to determine who gets what sorts of offers. Unfortunately, since the sales numbers are a historical perspective on spend and value, most organizations just create a rule of thumb that all customers get a flat rebate (5 percent) on whatever they spend. Boring.

However, what if you leveraged the Customer Loyalty and the Athletic Activity scores to create a maximum customer lifetime value (MCLTV) to predict which customers might have untapped sales potential and to which types of promotions or offers they might be most responsive (see Figure 10-9)?

Create maximum CLTV* score based on ***Loyalty*** and ***Athletic Activity*** scores to focus spend on customers with most upside potential

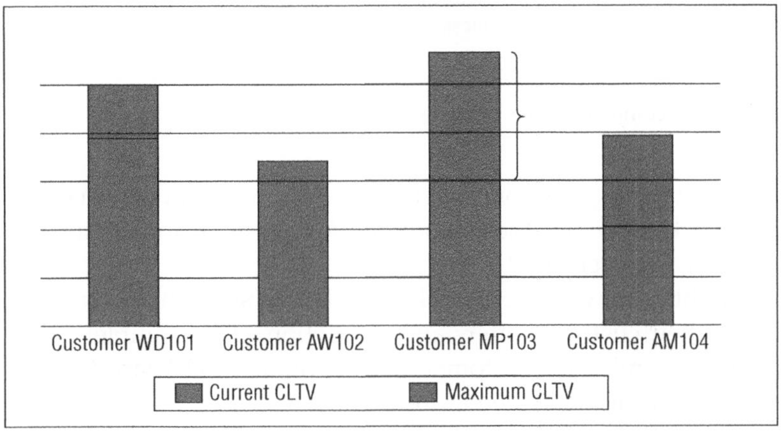

*CLTV = customer lifetime value

Figure 10-9: More predictive CLTV score

You could use this MCLTV score to guide key business decisions such as:

- Which customers get what sorts of promotions (in order to capture more of each customer's untapped potential value)
- What sorts of special events to offer to which customers (in order to drive loyalty and increase each customer's MCLTV)
- Which stores get a higher allocation of popular products based on the store maximum lifetime value score (where the "store maximum lifetime value" score is the sum of the "MCLTV" scores for the customers who come to that store on a regular basis)

Hopefully this is a simple but powerful example of how to leverage scores to create higher level maximum value scores that can be used to drive the analytics into action (via decisions) across the organization.

Summary

As you complete the "thinking like a data scientist" process, you can see how scores are a very important and actionable concept for business stakeholders who are trying to envision where and how data science can improve their decision making in support of their key business initiatives. As you saw from the FICO score example, scores aid in decision making by predicting the likelihood of certain actions or outcomes (e.g., likelihood to repay a loan, in the case of the FICO score).

The beauty of a score is its ability to integrate a wide range of variables and metrics into a single number. The power of the score is the ability to start small and then constantly search for new metrics and variables that might yield better predictors of performance.

Simple but powerful, exactly what big data and data science should strive to be.

Homework Assignment

Use the following exercises to apply what you learned in this chapter.

Exercise #1: Take the results from the "By" analysis conducted in Chapter 9 for your selected business initiative and look for common groupings or potential scores. It may be easier to write each of the metrics and variables onto a separate Post-it note and place them on a flip chart or whiteboard. That will make it easier to move the metrics and variables around as you look for common groupings or potential scores.

Exercise #2: Complete the recommendations worksheet for your selected business initiative. Validate that the scores uncovered in Exercise #1 support the decisions and recommendations that you need to support your selected business initiative.

Exercise #3: Contemplate how you might create a maximum lifetime value score that could be used to support the key decisions that you are trying to make about your targeted business initiative. I think you will find that the maximum lifetime value score can be used to prioritize spend and focus in business initiatives as diverse as marketing effectiveness, patient care, teacher retention, predictive maintenance, revenue protection, and network optimization.

CHAPTER

11

Monetization Exercise

Sometimes it is useful to work backwards in the "thinking like a data scientist" process. You can do this by first identifying the potential recommendations that the organization could deliver to its customers and frontline employees, and then working backwards to identify the supporting data and analytic requirements.

This chapter introduces a technique called the *monetization exercise* that seeks to understand how the organization's product or services are used by its customers, and then identify how the customer and product usage data can be used to create new monetization opportunities. The process works backwards to uncover the metrics, variables, data, and analytic techniques that you might need to support the new monetization opportunities.

The monetization exercise provides an opportunity to uncover new product and/or service opportunities through the identification and delivery of new customer and frontline employee recommendations. The monetization exercise works by first understanding the product usage patterns and customer usage behaviors associated with a particular product and service. The process then seeks to identify complementary or secondary recommendations that can be packaged and delivered along with that product or service (think the Data Monetization phase of the Big Data Business Model Maturity Index). Following is the monetization exercise process:

- Step 1: Understand product usage characteristics and behaviors
- Step 2: Develop personas for each customer type (including key decisions and pain points)

- Step 3: Brainstorm potential customer recommendations
- Step 4: Identify supporting data sources
- Step 5: Prioritize monetization opportunities (revenue)
- Step 6: Develop monetization plan

To get comfortable with this technique, you're going to use the monetization exercise to uncover new monetization opportunities for my new fitness tracker—a wearable device that monitors and provides feedback on my running and walking activities. The goal of this particular monetization exercise is to identify complementary or new monetization opportunities including:

- New products and/or services that can be sold to existing customers
- New products and/or services that can be used to acquire new customers
- New revenue opportunities for the fitness tracker manufacturer's current channel partners (e.g., Sports Authority, Dick's Sporting Goods, Foot Locker)
- New markets associated with fitness, exercise, and even potentially wellness
- New audiences who might find the new fitness and wellness services compelling
- New channels through which to sell the fitness tracker and the associated new services

Let's see the monetization exercise in action!

Fitness Tracker Monetization Example

In trying to stay true to my annual New Year's resolution to live a healthier and more athletically fit life, I was thinking about upgrading my current fitness tracker. The most important requirements for my ideal fitness tracker are the ability to add GPS tracking and new performance metrics to my workouts. In thinking about the fitness tracker marketplace, I saw that there seems to be lots of opportunities for fitness tracker manufacturers to provide additional products and services that would make their fitness trackers more valuable to the consumer, as well as provide dramatic business benefits to the fitness tracker manufacturer and its channel partners.

Let's walk through an example to see how the fitness tracker manufacturer could leverage the monetization exercise to create new products and services and uncover new monetization opportunities.

Step 1: Understand Product Usage

The first step in the monetization exercise is for the fitness tracker manufacturer to understand the key features and capabilities of the product or service being analyzed. For example, my ideal fitness tracker would have following functionality:

- Provides a complete history of my workouts including my start and finish times, time elapsed, distance, pace, and calories burned
- Measures my current speed, distance, time elapsed, pace, and calories burned
- Has a built-in GPS that delivers accurate speed and distance data readings and maps my workout
- Monitors my heart rate
- Records up to 50 runs and my personal bests
- Enables me to easily review and analyze my workout history
- Allows me to download my workout data for more detailed analysis (yeah, I know, I'm a nerd)
- Delivers recognition alerts when I beat a personal record
- Integrates performance results easily into my different social media networks (and supports gamification so I can rank my performance results versus those of my friends)

What is critically important to the fitness tracker manufacturer is how the fitness tracker is used and the decisions I am trying to make associated with those usage behaviors. From my own personal experience, the fitness tracker encourages different usage behaviors such as:

- Encourages me to take more walks including a lot more with the dog (poor Puffer)
- Encourages me to take the stairs instead of the escalator
- Encourages me to walk around the airport terminal as I wait for my delayed flight to finally depart
- Encourages me to park farther away from stores or restaurants so that I have longer to walk, or to walk to the furthest bathroom in the mall just to build up my steps
- Encourages me to ride my bike instead of drive the car for short trips

These behavioral changes, and the decisions associated with those behaviors (e.g., what shoes to wear, what running routes to take, how long to run, with whom to run), provide new monetization opportunities, which means that organizations need to go the extra mile to truly understand not only how their product is used but also the personal behaviors that are associated with their product usage.

Step 2: Develop Stakeholder Personas

Step 2 is for the fitness tracker manufacturer to identify and understand its different customer types. Identifying and understanding the organization's different customer types is a process that was covered in Chapter 8. For each of the customer types, the manufacturer would want to create a separate persona that captures the customers' tasks, decisions, and associated pain points with respect to their usage of the fitness tracker.

Figure 11-1 shows a persona for a key customer type that I have labeled the "Spirited Runner" (or at least that's how I would classify myself).

Overview: Average runner who runs 4 to 5 times per week for 25 to 40 minutes each. Occasionally participates in cycling and weightlifting workouts.

Quote: "Staying motivated gets harder and harder each year!"

Day	Key Tasks	Key Decisions	Pain Points
7am	• Early morning run around the neighborhood to jump-start the day	• What running shoes and gear do I wear? • How long do I run? • What route do I run? • Do I run alone or with a friend?	• Hard to set and monitor running goals • Don't know when to replace shoes • Always looking for new running routes
1pm	• Occasionally go to a Body Pump class or cycling class at the local YMCA	• Which class do I go to today? • What workout shoes and gear do I wear? • Do I run alone or with a friend?	• Don't know best shoes to wear to these workouts • Can't easily coordinate my workout plans with my friends • Can't find other classes that I might enjoy
9pm	• Late evening walk with the dog before retiring for the evening	• How long do I walk? • What route do I take? • Do I bring the dog or not?	• Hard to set and monitor walking goals • Don't know best walking shoes

Figure 11-1: "A day in the life" customer persona

As you have seen in the use of personas in the previous chapters, the "day in the life" persona seeks to provide a baseline understanding of the tasks, **decisions**, and pain points associated with the usage of the product or service. For example, in Figure 11-1, the "spirited runner" persona has the following decisions to contemplate for the "early morning run around the neighborhood to jump-start the day" task:

- What running shoes do I wear?
- What gear do I wear?
- How long do I run?
- What route do I run?
- Do I run alone or with a friend?

As you know from the previous exercises in this book, *understanding the decisions that the key users or business stakeholders are trying make is critical to uncovering new monetization opportunities.*

There are likely other decisions that could be captured for this persona, so it is worth the extra effort to put yourself in the person's *shoes* to better understand the decisions he or she is trying to make and the associated pain points.

Personas could also be developed for additional runners such as:

- Extreme runner (runs marathons, Ironman contests, and adventure races)
- Occasional runner (runs a couple of times a week but is not very serious about running)
- Reluctant runner (runs only at the beginning of each new year as part of his or her New Year's resolutions)

However, there are some other important business stakeholders for which the fitness tracker manufacturer would want to create additional personas. Those additional business stakeholder personas include:

- Fitness tracker manufacturer product development (which could also include product management and product marketing for completeness)
- Fitness tracker manufacturer sales and marketing
- Fitness tracker manufacturer channel partners (Foot Locker, Sports Authority, Big Five, Dick's)

As a homework exercise, you will be asked to create personas for one of these additional business stakeholders.

Step 3: Brainstorm Potential Recommendations

Step 3 is to brainstorm potential recommendations that could be delivered to each business stakeholder. That is, *what recommendations could the organization deliver to the different stakeholders that benefit or support the stakeholder's **decisions**?* There are two angles that you can leverage to help uncover potential recommendations:

- Understand the decisions the different stakeholders need to make and the associated pain points, and contemplate recommendations that might support the decisions and/or help to address the associated pain points
- Leverage your observations about the personal behavioral changes induced by the fitness tracker to identify other potential recommendations

You could use an old-fashioned facilitated brainstorming session (complete with lots of Post-it notes) to brainstorm potential recommendations for each of the key business stakeholders from the perspectives of the decisions that they are trying to make and the associated behavioral changes.

Table 11-1 shows some potential recommendations that the fitness tracker manufacturer could deliver to the customer persona based on the decisions that the customer is trying to make and the desired behavioral changes.

Table 11-1: Potential Fitness Tracker Recommendations

DECISION	POTENTIAL RECOMMENDATIONS
What running shoes do I wear?	**Optimal running shoes** given the consumer's running and walking behaviors, patterns, tendencies, routes, and physical attributes
	When to replace running shoes given how much the consumer has run on those particular shoes, how frequently the consumer runs, the type of terrain on which the consumer runs, and current "wear and tear" of the shoes
	Running accessories or apparel such as special running socks, thermal tights, stocking caps, and gloves for the cold weather when I travel to Iowa to visit my son
How long do I run?	**New performance metrics** such as elevation covered, workout effort level, circuit training metrics, calories burned, etc.
What route do I run?	**New local running routes** near the runner's home or favorite running routes
	New traveling running routes when the consumer is traveling to other areas of the country
Do I run alone or with a friend?[1]	**Potential running partners** based on social media contacts, running tendencies, and running locations

Step 4: Identify Supporting Data Sources

Step 4 is to brainstorm the different data sources that one *might* need in order to create the recommendations.

NOTE I use the term *might* frequently to convey that an important part of the exercise is to not pass judgment on the value or viability of the brainstormed data sources. You want to collect any and all ideas regarding potential data sources. All ideas are worthy of consideration. Determining the value or viability of the data source during the brainstorming process only inhibits the creative thinking process. We will determine the value and viability of the data sources later.

Table 11-2 provides an example of some of the data sources that you *might* want to consider to support the development of the recommendations.

[1] How about buying a fitness tracker for your dog's collar with an app that can tell you whether or not your dog needs exercise, what type, how much, etc.? That would be another product and service that, when coupled with data about your dog's breed, age, health, etc., could yield a more "fit" dog. You could call the product and service "FitBark" (hehehe).

Table 11-2: Recommendation Data Requirements

KEY STAKEHOLDER: END CONSUMER	
POTENTIAL RECOMMENDATIONS	**POTENTIAL DATA SOURCES**
Optimal running shoes	Exercise data: performance data about my exercises including length of time, effort level, calories burned, distance covered, points earned, etc. Workout GPS data: data about my workout route including a map of the route, route terrain, elevation, time of day, etc. Weather data: data about the weather conditions during my workout including temperature, precipitation, humidity, etc. Runner data: weight, height, age, gender, body mass index, shoe size, width of foot, high/low arch, preferred terrain type, etc.
When to replace running shoes	Shoe data: detailed data about my shoes including manufacturer, brand, type of shoe, size of shoe, when shoe was bought, where shoe was bought, where shoe was made, user reviews, etc. Note: the fitness tracker could provide an option that allows the runner to take a photo of the shoes and the app automatically provides data about the condition of the shoe. Workout GPS data: data about my workout route including a map of the route, route terrain, elevation, time of day, etc. Shoe wear data: ask consumer to take periodic photos of the soles in order for the manufacturer to track shoe wear and tear
Running accessories	Inventory of my running accessories: brand, type, size, where I bought it, when I bought it, what I bought it with Running accessories usage data: what I wear in what conditions, what I wear in combination with other workout items
New performance metrics	Allow users to create and share their own calculations and performance metrics (Schmarzo Performance Index = INTEGER(Steps/1000) + INTEGER(FuelPoints/1000)) Allow users to download the data to create and share new reports and analytics Integrate fitness tracker data with other exercise apps like MapMyFitness or MyFitnessPal

Continues

Table 11-2 (*continued*)

KEY STAKEHOLDER: END CONSUMER	
New local running routes	Analyze GPS and exercise data across all fitness tracker users in order to identify new routes to which I might be interested
	Integrate third-party apps like MapMyFitness and MyFitnessPal for capturing additional route, exercise, and workout data
New running routes while traveling	Collect all running and walking routes across all fitness tracker customers by location and exercise type (light walking, heavy running, etc.)
	Match my running and walking tendencies to the collection of running and walking routes in order to make new route recommendations
Potential running partners	Social media contacts from Facebook, Twitter, Instagram, etc.
	Relevant social media posts from my social media friends about their running behaviors and patterns and exercise habits
	Current location of my social media contacts (in order to make real-time running partner recommendations)

Step 5: Prioritize Monetization Opportunities

Step 5 is focused on prioritizing the recommendations from the perspectives of business value and implementation feasibility. For this exercise, you will use the prioritization matrix (which is covered in detail in Chapter 13), but with three dimensions:

- Value of the recommendation to the consumer
- Value of the recommendation to the fitness tracker manufacturer
- Implementation feasibility of the recommendation over the next 9 to 12 months (based on the availability of the supporting data)

Walking through a facilitation process to explore and triage these three dimensions is hard to do in a book; however, you can leverage brainstorming and polling techniques to get a high-level ranking or rating for the answers to these three dimensions as seen in Table 11-3.

Table 11-3: Recommendations Value Versus Feasibility Assessment

RECOMMENDATION	CONSUMER VALUE	MANUFACTURER VALUE	FEASIBILITY
A. Optimal new running shoes[2]	Medium	**High**	**High**
B. When to replace running shoes	**High**	**High**	Low
C. New local routes	**High**	Low	Medium
D. Running partners	Medium	Low	Low
E. Running apparel	Medium	**High**	**High**
F. Routes when traveling	Low	Low	Medium
G. New running metrics	**High**	Low	Medium

Since three dimensions don't work very well on a two-dimensional sheet of paper, you will leverage a visualization technique (shade of the dots) that allows you to mimic three dimensions in a two-dimensional environment. Figure 11-2 shows what the final results of the prioritization process might yield.

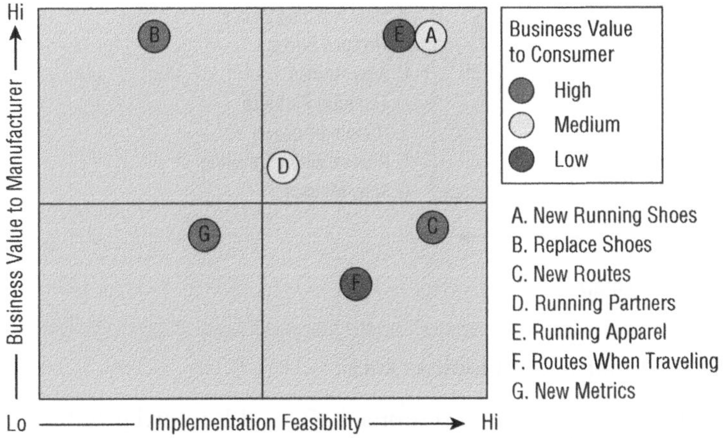

Figure 11-2: Fitness tracker prioritization

[2] Providing recommendations on optimal running shoes and running apparel creates new monetization opportunities from co-marketing with sporting shoe and apparel manufacturers.

Step 6: Develop Monetization Plan

As you can see from Figure 11-3, deciding on the "right" monetization opportunity is not always straightforward. The consumers prefer recommendations B (when to replace running shoes), C (recommending new routes), and G (creating new metrics), but only recommendation B is of high value to the fitness tracker manufacturer (since it leads to more direct sales). And unfortunately recommendation B isn't easy from an implementation feasibility perspective since it requires significant consumer-provided data.

Oh, what is one to do?

Maybe like a chess game, the answer lies a couple of moves beyond the obvious. Maybe the fitness tracker manufacturer would be best served to think about a road map that looks like Figure 11-3.

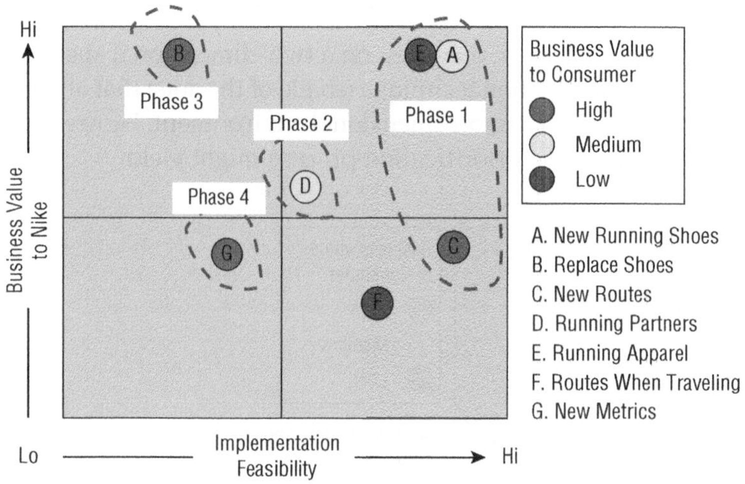

Figure 11-3: Monetization road map

The monetization road map would look as such:

- Phase 1 would focus on recommendations A, C, and E in order to build consumer interest in the fitness tracker products and start to collect more data about runners and their running behaviors (using consumer running behavioral and next best offering analytics).
- Phase 2 would then deliver recommendation D, which allows the fitness tracker manufacturer to build up its expertise in social media analysis in identifying and recommending potential running partners (using cohorts analysis).
- Phase 3 would then focus on recommendation B, which has the highest value to the fitness tracker manufacturer and builds on the analytic

expertise that it developed in phase 1 to move into the area of predictive maintenance and product replacement analytics.

- Finally, phase 4 would then deliver on recommendation G, which fosters community by building and sharing new performance calculations, metrics, analytics, and reports between fitness tracker community members.

This monetization road map has three big benefits for the fitness tracker manufacturer:

- Captures more and more data about runners' usage behaviors, patterns, and tendencies
- Captures more data about product usage and wear
- Gradually builds up the organization's data science capabilities in areas such as consumer behavioral analytics, next best offer, cohorts analysis, predictive maintenance, and product replacement analytics

Summary

This chapter introduced the monetization exercise as complementary to the "thinking like a data scientist" process to help organizations to uncover new product and/or service opportunities through the identification of new customer and employee recommendations. The monetization exercise is a non-technology, business-centric, organizational-alignment technique that uses the following process to uncover new monetization opportunities (phase 4 of the Big Data Business Model Maturity Index):

- Identify and understand how customers use your products and/or services
- Identify and understand key business stakeholders (customers, frontline employees, partners) including their key tasks, decisions, and associated pain points
- Brainstorm the types of recommendations that you could deliver to the stakeholders based on their usage of the product or service
- Identify the different data sources that *might* help support the recommendations
- Go through a valuation process where you contemplate three key variables for each recommendation: value of the recommendation to the customer, value of the recommendation to the manufacturer, and implementation feasibility
- Look for opportunities to cluster recommendations into similar groups in order to create a monetization road map

Homework Assignment

Use the following exercises to apply what you learned in this chapter:

Exercise #1: Develop a persona for one of your organization's key customers (stakeholders). Be sure to carefully contemplate that customer's key tasks, decisions, and associated pain points. I strongly recommend using the same template used in Figure 11-2.

Exercise #2: Brainstorm the recommendations your organization could deliver to that customer based on the customer's key decisions. Be sure to take into consideration the pain points as you brainstorm the recommendations. Use the template used in Table 11-1.

Exercise #3: Brainstorm the potential data sources for each of the identified recommendations. Again, all data source ideas are worthy of consideration, and you'll determine the value and feasibility of the different data sources later. Use the format in Table 11-2 to capture the data sources.

Exercise #4: Prioritize the recommendations from the perspectives of the value of the recommendation to the customer, the value of the recommendation to your organization, and the implementation feasibility over the next 9 to 12 months.

Exercise #5: Cluster the recommendations into similar or logical groups to create a monetization plan.

CHAPTER

12

Metamorphosis Exercise

Reaching the *Business Metamorphosis* phase of the Big Data Business Model Maturity Index is a significant accomplishment for most organizations. Even just contemplating what this end point might look like can be quite beneficial in the development of an organization's big data initiative. Beginning with an end in mind, to quote Stephen Covey, not only can help the organization's leaders to envision the potential of big data from a business transformation perspective but pragmatically can help the organization to identify where and how to start their big data journey.

In working with organizations to measure how effectively they leverage data and analytics within their key business processes using the Big Data Business Model Maturity Index (see Figure 12-1), I created an exercise to help organizations to envision what the business metamorphosis *might* look like. While it's not possible to start your big data journey at this phase, the exercise has helped my clients identify, prioritize, and develop their big data use cases.

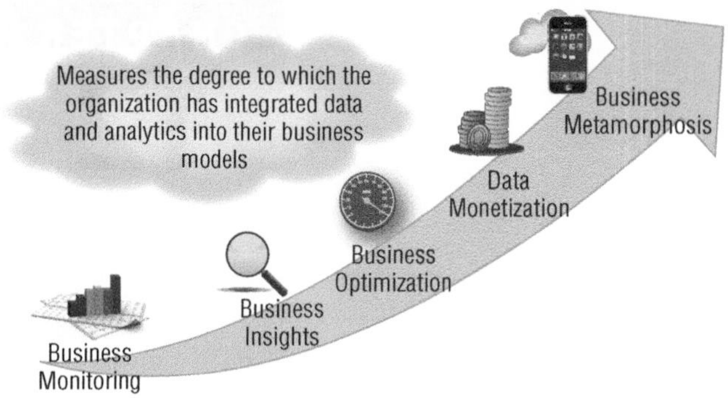

Figure 12-1: Big Data Business Model Maturity Index

Business Metamorphosis Review

As a refresher, the Business Metamorphosis phase is where organizations seek to leverage data, analytics, and the resulting analytic insights to transform the organization's business models. This includes areas such as business processes, organizational structures, products and services, partnerships, target markets, management, promotions, rewards and incentives, and others. The Business Metamorphosis phase is where organizations integrate the insights that they captured about their customers' usage patterns, product performance behaviors, and overall market trends to transform their business models. This business model metamorphosis might enable the organization to provide new services and capabilities to its customers in a way that is easier for them to consume. Perhaps it could enable third-party developers to proliferate on the organization's foundational platform, or facilitate the organization engaging in higher-value and more strategic services.

The Business Metamorphosis phase necessitates a major shift in the organization's core business model driven by the analytic insights gathered as the organization traverses the Big Data Business Model Maturity Index.

Here are some examples of what organizations could do to leverage data, analytics, and the resulting analytic insights to metamorphose their business models:

- Jet engine manufacturer transforming from selling jet engines to selling "thrust" and related high-value services to the airlines around service level agreements (on-time departures, on-time arrivals), product maintenance (minimizing aircraft down time), insurance, warranties, and upgrading product performance over time (improving fuel efficiency).
- Farm equipment manufacturer transforming from selling farm equipment to selling "farming yield optimization" to farmers by leveraging superior insights into seeds, soil conditions, weather, fertilizers, pesticides, irrigation techniques, and projected crop prices.

- Energy companies moving into the "Home Energy Optimization" business by recommending when to replace appliances (based on predictive maintenance) and even recommending which appliance brands and models to buy based on the performance of different appliances taking into consideration your usage patterns, local weather, local water quality and local water conservation efforts, and energy costs.
- Airlines moving into the "Travel Delight" business of not only offering discounts and upgrades on air travel based on customers' travel behaviors and preferences but also proactively recommending deals on hotels, rental cars, limos, sporting or musical events, and local sites, shows, restaurants, and shopping in the destination areas based on your areas of interest and preferences.

Continuing with the Foot Locker example from previous chapters, business metamorphosis for Foot Locker could mean shifting away from selling sporting shoes and apparel to providing "workouts as a service." Foot Locker could monitor all of your workouts and walking activities and automatically recommend the most appropriate shoes, workout apparel, workout routines, gym memberships, and exercise tips based on your unique workout habits, patterns, tendencies, and propensities. Foot Locker could even expand into "health and wellness services" to provide tips and recommendations about your diet, exercise, stress, cholesterol, and so forth, focused on improving your overall health and wellness (and maybe even helping to reduce your health insurance costs).

In all of these examples, these organizations couple new sources of customer, product, and operational data with data science to uncover new actionable insights that form the basis to metamorphose their business models.

Let's introduce an exercise that can help to strengthen your "thinking like a data scientist" methodology. The exercise begins with the Business Metamorphosis stage and works backwards to identify potential big data use cases and the supporting data and analytics.

Business Metamorphosis Exercise

I asked students in one of my MBA classes to pretend that they were management consultants that had been asked by a large airplane manufacturer to contemplate how big data could metamorphose the organization's future business model. In essence, the large airplane manufacturer wanted to metamorphose the business by transitioning from selling airplanes to selling "air miles."

The students, acting as management consultants, needed a process to uncover the analytic insights about passengers, airplanes, airlines, airports, and routes (the strategic nouns of this exercise) necessary to support the business metamorphosis—to transform business processes, people, organizational structures, products and services, partnerships, markets, organization, promotions, rewards, incentives, and so on. The management consultants would also need to identify the data, analytic, and business requirements necessary to encourage third-party developers to create value-added services and products based on the airplane manufacturer's new business platform.

Articulate the Business Metamorphosis Vision

The first step in the metamorphosis exercise is to articulate and understand the business ramifications of the airplane manufacturer's new business model vision. Use the following vision statement as your starting point:

> *Large airplane manufacturer wants to metamorphose its business model by transitioning from selling airplanes to selling air miles (transporting 250 customers 2,600 air miles from SFO to JFK on Sunday mornings at 9:00am) in order to create new high-value services for airlines (e.g., United, American, Delta, Southwest) and enable third-party developers to extend the airplane manufacturer's business model to airlines and potentially other customers, partners, and markets.*

As a starting point, this vision statement could have the following ramifications to the airplane manufacturer's business model:

- The airplane manufacturer would enjoy a dramatic competitive advantage over other airplane manufacturers by providing new business benefits to the airlines including significantly improved cash flow and financials (reduced capital expenditures), elimination of maintenance costs, elimination of parts inventory costs, and mitigation of flight delay risks.
- The airplane manufacturer would be responsible for owning and managing the fleets of airplanes (likely under their brand), and the airlines would contract with the airplane manufacturer to acquire (provision?) the air miles necessary to transport a specified number of the airline's passengers from one location to another at a specified time and date.
- The airplane manufacturer would assume all responsibilities for ensuring that planes are up and running (e.g., maintenance scheduling, maintenance technician training and management, maintenance and replacement parts inventory, component, and software upgrades). If the planes were not flying, then the airplane manufacturer would not be getting paid.

Understand Your Customers

The second step in the metamorphosis exercise is to identify and understand the airplane manufacturer's customers. It is clear that its current customers (airlines) would continue to be the future customers. However, this opens up opportunities to acquire new types of customers—airline passengers, for example.

For example, the airplane manufacturer is now in a unique position to know details about airline passengers who fly across different airlines and can now offer new services to those airline passengers that could be more compelling than any single airline could offer on its own. For example, create a new type of frequent flyer program that offers rewards, gifts, upgrades, recognition, and special privileges (airport club access, priority TSA pre-check) to passengers who fly on any of the airplane manufacturer's planes, regardless of the airline.

There may be other opportunities to leverage this new business model to address other customers, such as:

- Travel agents by virtue of having a more complete understanding of passenger demand and flight and seat availability
- Hotel operators who could work with the airplane manufacturer to direct customers to available rooms
- Ground transportation companies (car rental companies, Uber, Lyft, taxis, airport shuttles) by sharing passenger forecasts into specific airports
- Sporting, casinos, and entertainment companies by directing passengers to sporting events and entertainment that may match the passengers' areas of interest

And there are surely others. The business potential to reach new customers and new markets with new services is only limited by the creative thinking of the organization.

Articulate Value Propositions

The next step is to brainstorm what this business metamorphosis would mean to the airplane manufacturer's customers (United, American, Delta, Southwest, Virgin Atlantic, etc.). Let's contemplate the value propositions that the airplane manufacturer's new business model might provide to these airlines customers. These value propositions to the airlines could include:

- Significantly improve airline cash flow by converting the fixed monthly airplane lease payments to a variable cost based on the number of passengers and air miles. This gives the airlines significant flexibility in defining, scheduling, and managing passengers, routes, and crews.

- Dramatic reduction in maintenance costs including spare and maintenance parts inventory and maintenance personnel (including hiring, training, and managing of maintenance personnel).
- Reduction in unplanned and overtime costs associated with flight delays due to mechanical issues, as these issues would now become the airplane manufacturer's responsibility.
- Airlines could then focus on differentiating themselves in areas other than airplane configuration (because the same models of airplanes would likely be used to serve multiple airlines) including: on-plane customer service and amenities, onboard meals (yeah, right), gate area customer service and amenities (lounge chairs instead of today's stadium rejected seats), frequent flyer reward programs (with miles that you can actually use), club locations and amenities, ticket pricing, travel convenience, trip duration times (e.g., reduce number of connections), and so on.

While this could be a scary proposition for some airlines, for other airlines it provides an opportunity to provide new high-value services to high-value customers in order to build loyalty in new and creative ways outside of just fight schedules and seat availability.

Define Data and Analytic Requirements

The final step in the metamorphosis exercise is to brainstorm the airplane manufacturer's data and analytic requirements. You will brainstorm these requirements via a three-step process: (1) identify key business and operational decisions, (2) identify the analytics to support the decisions, and (3) identify data to support the analytics.

Step 1: Identify Business and Operational Decisions

The first step is to identify the key operational and business decisions that the airplane manufacturer needs to make in order to support the new business model. It is critical to the success of your big data initiative to thoroughly understand the business and operational decisions that the key business stakeholders are responsible for making. Decisions (and some supporting questions) for the airline manufacturer could include the following:

- Decisions about pricing and their supporting questions:
  - How do I price considering surge demand driven by special events (bowl games, Final Four tournament, holidays)?

  - How directly does my pricing impact the airlines' pricing and their ability to be profitable?
  - Can I support surge pricing?
  - Can I provide pricing discounts for packages of air miles?
- Decisions about sales and marketing and their supporting questions:
  - How can I leverage a loyalty program to drive usage and capture more passenger data?
  - What promotional packages are most effective at driving passenger demand?
  - Can I leverage social media and influencers to drive families and groups to fly?
  - In what markets and routes do what types of promotions work best?
- Decisions about in-flight airplane performance and their supporting questions:
  - Which airplane configurations yield the best fuel efficiencies?
  - What pilots are most fuel efficient?
  - What are the optimal crew configurations?
  - How do I best distribute baggage and cargo to optimize fuel efficiencies?
  - Which in-flight MVP passengers are unhappy, and what should I do about that?
- Decisions about passenger and baggage management and their supporting questions:
  - How can I speed loading and unloading passengers and baggage (in order to speed airport turns)?
  - What airplane configurations are most effective on getting passengers and baggage on and off the planes faster?
  - How do I incent more passengers to check bags so that less time is spent in boarding planes (again, to speed airplane turns)?
  - Should I create a ramp management service where I take responsibility for loading and unloading the airplane baggage?
- Decisions about airplane maintenance and their supporting questions:
  - How do I select which airplanes and/or jet engines to replace with more efficient models?
  - How do I balance the jet engine fuel efficiency with jet engine maintenance costs?
  - Which jet engines are most cost-effective from a fuel efficient and maintenance perspective?

- Decisions about parts and logistics management and their supporting questions:
  - How can I reduce spare parts and maintenance costs?
  - What is the optimal number and type of airplane configuration in order to reduce spare parts and inventory costs?
  - Can I design planes with more interchangeable parts to reduce parts inventory costs?
  - How can I leverage low-cost, centralized parts depots to support the maintenance and inventory needs of the high-volume airports (e.g., Cedar Rapids, IA servicing ORD, MSP, MCI, and STL)?
- Decisions about airplane design and their supporting questions:
  - How can I design/build/configure airplanes to get passengers on and off the plane more quickly?
  - How can I design/build/configure airplanes that reduce parts maintenance costs?
  - How can I design/build/configure airplanes that reduce operational costs (gate agents, baggage workers, flight attendants, pilots)?
  - How can I design/build/configure airplanes that reduce parts inventory costs?

Step 2: Identify Analytic Requirements

Next you need to identify the analytics that the airplane manufacturer would need to support the operational and business decisions. **In this step you want to work backwards from the decisions and supporting questions to identify the potential analytics necessary to support the decisions. Table 12-1 contains a starter set of these analytics.**

Table 12-1: Decisions to Analytics Mapping

DECISIONS	POTENTIAL ANALYTICS
Pricing	Passenger (demand) forecast
	Fuel costs forecast
	Maintenance costs forecast
	Pilot / flight attendant performance optimization
	Pilot / flight attendant retention effectiveness

DECISIONS	POTENTIAL ANALYTICS
Sales and marketing	Passenger lifetime value score
	Passenger loyalty score
	Passenger net promoter score
	Passenger acquisition effectiveness
	Passenger retention effectiveness
	Marketing campaign effectiveness
	Personalized promotions effectiveness
In-flight performance	Airplane fuel optimization
	Crew scheduling optimization
	Cargo distribution optimization
	Baggage distribution optimization
	Passenger distribution optimization
Passenger and baggage management	Baggage handler / agent scheduling optimization
	Baggage handler / agent cost optimization
	Baggage handler / agent performance monitoring
	Baggage handler / agent retention
	Flight turnaround effectiveness
Airplane maintenance	Airplane and parts predictive maintenance
	Weather forecasts
	Airplane / component upgrades
	Optimize inventory costs
	Optimize logistics costs
	Maintenance worker effectiveness
Parts and logistics management	Airplane and parts predictive maintenance
	Maintenance scheduling optimization
	Crew scheduling optimization
	Parts demand forecast
	Parts inventory optimization
	Parts logistics optimization

Continues

Table 12-1 (*continued*)

DECISIONS	POTENTIAL ANALYTICS
Airplane design	Long-term fuel costs forecast Airplane design fuel efficiency Passenger board / de-board optimization Baggage load / unload optimization

Step 3: Identify Data Requirements

In step 3 you identify the data that the airplane manufacturer might need to support the pricing, sales, marketing, maintenance, logistics, and other analytics. You want to brainstorm the different data sources that might be useful in helping you develop the analytics to support your key decisions. Let's expand Table 11-1 to include the different data sources you might need to support the analytics (see Table 12-2):

Table 12-2: Data-to-Analytics Mapping

DECISIONS	POTENTIAL ANALYTICS	POTENTIAL DATA SOURCES
Pricing decisions	Passenger (demand) forecast Fuel costs forecast Maintenance costs forecast Pilot / flight attendant performance optimization Pilot / flight attendant retention	Passenger flight history Airplane flight history (routes, airports, miles flown, fuel consumed, passengers carried, % empty seats) Airplane flight sensor data Airplane physical data (age, last upgrade date, configuration, weight, fuel consumption, capacity, max airspeed) Airplane maintenance history Pilot / flight attendant demographics Pilot / flight attendant flight history Pilot / flight attendant notes and comments Airport physical data (number of runways, age of runways, operation hours) Airport weather Economic data History of fuel costs

DECISIONS	POTENTIAL ANALYTICS	POTENTIAL DATA SOURCES
Sales and marketing programs decisions	Passenger lifetime value score Passenger loyalty score Passenger net promoter score Passenger acquisition Passenger retention Marketing campaign effectiveness Personalized promotions effectiveness	Passenger demographics (age, height, weight, family members, job type) Passenger flight history Passenger social media data (posts, likes, tweets, shares) Passenger comments Passenger social media sentiment
In-flight airplane performance decisions	Airplane fuel optimization Crew scheduling optimization Cargo distribution optimization Baggage distribution optimization Passenger distribution optimization	Route data (departure, destination, distance, wind patterns) Weather conditions Airport data (number of runways, landing traffic patterns and demand) Weight of baggage Weight of passengers (ouch!) Weight of cargo Airplane fuel consumption history
Passenger and baggage management decisions	Baggage handler / agent scheduling optimization Baggage handler / agent cost optimization Baggage handler / agent performance monitoring Baggage handler / agent retention Flight turnaround effectiveness	Baggage loading and unloading performance data (flight, airplane configuration, airport, size of crew, experience of crew) Baggage handler /agent demographics (age, experience, training, recognitions) Baggage handler / agent work history Baggage handler / agent notes and comments Flight data (departure time, actual departure time, departure airport, destination airport, air miles, etc.)

Continues

Table 12-2 (*continued*)

DECISIONS	POTENTIAL ANALYTICS	POTENTIAL DATA SOURCES
Airplane maintenance decisions	Airplane and parts predictive maintenance Airplane / component upgrades Optimize inventory costs Optimize logistics costs Maintenance worker effectiveness	Airplane physical data (age, last upgrade date, configuration, weight, fuel consumption, capacity) Airplane flight history of number of passengers flown by route, day of week, holiday and seasonality Airplane maintenance history (date, work done, parts replaced, technician, costs) Maintenance worker data (age, experience, areas of expertise, certifications) Maintenance worker comments and notes Average mean-time-to-failure (air miles) by maintenance types Average maintenance parts and personal costs by maintenance types
Parts and logistics management decisions	Airplane and parts predictive maintenance Maintenance scheduling optimization Crew scheduling optimization Parts demand forecast Parts inventory optimization Parts logistics optimization	Replacement parts data (costs, manufacturer, associated parts, special certification) Maintenance parts (costs, manufacturer) Logistics center data (location, costs, capacity, access points) Inventory levels
Airplane design decisions	Long-term fuel costs forecast Airplane design fuel efficiency Passenger board / de-board optimization Baggage load / unload optimization	Forecast fuel costs / fuel price index Average weight and age by passenger Optimal airplane flow (load and unload) by airplane configuration

Using this approach, my MBA students were able to quickly determine the insights, analytics, and potential data sources necessary to support the airplane manufacturer's business metamorphosis *without having any working experience with either the airplane manufacturer or any airline company*. I think they impressed themselves!

Business Metamorphosis in Health Care

I'm struck by what's happening with the United States health care industry and the power struggle between health care providers and health care payers. The health care industry is ripe for a metamorphosis into something much more efficient, effective, and customer (patient) centric. This health care business metamorphosis could create new power brokers; health care players who will leverage new sources of patient, physician, clinical, medication, wellness, and care data to improve the quality of care and outcomes, more effectively manage costs, dramatically reduce or eliminate inefficient and unnecessary processes and procedures, and provide a much more compelling patient and physician experience. Think about it as the Uber-ification of the health care industry by simplifying the overall health care process in order to reduce costs, improve patient care, and improve overall population wellness.[1]

Today there is friction between health care providers (doctors, hospitals, clinics) and the health care payers (insurance companies, government agencies). The health care payers want to cap the cost of medical services by dictating how much they are willing to reimburse for particular types of care under particular conditions. However, the health care providers are starting to capture and analyze a wider variety of patient, care, and treatment data. This includes structured data from operational systems (Epic, Cerner, Lawson, Kronos), unstructured data (nurse and physician notes, patient comments, e-mail conversations), and external data sources (WebMD, Fitbit, MyFitnessPal, Yelp, Lumosity, and a growing variety of other health care-related websites and mobile apps). Leading health care providers are integrating these data sources to create actionable scores about their patents' overall wellness (diet, exercise, stress), as well as scores about the patients' likelihood for strokes, heart attacks, diabetes, and other maladies (see Figure 12-2).

---

[1] I use the term "Uber-ification" to describe the metamorphosis of traditional industries by new business models that simplify the consumer's decision process. The company Uber is threatening the traditional taxi, limousine, and transportation industries with a smartphone app that greatly simplifies the user's transportation decisions. Uber has created a new marketplace that matches riders with drivers and has turned every driver into a potential limo or taxi driver.

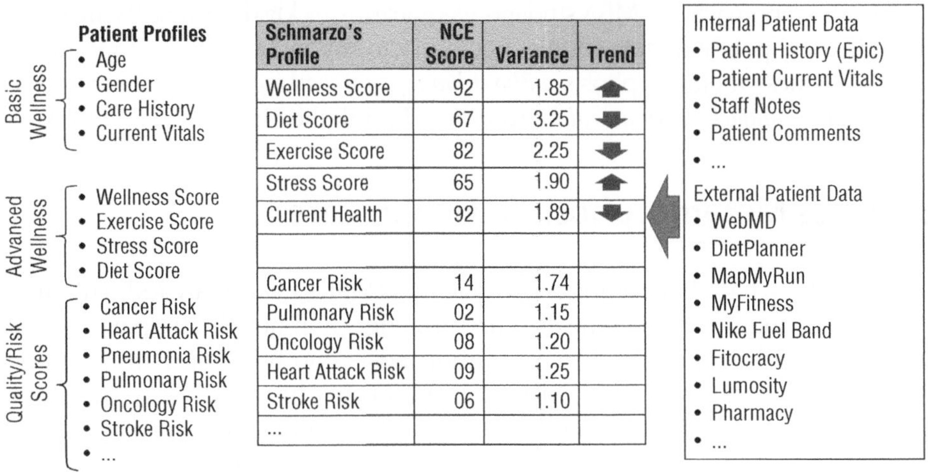

Figure 12-2: Patient actionable analytic profile

Health care providers are in a position of strength with respect to their ability to leverage superior insights about patients, physicians, medications, procedures, treatments, diseases, therapy, maladies, etc. in order to exert significant pressure on the insurance companies with respect to what procedures should be reimbursed and for how much. The health care providers will know which procedures and medications work best for which patients in what situations and can leverage those insights to exert more influence on the health care industry.

Health care providers need to contemplate the business metamorphosis potential, and how they will transition from providing just patient care to how they become the maintainer of the population's overall wellness. Preventive care opportunities fueled by superior patient, medication, exercise, diet, and stress insights could ultimately be the most important (and profitable) part of the health care value chain!

Let's drill into this potential health care industry metamorphosis in more detail. You'll use the same approach discussed with the airplane manufacturer example by first understanding the key decisions that need to be made to support the health care industry metamorphosis, and then identifying the analytics (or insights) and data necessary to support the decisions.

Business decisions → Supporting analytics → Potential data sources

First, you want to capture the decisions that the health care providers need to make about patients, quality of care, cost of care, procedures, medications, etc. Those decisions could include:

- Decisions about which medical procedures and medications to use with which patients in what medical situations
- Decisions about the appropriate level of medical care versus costs given the patient situation and prognosis

- Decisions (recommendations) for patients regarding diet, sleep, stress level, exercise, etc. in order reduce the risk of diabetes, strokes, heart attacks, etc.
- Decisions about what combinations of doctors, nurses, and technicians are most cost-effective in different surgical situations
- Decisions about what medications and treatments are most cost-effective in treating different patient health care situations
- Decisions about the optimal combinations of rehab, exercise, sleep, medication, therapy, and diet that can accelerate a patient's recovery

After you have identified the business and operational decisions, then you want to capture the analytics necessary to support the decisions. Some of those analytics could include:

- Patient wellness score
- Patient exercise score
- Patient stress score
- Patient diet score
- Medication, procedures, and treatment effectiveness
- Hospice versus hospital cost and care effectiveness
- Physician and nurse effectiveness
- Emergency room demand forecasting
- Population health forecasting
- Physician and nurse retention
- Hospital acquired infections reductions
- Unplanned readmissions reductions

Finally, you want to brainstorm data sources (patients, physicians, outcomes, cost of care, procedures, treatments, medications, etc.) that could support your analytics. Following is a list of potential data sources that might be of value in developing your analytics:

- Hospital care data (Epic, Cerner)
- MapMyRun
- Financials (Lawson, Oracle)
- MyFitnessPal
- Hours worked (Kronos)
- Strava
- Physician notes
- Smart toilets

- Nurse and technician notes
- Smart blood pressure monitors
- Pharmacy and prescriptions
- Smart glucose monitors
- Medication usage
- Apple Health
- Patient comments
- Indeed.com
- HCAHPS and surveys
- CDC
- Social media comments
- Healthcare.gov
- Yelp ratings
- Google Trends
- WebMD
- Traffic patterns
- Lumosity
- Weather forecasts
- Nike FuelBand, Fitbit, and Garmin
- Holiday schedules
- Apple Watch
- Special events schedules

At the end of this metamorphosis exercise process, health care providers will be in a better position to have identified the decisions, analytics, and data necessary to claim a bigger portion of the health care value chain, including:

- What are the optimal treatments and medications given a patient's conditions and history and how much the payer should reimburse?
- What is the value of preventive care (diet, exercise, sleep, medication, therapy), and how much should health care payers cover to incent more healthy and more profitable patient behaviors?

Summary

Industries as diverse as professional sports, manufacturing, consumer package goods, retail, education, social services, and health care are going through business model metamorphoses by leveraging the wealth of rich data sources about their customers, products, and operations. And leading organizations are learning to leverage the resulting analytic insights to change the balance of power within their industry.

In the health care industry, health care providers that know the most about their patients' and physicians' behaviors, tendencies, and usage patterns are in the best position to correct the fuzzy math that health care payers have been using to set their reimbursement rates.

No matter what your organization's ultimate business vision, going through the business metamorphosis exercise can uncover big data requirements around decisions, analytics and data sources that can be leveraged to transform or metamorphose your organization's business model. And it is an easier exercise to do than one might think, as the students in my MBA class discovered.

The bottom line across all industries is this: the organizations that know the most about their products, operations, and customers' behaviors, tendencies, and usage patterns are in the best position to monetize those insights and exert control over those organizations within their value chains that lack those customer, product, and operational insights. In the end, that's the ultimate goal of the Business Metamorphosis phase of the Big Data Business Model Maturity Index.

Homework Assignment

Use the following exercises to apply what you learned in this chapter:

- **Exercise #1:** Build on the airplane manufacturer example by applying the metamorphosis exercise techniques to another business stakeholder such as travel agents, hotel operators, or ground transportation companies.
- **Exercise #2:** Pick an organization (preferably your own organization) and apply the metamorphosis exercise to brainstorm the decisions, analytics, and data necessary to support your organization's business metamorphosis. As always, it is more productive and more fun to do this exercise with a small group. Maybe fly someplace cool (like Las Vegas, Austin, Charles City, or Nashville) to put everyone in the right frame of mind!

Part

IV

Building Cross-Organizational Support

Chapters 13 through 15 lay the organizational and cultural foundation for metamorphosing the organization. These chapters cover many of the people, processes, roles, and responsibilities that need to be addressed as organizations look to integrate data and analytics into their business models and complete the big data journey to the Business Metamorphosis phase of the Big Data Business Model Maturity Index.

In This Part

CHAPTER

13

Power of Envisioning

The business potential of big data is only limited by the creative thinking of your business stakeholders. So in a sense, this may be the most important chapter supporting the "thinking like a data scientist" process and the most fundamentally critical guidance within the book.

Opportunities abound for organizations to analyze the "dark" data that is buried within their operational systems and data warehouses and identify other internal and external data sources that they could leverage to optimize key business processes, differentiate their customer engagement, and uncover new monetization opportunities. However, getting the business stakeholders to envision what might be possible with respect to their currently under-utilized internal data and the wealth of external data sources is a significant challenge. Sounds like the perfect time for an envisioning engagement such as EMC's Big Data Vision Workshop.[1]

NOTE **I am the creator of EMC's Big Data Vision Workshop methodology. I have personally experienced the powerful business ideas that the Big Data Vision Workshop can unleash from participants when the proper creative environment and processes are put into place. Consequently I am a very bullish on the Big Data Vision Workshop and the game-changing power of envisioning.**

---

[1] EMC Corporation is the world's leading developer and provider of information infrastructure technology and solutions that enable organizations of all sizes to transform the way they compete and create value from their information.

In this chapter, I am going to discuss EMC's Big Data Vision Workshop as an example of an envisioning engagement that can fuel the organization's creative thinking for identifying where and how to leverage big data to power the organization's business models. The Big Data Vision Workshop leverages the "thinking like a data scientist" techniques to help the business stakeholders understand how big data can optimize their key business processes and uncover new monetization opportunities.

Envisioning: Fueling Creative Thinking

The Big Data Vision Workshop is an envisioning engagement designed to drive organizational alignment and fuel creative thinking about where and how an organization can leverage data and analytics to power its business models. The Big Data Vision Workshop helps organizations that don't know how to analyze the data they already collect or how to identify additional data worth collecting. Specifically, the Big Data Vision Workshop:

- Provides a formal process for identifying where data and analytics can drive material business impact that affects the organization's key business initiatives over the next 9 to 12 months.
- Ensures business relevance by focusing on the organization's most impactful business opportunities.
- Facilitates group exercises to encourage business and IT stakeholders to envision the "realm of what's possible" from the organization's internal data, as well as explore the potential of external data.
- Drives business and IT alignment around those "best" analytic opportunities with a clear road map of what needs to be done over the next 9 to 12 months.

The Big Data Vision Workshop process is ideal for organizations who:

- Have a desire to leverage big data to transform their business but do not know where and how to start.
- Have a wealth of data that they do not know how to monetize.

Organizations of all sizes have successfully leveraged the Big Data Vision Workshop to identify where and how to leverage data and analytics to power their business models. No organization is too small, and yes, your data is "big" enough.

Big Data Vision Workshop Process

The Big Data Vision Workshop typically spans two to three weeks. It concludes with a half-day, facilitated, on-site interactive workshop that prioritizes the high-value business use cases and identifies the supporting data and advanced analytic recommendations. However, a substantial amount of work needs to be done prior to the workshop to drive the cross-organizational collaboration and fuel the creative thinking processes. Figure 13-1 outlines the Big Data Vision Workshop process and timeline.

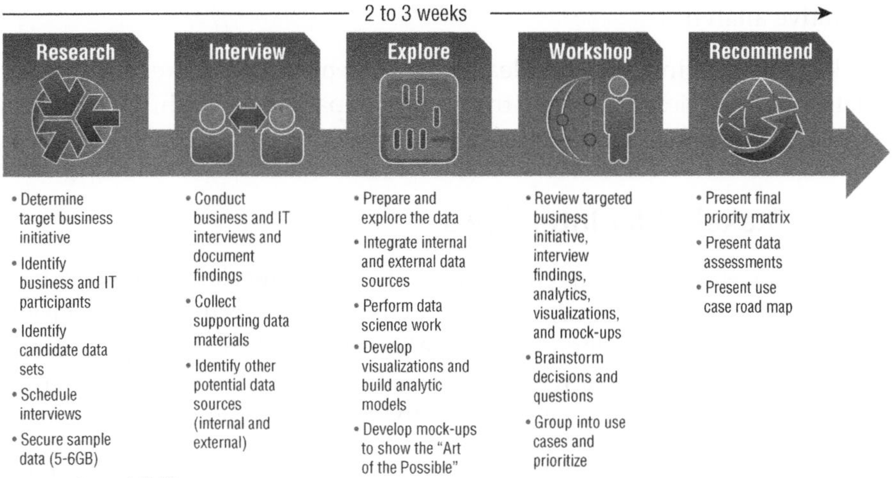

Image courtesy of EMC

Figure 13-1: Big Data Vision Workshop process and timeline

Let's examine the stages of the Big Data Vision Workshop process to help you understand how to stimulate creative thinking and generate the actionable analytic recommendations that best support the advancement of your organization's key business initiatives.

To make this envisioning process more real, I am going to walk through the process using a health care organization (group of hospitals) as an example. I will refer to the organization as *Healthcare Systems*.

Pre-engagement Research

For the engagement to be successful, there are several key activities that need to happen prior to the envisioning engagement to ensure that it is impactful to the organization. Following are the key steps in the pre-engagement phase of the Big Data Vision Workshop:

- Identify the organization's business initiative or business challenge on which to focus the engagement.
- Identify the business stakeholders who impact or are impacted by the targeted business initiative. There are typically three to five different business

functions engaged in the envisioning process. A wide variety of business stakeholders ensure a comprehensive collection of decisions, questions, metrics, and data sources that support the targeted business initiative.

- Gather information about the sample data sets including file formats, data location, data dictionary, and small sample of the data (5 to 6 gigabytes). Ultimately, the data scientists will use the small data sets to create illustrative analytics.

The key business initiative for Healthcare Systems is to explore how to leverage data and analytics to improve the quality of patient care while controlling costs, or to "improve cost/quality of patient care."

Business Stakeholder Interviews

The Big Data Vision Workshop engagement starts by interviewing the key business stakeholders. The interview process focuses on (1) capturing the decisions that the business stakeholders need to make to support the targeted business initiative and (2) capturing a wide range of questions that support those decisions. Key steps in the interview phase of the Big Data Vision Workshop are:

- Conduct interviews with business and IT stakeholders to capture key business objectives, the decisions that they are trying to make, and the types of questions that they need to answer in support of those decisions.
- Collect supporting materials such as sample reports and dashboards. Also collect any examples of the business stakeholders downloading data into spreadsheets. Those spreadsheets can be gold in understanding the decisions that the business stakeholders are trying to make.
- Identify or brainstorm other potential data sources (internal and external) that might be of value in supporting the key decisions.

It is always best to create and share an interview questionnaire with interviewees prior to the interviews. The interview questionnaire should address the following:

- What are their key objectives and responsibilities?
- What decisions must the interviewees make with respect to the targeted business initiative?
- What questions do they need to answer in support of those decisions?
- What are the metrics or key performance indicators against which success will be measured?
- What are the organization's value drivers (e.g., the key activities that help the organization make money related to the targeted business initiative)?

The Healthcare Systems key business stakeholders for the "improve cost/quality of patient care" initiative are the following:

- Physicians and nurses
- Clinical
- Operations
- Finance
- Human resources
- Population health

Explore with Data Science

A very powerful part of the Big Data Vision Workshop engagement is the data science work to create illustrative analytics on the sample data sets. This part of the envisioning engagement might not be possible if your organization does not have access to a data science team. But if you do, the data science team should explore different analytic techniques (like the ones covered in Chapter 6) to help the business stakeholders to envision the realm of what is possible using data science. Key tasks in the data science explore phase are:

- Prepare, transform, and enrich the data.
- Explore the data using different data visualization techniques.
- Explore opportunities to integrate external data sources such as social media (Twitter, Facebook, LinkedIn), app-generated (Zillow, Eventbrite), and public domain data (data.gov).
- Build illustrative analytics using different analytic techniques to determine which analytic techniques yield the most relevant insights.
- Package data visualizations and analytic models for consumption by the business and IT stakeholders.
- Develop simple user experience mock-ups to validate how the analytics will support the business stakeholders' key decisions.

At Healthcare Systems, a small sample set of data from Epic (hospital operations), Kronos (time and attendance), and Lawson (finance and costs) were pulled together, and illustrative analytics were created around the following business areas (see Figure 13-2):

- Emergency room volume variances
- Operating room patient volume forecasting
- Diagnostic code relationships
- Knee replacement cost clusters

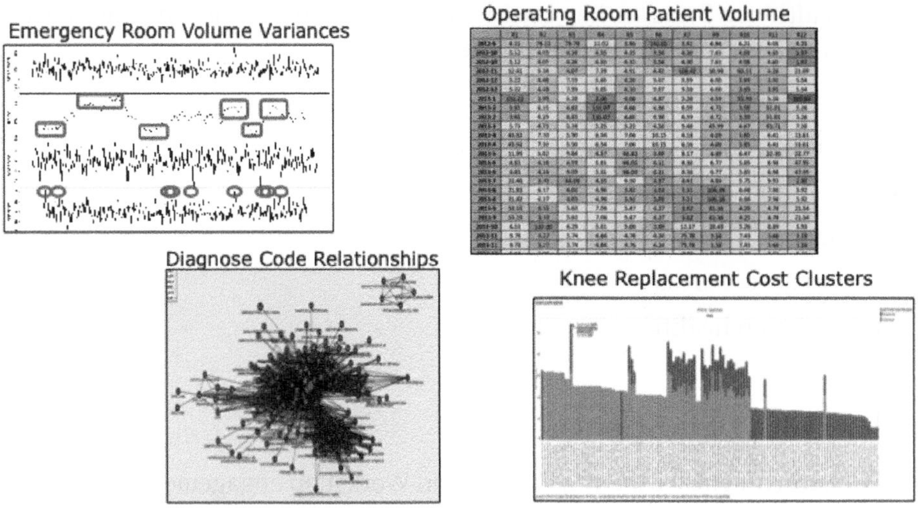

Figure 13-2: Big Data Vision Workshop illustrative analytics

At Healthcare Systems, simple mock-ups were also developed so that the workshop participants could envision how the analytic results could be presented to frontline workers (physicians, nurses, admissions) and patients (see Figure 13-3).

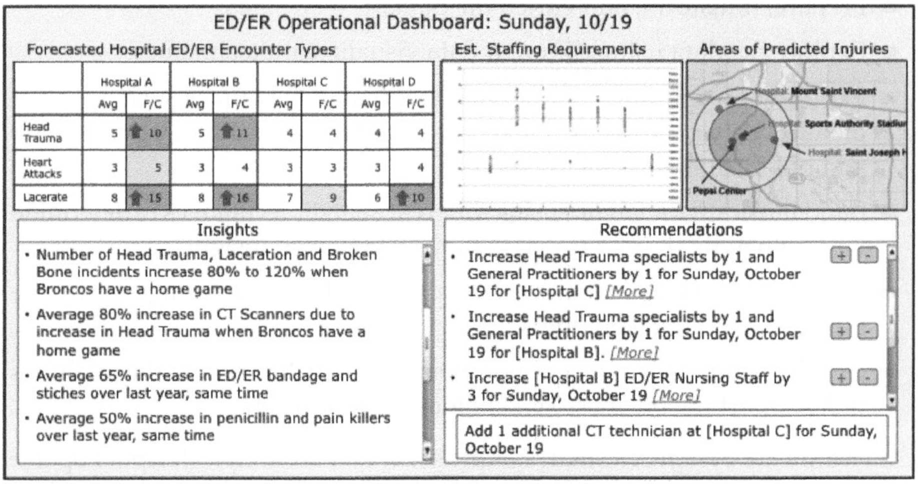

Figure 13-3: Big Data Vision Workshop user experience mock-up

Workshop

Once the above activities have been completed (which typically takes about two to three weeks of work), you are now ready for the half-day workshop. The goal of the facilitated, on-site, interactive workshop is to help the participants:

- Go beyond descriptive reporting to brainstorm the applicability of predictive (what is likely to happen) analytics and prescriptive (what should I do) analytics.
- Brainstorm, identify, and prioritize additional data sources (both internal and external data sources) that may be worthy of collecting for the targeted business initiative.
- Use a prioritization process to identify the best analytic opportunities based on business value and implementation feasibility over the next 9 to 12 months.

Following are some specific tasks that should be accomplished during the workshop.

Fuel the Creative Thinking Process

You want to stimulate creative, "out of the box" thinking during the workshop. To fuel the creative thinking process, do the following:

- Share the illustrative analytics that the data science team created from the client's data to stimulate creative thinking regarding how advanced analytics could energize the business.
- Review examples from other industries of advanced analytics applied to different business scenarios.
- Share the mock-ups in order to stimulate creative thinking (PowerPoint works great as your mock-up and user experience development tool).

Brainstorm Business Decisions and Questions

After walking through the illustrative analytics and mock-ups, lead the workshop participants through a series of facilitated brainstorming scenarios including:

- **Scenario 1.** Brainstorm the insights that you want to uncover about your targeted business initiative if you could get access to ALL the organization's operational and transactional data. For Healthcare Systems, what insights would you want about your key business initiative if you had 10 to 20 years of patient care data, hospital operations data, time and attendance data, and finance data? Heck, I'm starting to sound like the NSA!
- **Scenario 2.** Brainstorm the insights that you would want to uncover about your key business initiative if you had access to all of the organization's internal unstructured data (physician or nurse notes, patient comments, e-mail threads) and external unstructured data (social media, mobile, blogs, newsfeeds, weather, traffic, economic, population health, Centers for Disease Control).

- **Scenario 3.** Decompose the key business initiative into the different events that compose that initiative, and brainstorm what insights you would want to capture if you had access to that data in real-time. For Healthcare Systems, are there opportunities to "catch the patient at the time of need" interacting with your organization in order to provide preventive care recommendations?
- **Scenario 4.** Brainstorm how you would leverage predictive analytics and prescriptive analytics to uncover new actionable insights about your targeted business initiative. For Healthcare Systems, build on the learnings from the stakeholder interviews to create questions about the "improve cost/quality of patient care" business initiative that start with verbs such as predict, forecast, recommend, score, or correlate.

Be sure to capture the decisions and questions on separate sticky notes and place the sticky notes on flip charts.

Group Decisions and Questions into Common Themes

Next, have the workshop participants group the decisions and questions into use cases that share common business and/or financial objectives. Have participants gather around the flip charts and group the sticky notes into use cases on the flip chart sheets. Once the sticky notes are grouped into common use cases, use a marker to draw a circle around each of the groupings and give each grouping a descriptive short name. For Healthcare Systems, brainstorming the "improve cost/quality patient care" business initiative could yield use cases such as unplanned readmissions analysis, hospital acquired infections, service variance analysis, staffing/cost/outcomes analysis, staff retention, procedures cost analysis, volume forecasting, and population health.

Prioritize the Groupings

Next, have the workshop participants prioritize the use cases using the *prioritization matrix* (see Figure 13-4). The use of the prioritization matrix is covered in depth later in this chapter.

Summarize Workshop Results

Finally, summarize the results of the workshop including:

- Review of the prioritized list of potential "Analytics Opportunities." Verify that everyone buys off on the end result.
- Review of "Parking Lot" items and discussion of any potential follow-up steps.
- Discussion of next steps.

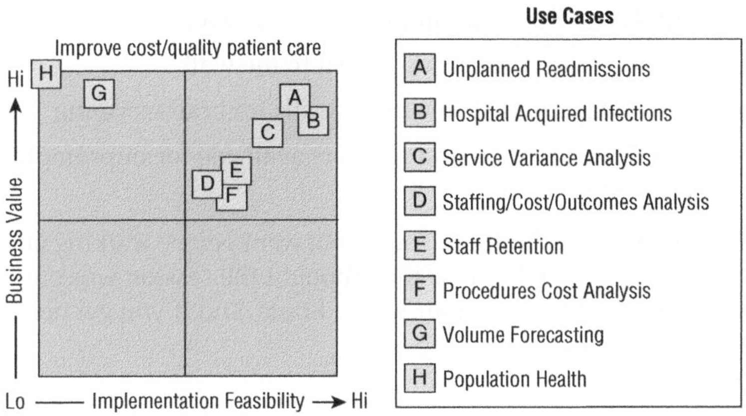

Figure 13-4: Prioritize Healthcare Systems's use cases

The Big Data Vision Workshop deliverables include:

- Prioritization matrix with the prioritization of the use cases
- The sticky note content for each use case
- Interview takeaways
- Data scientist illustrative analytics
- User experience mock-ups
- Documentation of the Parking Lot items (for potential follow-up)
- Data assessment worksheets that assess the business value and implementation feasibility of each data source

Setting Up the Workshop

There are many "little" things that need to be done prior to the workshop. And while you may be tempted to skip over these seemingly superficial tasks, they are critical to the workshop success because they set the proper stage for the desired "out of the box" thinking….yes, thinking differently!

Pick a creative, out-of-the box location. I have done workshops in the middle of an Iowa cornfield (for a wind turbine energy company), in a grade school classroom complete with those little chairs and tables (for a charter school), in a comedy club (for a gaming establishment), and in a technology museum (for a high-tech manufacturer).

Set up the room for facilitated conversations, which can include the following:

- Arrange chairs in a horseshoe shape
- Create a "Parking Lot" flip chart and tape it to the wall

- Create a "Ground Rules" flip chart and tape it to the wall
- Create a prioritization matrix chart and tape it to the wall
- Tape five to six blank flip chart sheets to the walls for brainstorming
- Have plenty of 3 × 5 sticky notes and markers available for impromptu capturing of ideas and thoughts

Confirm the meeting time and duration. You do not want people walking out of the workshop halfway through because they thought the session was only two hours. Have participants block out four to five hours, and if you get done sooner, give them the time back.

Kick off the meeting by:

- Explaining why the participants are there and the objectives of the workshop.
- Sharing the roles of the workshop team (facilitator, data scientist, subject matter expert, and scribe).
- Having everyone share their name, their responsibilities and their expectations for the workshop.

Establish the workshop ground rules including:

- Only one conversation at any given moment.
- No hierarchy in the room; everybody and their ideas are equal.
- Turn off cell phones, tablets, and computers (or at least put them into buzz or stun mode).
- Share any and all ideas (the only bad idea is the one that isn't shared).
- Breaks are planned throughout the workshop, so please stay with the group.

Use icebreakers to kick off the workshop to get everyone participating. There are several different types of icebreakers. Be creative and relevant to the client's environment. For example:

- Have everyone share with the group something about themselves that you don't think anyone else knows.
- With a movie chain client, we asked each participant to identify a movie character that they are most like and why.
- Have participants pick their favorite superhero and explain why that superhero is their favorite.

Use a Parking Lot flip chart to control the workshop. Explain the purpose of the "Parking Lot" (i.e., captures topics that are outside the scope of the workshop and keeps the workshop moving in the right direction).

During the workshop, use the following techniques to help fuel the participants' creative thinking process:

- Have the workshop participants capture one idea or thought per sticky note throughout the scenarios.
- Have the facilitators place the sticky notes on the flip charts as the ideas or thoughts come up.
- Have the facilitators read aloud the idea or thought as they are posting it to the wall; this helps to fuel the creative thinking process.
- Ensure that participants brainstorm individually. If you brainstorm in groups, good ideas can get lost when there are overpowering personalities in the groups.

The Prioritization Matrix

One big obstacle to a successful big data journey is gaining consensus and alignment between the business and IT stakeholders in identifying the big data use cases that deliver sufficient financial value to the business while possessing a high probability of implementation success over the next 9 to 12 months. You can identify multiple use cases where big data and advanced analytics can deliver compelling business value. However, many of these use cases have a low probability of implementation success over the next 9 to 12 months because of:

- Lack of availability of timely, accurate data.
- Inexperience with new data sources such as social media, mobile, unstructured, and sensor data.
- Limited data or analytic people resources.
- Lack of experience with new technologies like Hadoop, MapReduce, Spark, Mahout, MADlib, text mining, etc.
- Weak business and IT collaborative relationship.
- Lack of management fortitude to stick with the engagement.

One of my favorite organizational alignment tools for addressing this issue is the *prioritization matrix*. The prioritization matrix is a marvelous tool for:

- Identifying the "right" use case to pursue with big data based on a balance of business value and implementation feasibility.
- Ensuring that both IT and business stakeholders have a voice in discussing the relative value and implementation challenges for each use case.

- Capturing the business drivers and implementation risks for each of the use cases.
- Catalyzing the decision on the "right" use cases so that everyone (business and IT) can agree on a path forward.

The prioritization matrix is the capstone of the Big Data Vision Workshop process. The prioritization matrix facilitates the discussion (and debate) between the business and IT stakeholders in determining the "right" use case on which to focus the big data initiative. The "right" use case has both meaningful business value (from the business stakeholders' perspectives) and reasonable feasibility of successful implementation (from the IT stakeholders' perspectives) over the next 9 to 12 months.

Focusing the prioritization matrix process on a key business initiative—such as reducing churn, increasing same store sales, minimizing financial risk, optimizing market spend, or reducing hospital readmissions—is critical as it provides the foundation and the guardrails for meaningful business value and implementation feasibility discussions.

The prioritization matrix process starts by placing each identified use case (identified in the Big Data Vision Workshop) on a sticky note. The workshop participants then decide the placement of each use case on the prioritization matrix (weighing business value and implementation feasibility) vis-à-vis the relative placement of the other use cases (see Figure 13-5).

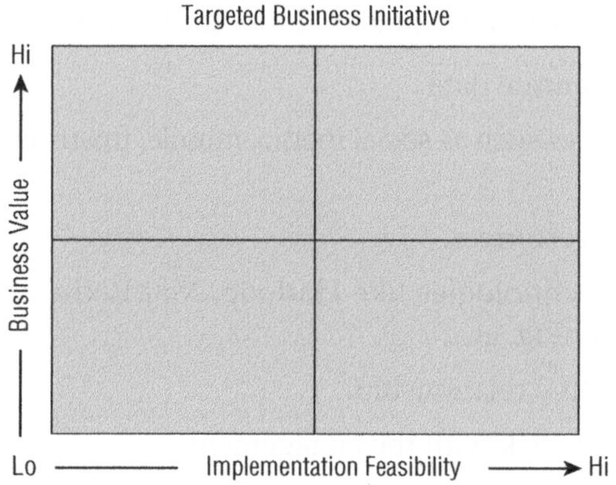

Figure 13-5: Prioritization matrix template

The business stakeholders are responsible for the relative positioning of each business case on the business value axis. The IT stakeholders are responsible for relative positioning of each business case on the implementation feasibility axis (considering data, technology, skills, and organizational readiness).

The heart of the prioritization process is the discussion that ensues about the relative placement of each of the use cases. Issues discussed could include (see Figure 13-6):

- Why is use case [B] more or less valuable than use case [A]? What are the specific business drivers or variables that make use case [B] more or less valuable than use case [A]?
- Why is use case [B] less or more feasible from an implementation perspective than use case [A]? What are the specific implementation risks that make use case [B] less or more feasible than use case [A]?

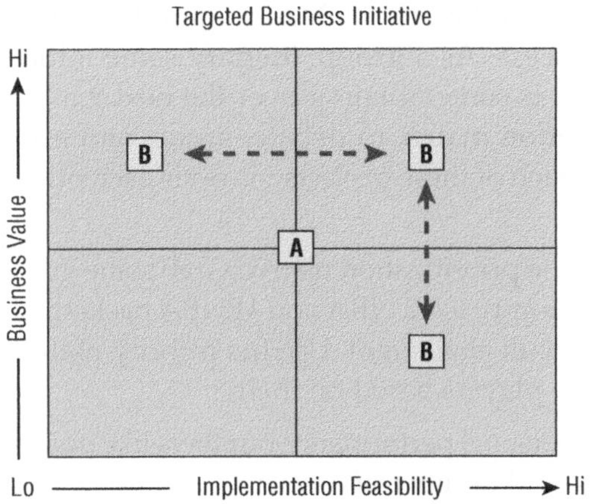

Figure 13-6: Prioritization matrix process

It is critical to the organizational alignment process to capture the reasons for the relative positioning of each use case during the prioritization process. These discussions provide the financial guidelines necessary to achieve the use case business value and flag potential implementation risks that need to be addressed during the project.

Summary

The Big Data Vision Workshop and the prioritization matrix are marvelous tools for driving organizational alignment between the business and IT stakeholders about where and how to start the organization's big data journey. These tools provide a framework for identifying the relative business value of each use case vis-à-vis its implementation risks over the next 9 to 12 months. As a result of the prioritization process, both the business and IT stakeholders know what use cases they are targeting, understand the potential business value of each use case, and have their eyes wide open to the implementation risks against which the project needs to manage.

The bottom line is that the Big Data Vision Workshop and prioritization matrix ensure that the full force of the organization can be brought to bear in capturing the business potential of the organization's big data initiative.

Homework Assignment

Use the following exercises to apply what you learned in this chapter.

Exercise #1: Grab some coworkers and block off 30 to 45 minutes to test out the prioritization matrix process. As a group, identify some initiatives or projects the organization is contemplating over the next 9 to 12 months. Then use the prioritization matrix to debate, argue, and arm wrestle about where to position each of these projects vis-à-vis each other on the priority matrix.

Exercise #2: Have some fun with the prioritization matrix! Grab some guys and gals and identify the current top 10 to 12 NBA and WNBA basketball players (that alone may be a difficult challenge). Use the priority matrix process to decide the value of the players based on their:

- Personal performance—their personal performance numbers like points scored, number of rebounds, and number of assists
- Importance to the team—their ability to make their teammates better (I wonder how one would compare Stephen Curry to Elena Delle Donne. Man, that should be a fun discussion!)

CHAPTER

14

Organizational Ramifications

Now comes the hard part. No, it's not the technology and knowing what technologies to back and which ones might fade. No, it's not the lack of data science talent. And no, it's not even gaining the buy-in of the business stakeholders, though that can be a huge issue, as we have discussed throughout this book.

The biggest threat to the success of any organization's big data initiative is the organizational impediments. More accurately put, it is overcoming the organizational inertia and implementing the organizational and cultural changes necessary to advance from business monitoring to business optimization, monetization, and ultimately metamorphosis. It's tough to get the organization to "think differently." As Pogo famously said, "We have met the enemy and he is us."

In this chapter, you will explore the role of the Chief Data Officer, which I prefer to call the Chief Data Monetization Officer. You are going to consider the trio of privacy, trust, and decision (not data) governance. And finally, the chapter concludes with guidance for liberating the organization and unleashing the only thing standing between big data mediocrity and big data metamorphosis—creative thinking.

Chief Data Monetization Officer

There's a new sheriff in the big data world and that's the Chief Data Officer (CDO). A more accurate title for this role is Chief Data Monetization Officer (CDMO), as this person should focus on driving and deriving value from the organization's data and analytic assets. The CDMO should own the organization's investment decisions with respect to data and analytics and own the charter for identifying and managing the organization's data and analytics monetization initiatives.

An ideal CDMO candidate should have a background in economics. The CDMO doesn't need an information technology background (that's the CIO's job). I recommend an economics education because economists have been trained to assign value to *abstract* concepts and assets. An economist is an expert who studies the relationship between an organization's resources and its production or value. And in today's world, assigning value to data can be extremely abstract.

CDMO Responsibilities

The CDMO owns quantifying the value of data and championing the organization's efforts to monetize the organization's data (by applying analytics in order to optimize key business processes and uncover new revenue opportunities). The CDMO must collaborate with business management to determine the costs, benefits, and Return on Investment (ROI) for data and data-related business initiatives.

The CDMO should sit between the business leaders (who have profit or margin responsibilities) and the CIO (who owns the technology decisions) in order to drive the identification, valuation, and prioritization of data acquisition and data monetization projects. The CDMO should report to the COO or CEO because the CDMO should also have revenue and margin responsibilities. Reporting to the COO or CEO also ensures the CDMO has the organizational clout to drive collaboration between business management and the CIO and to lead the organization's data monetization efforts.

CDMO Organization

As organizations build out their data science teams, the data science teams should fall under the purview of the CDMO. The data science team needs a senior management champion, and the CDMO is the best choice. Heck, I'd even put the Business Intelligence (BI) teams under the purview of the CDMO in order to drive closer collaboration and share learnings between the BI and data science teams. (See Chapter 5 for a review on the differences between BI and data science.)

I would have the data scientists (and BI teams) hardline to the business functions and dotted line into the CDMO (see Figure 14-1).

To drive data monetization success, the BI and data science teams must thoroughly understand the organization's key business initiatives, the decisions that the business needs to make and the questions that the business needs to answer to support those business initiatives. The BI and data science teams need to be accountable to the line of business because that's where value (revenue, profit, margin) is being created.

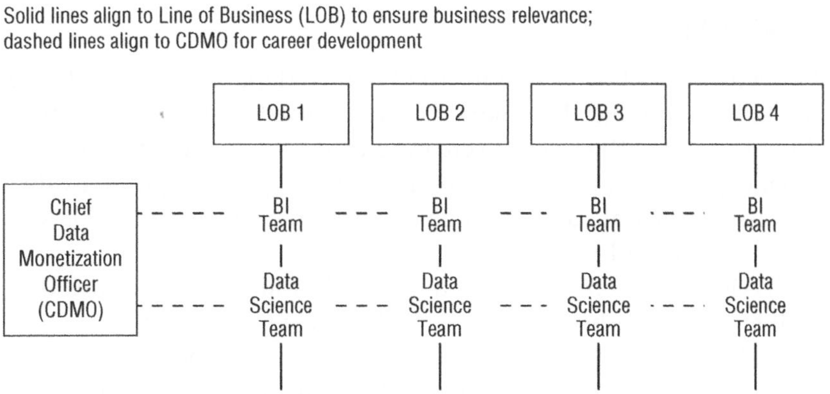

Figure 14-1: CDMO organizational structure

By the way, the CDMO should NOT own the data lake, the data warehouse, or any of the underlying data architecture or technologies. These data architectures and technologies need to be owned by the CIO. Consequently, the CDMO must collaborate with the CIO to create a data architecture and technology road map that supports the CDMO's monetization efforts.

Analytics Center of Excellence

The analytics Center of Excellence (COE) is critical to the success of the CDMO's data monetization charter and needs to be the responsibility of the CDMO. Key CDMO tasks with respect to the COE include:

- Hiring, development, promotion, retention, and talent management of the data science and Business Intelligence teams (even if they do sit within the business units)
- Continuous training program and certification on new technologies and analytic algorithms
- Active industry and university monitoring to stay on top of most current data and data science trends
- Business Intelligence, data visualization, statistical, predictive analytics, machine learning, and data mining tool evaluations and recommendations
- Capturing, sharing, and management (i.e., library function) of the Business Intelligence, data warehousing, and data science best practices across the organization
- Identifying analytic processes worthy of legal or patent protection

The analytics COE becomes the sun around which the data science and Business Intelligence personnel "orbit" from a skills and career development perspective.

CDMO Leadership

The CDMO needs to work closely with the Finance department in order to develop data acquisition and data monetization ROI estimates. Finance will keep the CDMO honest with respect to creating value, but expect that relationship to be "challenging" because Finance will likely struggle with putting value on intangible assets like data and analytic insight. That's where the CDMO's economics background will help.

Also, the CDMO will need to become a master facilitator (by the way, this is a good skill for anyone who is trying to bridge the gap between IT and the business). The CDMO is going to need to leverage teamwork and collaboration to be successful in the job. He or she also must be in the front of these data and analytic enablement discussions. The CDMO must take the initiative to lead the cultural change necessary to get the organization to more readily embrace data and analytics in the operations of the business.

Infusing a CDMO role can be a significant challenge. Not only is it new, so there are no predefined best practices to leverage, but also trying to determine the value of data and analytics is something at which few organizations have mastered. The CDMO will have to continually prove him- or herself to the rest of the organization. The CDMO will have to evangelize the role that data and analytics can play in improving the entire organization's decision-making capabilities and empowering frontline employees and customers.

Privacy, Trust, and Decision Governance

By now, we've all heard the story. A retailer, by virtue of its advanced analysis of website activities, determined with some level of confidence that a particular website visitor was a pregnant woman. On the basis of this insight, the retailer started mailing baby-related coupons (prenatal care, baby room furniture, nursing products, etc.) to the woman, who was actually a *16-year-old girl*. The girl's father became outraged when he saw the coupons addressed to his *daughter*. He complained to the local store manager, only to learn two weeks later that his daughter was indeed pregnant.

Many in the data science community might perceive this as a huge success—the merchandiser's superior data science skills were able to determine that a female customer was pregnant even before her father knew! However, the retailer created a public relations fiasco, because just as the retailer knew with some level of confidence that the customer was pregnant, the retailer also likely knew with some level of confidence that she was underage.

There are numerous other examples where an organization may uncover (with some level of confidence) insights about its customers but should not to act on those insights. Examples include:

- Customer is researching cancer or some other serious ailment
- Customer is researching a new job (if he or she has an existing job)
- Customer is researching dating sites (if he or she has married)
- Customer is researching divorce lawyers (if he or she got busted visiting dating sites)

All of these situations can probably can be ascertained (with some level of confidence) by mining a customer's keyword searches, social media postings and exchanges, e-mail communications, and website and blog visits (e.g., time on a site, frequency of visits, recency of visits, etc.). However, acting on these suspected situations could be catastrophic from an organizational goodwill and public relations perspective. Which brings us to what I believe should be the "golden rule" for big data and data science:

Just because you know or suspect something about a customer does NOT necessarily mean that you should act on that knowledge.

Reluctance to adhere to this rule can be catastrophic for an organization, leading to privacy issues, fines, and potentially even lawsuits.

Privacy Issues = Trust Issues

Customer loyalty programs thrive because organizations give their customers something in return for purchase information and information about the customer. I'm a member of numerous loyalty programs, and these loyalty programs reward my loyalty with discounts, free coffee and pastries, free airline trips and hotel stays, and cash. I give them information about my shopping and travel activities, and in return they pay me back in rewards and discounts.

However, I'm hesitant to share any additional personal information because (1) these organizations have not given me a compelling reason to share more personal information, and (2) I do not trust them to use that data in my best interests. Let me walk you through an example.

Let's say that you are a grocery chain and you would love to know the following information as a customer walks into your store:

- What's on her shopping list?
- What's her budget?
- If there is any particular event (birthday, barbeque, party) for which she is planning?

With that information, the grocery chain could create a set of recommendations that would allow the customer to optimize her budget, as well as recommend items that might be useful for the upcoming event. That would be a real win for both the customer and the grocer. In fact, I would be willing to share that information with my grocer as long as I could be confident that the grocer was making recommendations that were in my best interest.

However, the minute the retailer recommends something that is not of value to me but is of value to it (i.e., recommends one of the retailer's more profitable private label products as a replacement for the branded product that I have used for years), then it will have violated my trust that it would only use my data in my best interests.

Trust is the heart of the privacy issue from a customer's perspective:

- Customers don't trust the organization to have the guidelines and governance in place to know when it should act, and when it should NOT act, on insights that it has gleaned about them.
- Customers don't trust the organization to focus on the customer's best interests and instead of the organization's best interests.
- Customers don't trust the organization to refrain from selling their personal data to others for its own gain.

This privacy issue is only going to become bigger and bigger, especially as organizations become more proficient at mining big data and uncovering new insights about their customers' interests, passions, affiliations, and associations.

One simple way to test whether or not you should act on the insights that you have gained about your customers is the "Mom" test. That is, what would your mom think of your decision about how you use that information about a customer? In most cases, the Mom test would quickly identify those things that are just not the right thing to do.

However, organizations can't rely on the Mom test, so they need a more formal decision governance organization.

Decision Governance

Organizations need a formal decision governance organization and processes that clearly articulate the rules, policies, and regulations with respect to how organizations will and will not use information about their customers. Decision governance is different from data governance in the following ways:

- Data governance provides policies, procedures, and rules that manage the availability, usability, integrity, security, and accessibility of an organization's data.
- Decision governance provides policies, procedures, and rules that manage the capture, privacy, and use of the insights to drive interactions or decisions that might impact a particular customer.

Most organizations already have a data governance organization, so they likely already have the experience, policies, procedures, and people on which they could build their decision governance organization.

The decision governance team must work with the business stakeholders to decide what information they are seeking on their customers and clearly define when and where they will use that information. And if there ever is a situation that is not covered by the decision governance policies, then no action should be taken until the decision governance organization has decided what the proper action should be.

Decision governance has become a priority for organizations because the advent of big data is enabling organizations to gather detailed insights about their customers' behaviors, tendencies, propensities, interests, passions, affiliations, and associations that can easily be used for both appropriate and inappropriate decisions and actions. Lack of decision governance is a clear and present danger to organizations that are trying to mine actionable insights out of their bounty of consumer data. Organizations need to act to ensure the proper and ethical use of their customers' data and the resulting analytic insights, otherwise they risk opening themselves to significant privacy issues and lawsuits.

Unleashing Organizational Creativity

Ah, the anguish of not knowing the "right" answers. Organizations struggle with the process of determining the "right" answers, resulting in wasted debates and divisive arguments regarding whose answers are more right. They even have a name for this debilitating process—*analysis paralysis*—where different sides of the argument bring forth their own factoids and antidotal observations to support the justification of their "right" answer. However, the concepts of experimentation and instrumentation can actually liberate organizations from this "analysis paralysis" by providing a way out—a way forward that leads to action versus just more debates, more frustrations, and more analysis paralysis.

For many organizations, the concepts of experimentation and instrumentation are a bit foreign. Internet companies and direct marketing organizations have ingrained these two concepts into their analytics and customer engagement processes through concepts like A/B testing.[1] They have leveraged the concepts of experimentation and instrumentation to free up the organizational thinking—to freely explore new ideas and test "hunches"—but in a scientific manner that results in solid evidence and new organizational learning.

[1] A/B testing (also known as split testing) is a method of comparing two versions of a webpage against each other to determine which one performs better. By creating an A and B version of your page, you can validate new design changes, test hypotheses, and improve your website's conversion rate. Source: `https://www.optimizely.com/ab-testing/`

Let's examine how your organization can embrace these same concepts as part of your big data business strategy. Let's start by defining two key terms:

- **Experimentation** is the act, process, practice, or instance of making experiments, where an experiment is a test, trial, or tentative procedure; an act or operation for the purpose of discovering something unknown or of testing a principle, supposition, or hypothesis.
- **Instrumentation** is the process of measuring the experimentation results within a production or operational environment.

Taken together, these two concepts can liberate organizations that are suffering from analysis paralysis and are struggling when they are not certain what decision to make. The concepts of experimentation and instrumentation can empower the creative thinking that is necessary as organizations look to identify how to integrate data and analytics into their business models. This "empowerment" cycle empowers organizations to freely consider different ideas without worrying about whether the ideas are correct ahead of time. Organizations can let the tests tell them which ideas are "right" and not let the most persuasive debater or most senior person make that determination. It empowers the organization to challenge conventional thinking and unleashes creative thinking that can surface new monetization ideas. No longer do you have to spend time debating whose idea is right. Instead, put the ideas to the test and let the data tell you!

Let's walk through an example of how the empowerment cycle works (see Figure 14-2):

Liberate organization's creative thinking process

- Step 1: Develop hypothesis or hunch to test
- Step 2: Develop test cases to test hypothesis or hunch
- Step 3: Instrument all test cases to measure results
- Step 4: Execute and measure test results
- Step 5: Learn and move on

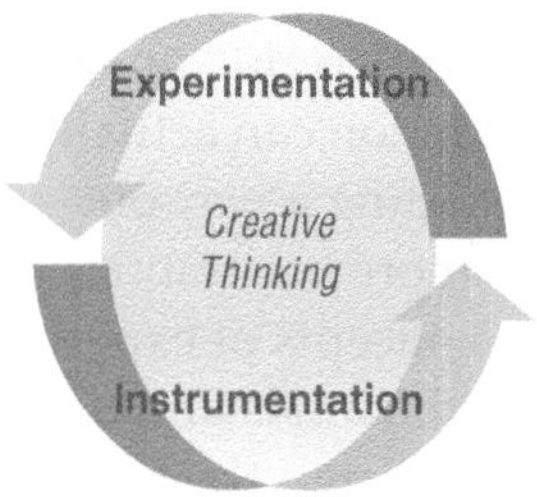

Figure 14-2: Empowerment cycle

Step 1: Develop a hypothesis or hunch that you want to test. For example, I believe that my target audience will respond more favorably to a "Buy One Get One Free" (BOGOF) offer, while my colleague believes that a "50% off" offer is more attractive to our target audience.

Step 2: Develop the different test cases that can prove or disprove the hypothesis. You want to be clear as to the metrics you would use to measure the test results (e.g., click through rate, store traffic, sales, market sentiment). In this example, we would create three test cases: "BOGOF" offer, "50% off" offer, and a control group. We would randomly select our test and control audiences and ensure that other variables are being held constant during the test (e.g., same time of day, same audience characteristics, same channel, same time frame, etc.).

Step 3: Measure the results of the test cases in order to determine the effectiveness of the test cases. In this example, we'd want to ensure that each of the three test cases was appropriately instrumented or "tagged" and that we were capturing all the relevant data to determine who responded to which offers, who didn't respond, and the ultimate outcomes of their responses.

Step 4: Execute the tests. We would now start the tests, capture the data, end the test, and quantify the test results.

Step 5: Learn and move on. We'd look at the test results, examine who responded to what offers, determine the final results, and declare a winner. We would then package or share the learnings with other parts of the organization and then move on to the next test.

The empowerment cycle leverages experimentation and instrumentation to empower organizations to freely explore and test new ideas, and it empowers organizations to get moving and not get bogged down in analysis paralysis. Experimentation and instrumentation are the anti-analysis paralysis ointment, because they provide organizations with the tools and concepts to test ideas, learn from those tests, and move on.

Summary

There are several organizational issues that need to be addressed in order to help organizations integrate data and analytics into their business models. This chapter addressed some concepts to help the organization more effectively adopt data and analytics:

- The role of the Chief Data Monetization Officer to lead the organization's data and analytics investment and monetization efforts
- Addressing the issues of privacy and trust through a formalized decision governance organization
- How to unleash the organization's creative thinking, which is the only thing standing between big data mediocrity and big data metamorphosis

Finally, don't forget this critical customer golden rule:

Just because you know or suspect something about a customer does NOT necessarily mean that you should act on that knowledge.

Make your mom proud.

Homework Assignment

Use the following exercises to apply what you learned in this chapter.

Exercise #1: Document the biggest organizational challenges that a CDMO would face within your organization. For each challenge, brainstorm some ideas as to what the CDMO could do to address those issues.

Exercise #2: Identify some business partners with whom you could discuss and ultimately test the empowerment cycle. Identify some hypotheses or rules of thumb that your business partners would like to challenge. Brainstorm the decisions, analytics, and data requirements necessary to challenge that conventional thinking.

CHAPTER
15
Stories

Everyone loves stories to which they can relate, which probably makes it the ideal way to conclude this book. While stories can be fun and funny, the most valuable stories are those that motivate us to think differently and take action, where the story is so compelling that the reader can't wait to put the ideas into action!

The goals of this chapter are to share some big data stories and to help you, the reader, develop inspiring stories that are relevant to your organization and motivate the organization into action.

Instead of providing a long list of the different analytics that are occurring within different industries, I'm offering a "think differently" approach for how you find and construct big data stories that are the most relevant to your organization. Instead of looking at the big data stories from the traditional industries perspective, let's look at stories from the perspective of the organization's strategic nouns, or key business entities. I find that most big data and data science stories fall into three categories of business entity analytics (regardless of industry):

- Customer and employee analytics
- Product and device analytics
- Network and operational analytics

The advantage of looking for stories across these three categories is that it prevents organizations from artificially limiting themselves in searching for relevant big data stories. Many organizations are only interested in hearing about big data stories that are happening within their industry. That's the "safe" way to go. But sometimes the most powerful opportunities are realized from stories from other industries. Having a broader view of these big data stories can open the eyes of the business executives as to the potential of big data within their organizations.

For example, digital media organizations use "attribution analytics" to quantify the impact of different digital media treatments (messaging, websites, impressions, display ad type, display ad page location, keyword searches, social media posts, day parting, etc.) on a conversion or sales event. Think about how many different websites, display ads, and keyword searches you interact with as you decide to do something (e.g., buy a product, request some collateral, download an article, play a game, research an event, etc.). Attribution analysis looks at "baskets" of digital media treatments and activities that lead to particular conversion events across a large number of visitors and creates complex data enrichment calculations (frequency, recency, and sequencing of marketing treatments) in order to attribute sales credit to these different digital media treatments. Think "hockey assist" as in trying to measure the impact that a wide variety of digital media treatments had over a period of time to drive a conversion or sales event.[1] Following is an example of how organizations use attribution analysis to maximize campaign return on marketing investment (ROMI):

Digital media attribution analysis

1. **Track Activities Leading to Conversion Events.** Create market baskets of keyword searches, site visits, display impressions, display clicks, and other media treatments associated with each conversion event
2. **Enrich Data to Create New Metrics to Understand Drivers of Visitor Behaviors.** Create metrics around frequencies, ordering, sequencing, and latencies
3. **Analyze Metrics to Quantify Cause and Effect.** Identify commonalities in baskets, calculate correlations and strength of correlations, and build "conversion path" models
4. **Operationalize Actionable Insights.** Operationalize insights into media planning and buying systems, and guide in-flight campaign execution

That same attribution analytics would work perfectly in the area of health care where physicians, nurses, and other caregivers are trying to determine or attribute the impact on a patient's wellness across a wide variety of health care "treatments" including medications, surgery, supplements, therapy, diet, exercise,

[1] In hockey, a "hockey assist" or credit is given to the player who gives an assist to the player who gets the ultimate assist that leads directly to another player scoring a goal. Think of this as an "assist to an assist" statistic.

sleep, stress, religion, consoling, and many other health-impacting variables. Using the digital media attribution analytics, health care organizations could determine which combinations, frequency, recency, and sequencing of health care treatments are most effective for which types of patients in what types of wellness situations. But if health care organizations only look within their own industry, they are likely to miss opportunities to learn from other industries' analytic stories and miss the opportunity to apply those stories to optimize their own key business processes, uncover new monetization opportunities, and gain a competitive edge within their industry.

These three business entity analytics buckets will help you see that the use case type is more relevant than the industry from which it came; that it provides a "think differently" moment to borrow analytic best practices from other industries. Let's discuss each of these three categories in more detail to see what stories you might uncover that could be meaningful to your organization:

- Customer and employee analytics
- Product and device analytics
- Network and operational analytics

Customer and Employee Analytics

For organizations in business-to-consumer (B2C) industries, understanding and taking care of customers is job #1. Understanding in detail the propensities, tendencies, patterns, interests, passions, affiliations, and associations of each of your individual customers is key to increasing revenue, reducing costs, mitigating risks, and improving margins and profits.

Customers can take many forms including visitors, passengers, travelers, guests, lodgers, patients, students, clients, residents, citizens, constituents, prisoners, players, and more. Many B2C industries can benefit directly from data and analytics that yield superior insights into the behaviors of their customers including:

- Retail
- Restaurants
- Travel and hospitality
- Airlines
- Automotive
- Gaming
- Entertainment
- Banking

- Credit cards
- Financial services
- Health care
- Insurance
- Media
- Telecommunications
- Consumer electronics (e.g., computers, tablets, digital cameras, digital media players, GPS devices)
- Primary and higher education
- Utilities
- Oil and gas
- Public service agencies
- Government agencies

The foundation of customer analytics is identifying, quantifying, and predicting the individual customer's behavioral characteristics (propensities, tendencies, patterns, trends, interests, passions, associations, and affiliations) to identify opportunities to engage the customer to influence his or her behaviors. Some call this "catching the customer in the act." The more timely the identification of these customer interactions, the better the chances of uncovering new revenue or monetization opportunities. Customer analytics include the following:[2]

- **Customer acquisition** measures the effectiveness of different sales and marketing techniques to get customers to sample or trial your product or service.
- **Customer activation** measures the effectiveness of different sales and marketing techniques to get customers to regularly use and/or pay for your product or service.
- **Customer cross-sell and up-sell** measures the effectiveness of different sales, marketing, and merchandising techniques to get customers to upgrade the products and services that they already use or buy and/or get customers to use or buy complementary products and services.
- **Customer retention** measures the effectiveness of sales, marketing, and customer service treatments to identify customers likely to attrite and the subsequent efforts to retain those customers.

[2] This is not intended to be a comprehensive list of customer analytics, but it instead represents a sample of the types of customer analytics for which organizations in business-to-consumer industries should be aware.

- **Customer sentiment** monitors the sentiment of customers across multiple social media sites, blogs, consumer comments, and e-mail conversations to flag product, service, or operational problem areas and recommend corrective action.
- **Customer advocacy** measures how effective particular customers are at influencing other customers' actions or behaviors.

NOTE Some industry estimates show that just 3 percent of the participants in an online conversation yield over 90 percent of the results—such as likes, views, retweets, linkbacks—within a particular subject area.

- **Customer lifetime value** determines the current (and future or maximum) value of a particular customer.
- **Customer fraud** monitors and flags potential fraudulent activities in real-time in order to recommend timely corrective or preventive action.
- **Cohort analysis** determines the impact that one particular customer has on other customers in driving particular customer and/or group behaviors.

There is also a set of customer analytics around marketing. These marketing analytics include:

- **Targeting effectiveness** measures the effectiveness of marketing's targeting efforts to reach the "right" or highest qualified prospects.
- **Re-targeting effectiveness** measures the effectiveness of re-targeting efforts to re-target prospects that have shown an interest in a particular product or service.
- **Segmentation effectiveness** measures the effectiveness of segmentation efforts to identify high-value prospect clusters.
- **Campaign marketing effectiveness** measures the effectiveness of general marketing campaigns at driving customer or prospect actions.
- **Direct marketing effectiveness** measures the effectiveness of direct-to-consumer marketing campaigns to get customers to respond to marketing requests or buy particular products or services.
- **Promotional effectiveness** measures the effectiveness of channel or partner promotional activities, events, packages, and offers.
- **A/B testing** tests the effectiveness of two different marketing treatments (messaging, ad types, websites, keywords, day part, and page location) to determine which marketing treatment is most effective in driving the desired customer action or behavior.

- **Market basket analysis** determines the propensity of products or services to sell in combination with other products and services (within same basket or shopping cart). Market basket analysis also can identify time lags between purchase events (buy a boat and then two weeks later, buy water skis).
- **Attribution analysis** quantifies the contribution of different digital marketing or media treatments in driving a customer event or activity (e.g., buy a product, download an app, play a game, request collateral, research an event).
- **Omni-channel marketing analysis** quantifies the inter-play of marketing effectiveness across multiple retail or business channels (e.g., physical store, catalog, call center, website, social media) in driving sales results.
- **Trade promotion effectiveness** measures the effectiveness of channel or partner promotions to drive end consumer sales.
- **Pricing and yield optimization** determines both the timing and the "optimal" prices in order to maximize revenue and profitability for perishable products or services (vegetables, meat, airline seats, hotel rooms, sporting events, concerts).
- **Markdown management optimization** determines the timing and amount of price reduction and promotions to reduce obsolete and excess inventory while balancing revenue, margin, and cost variables.

By the way, many of these customer analytics have a corollary for employee analytics (teachers, police officers, parole officers, case workers, physician, nurses, technicians, mechanics, pilots, drivers, entertainers, etc.). These analytics include:

- **Employee acquisition** (hiring) measures the effectiveness of different hiring practices and recruiting personnel to identify and hire the most productive and successful employees.
- **Employee activation** (productivity or performance) measures the effectiveness of training programs and managers to engage employees and drive more productive and effective performance.
- **Employee development** (promotions, firing) measures the effectiveness of reviews, promotions, training, coaching, interventions, and management to identify and promote high potential employees and release low productivity employees at the lowest cost and lowest risk.
- **Employee retention** measures the effectiveness of promotions, raises, awards, stock options, etc. to retain the organization's most valuable and productive employees.
- **Employee advocacy** (hiring referrals) measures the effectiveness of advocacy and referral programs to acquire high potential job candidates.

- **Employee lifetime value** determines or scores the current (and future or maximum) value of employees to the organization.
- **Employee sentiment** (employee satisfaction, "best places to work" surveys, etc.) identifies, measures, and recommends corrective action on the drivers of employee and departmental dissatisfaction.
- **Employee fraud** (shrinkage) monitors and flags shrinkage problems and triages those situations to identify root causes of fraud and shrinkage.

It can be useful to look at what other organizations in other industries are doing to better understand their customers and employees. For example, your organization could identify which organizations are best at leveraging customer loyalty programs to drive customer acquisition, maturation, retention, and advocacy. Then identify what data they are capturing about their customers and what analytics they are leveraging to improve the customer experience. There are many examples of organizations that understand how to optimize their loyalty programs. Just go grab a venti non-fat, no water chai latte at a certain coffee chain to experience that for yourself.

Product and Device Analytics

The second area of business entity analytics focuses on physical items—products and machines. Many of the same behavioral analytic basics that are used in customer analytics are applicable for products and machines. Like humans, products and machines exhibit different behavioral tendencies, especially over time. Two wind turbines manufactured by the same manufacturer, installed at the same time, and located in the same cornfield could develop very different behaviors and tendencies over time due to usage, maintenance, upgrades, and general product wear and tear.

Analytics about products and machines (airplanes, jet engines, cars, delivery trucks, locomotives, ATMs, washing machines, routers, traffic lights, wind turbines, power plants, etc.) could include any of the following:

- **Predictive maintenance** predicts when certain products or devices are in need of maintenance, what sort of maintenance, the likely maintenance and replacement materials, and technician skill sets.
- **Maintenance scheduling optimization** optimizes the scheduling of resources (technicians with the right skill sets, replacement parts, maintenance equipment, etc.) in order to optimize the replacement and/or upgrading of failing or under-performing parts or products.
- **Maintenance, repair, and operations (MRO) inventory optimization** balances MRO inventory with predicted maintenance needs in order to reduce inventory costs and minimize obsolete and excessive inventory.

- **Product performance optimization** optimizes product performance and mean time between maintenance (MTBM) by understanding the product's or device's optimal operation performance ranges, tolerances, and variances.
- **Manufacturing effectiveness** reduces manufacturing costs while maintaining product quality levels and production schedules through the optimal mix of supplies, suppliers, and in-house and contract manufacturing capabilities.
- **Supplier performance analytics** quantify supplier product quality and delivery reliability in order to minimize manufacturing line downtown.
- **Supplier decommits/recommits analytics** understand optimal production capacities of suppliers and contract manufacturers in order to properly rebalance manufacturing needs caused by supply chain disruptions (strikes, storms, wars, raw material shortages).
- **Supplier network analytics** triage product and supplier problems more quickly by understanding the dynamics of the underlying supplier and contract manufacturer relationships and inter-dependencies.
- **Product testing and QA effectiveness** accelerates product quality assurance testing by optimizing the tests and/or combinations of tests that cause products, components, suppliers, and contract manufacturers to fail more quickly.
- **Supply chain optimization** optimizes supply chain delivery and inventory levels while minimizing supply chain costs and risks associated with obsolete and excess inventory.
- **Optimize MRO parts inventory** to determine the appropriate level of MRO parts inventory based on predicted maintenance needs.
- **New product introductions** optimize product and marketing mix to increase the probability of success when launching new products, product extensions, and/or new product versions.
- **Product rationalization/retirement** determines which products to divest or retire, and when, based on that product's impact on customer value and inter-related profitability of other products (market basket analysis).
- **Brand and category management analysis** determines optimal pricing, packaging, placement, and promotional variables of individual brands

and products within brands to drive overall brand and category revenues, profitability, and market share.

Product-centric industries most impacted by product and device analytics include:

- Consumer packaged goods
- High-tech manufacturing
- Appliance and electronics manufacturing
- Sporting goods manufacturing
- Food and beverage
- Automotive
- Agriculture
- Farm machinery manufacturing
- Heavy equipment manufacturing
- Pharmaceuticals
- Financial services
- Banking
- Credit cards
- Insurance

Network and Operational Analytics

The third area of business entity analytics focuses on network and operational analytics. The "internet of things" (IoT) and wearable computing (Fitbit, Jawbone, Garmin) has increased the level of interest (and the volume and variety of data) about what is happening across vast and complex human and machine/device networks. More than ever, we are an interconnected world where the actions of one person or device in a social or physical network can have a "butterfly effect" on all of the people and devices across that network.[3]

[3] In chaos theory, the "butterfly effect" is the sensitive dependence on initial conditions in which a small change in one state of a deterministic nonlinear system can result in large differences in a later state.

Networks can take many different shapes and forms including ATM networks, retail branches, supplier networks, device sensors, in-store beacons, mobile devices, cellular towers, traffic lights, slot machines, and communication networks. Analytics about networks and operations could include any of the following:

- **Demand forecasting** forecasts network demand (average demand, surge demand, minimal viable demand) based on predicted network usage behaviors, patterns, and trends.
- **Capacity planning** predicts network capacity requirements in all potential (what if) working situations.
- **Reduce unplanned downtime** to identify, monitor, and pre-emptively predict the failure of the drivers of unplanned network downtime.
- **Network performance optimization** predicts and optimizes network performance across multiple usage scenarios (network traffic, weather, seasonality, holidays, special events) in real-time.
- **Network layout optimization** optimizes network layout in order to minimize traffic bottlenecks and optimize network bandwidth and throughput.
- **Reduce network traffic** to triage network traffic bottlenecks and provide real-time incentives and/or governors to reduce or re-route traffic during overload situations.
- **Load balancing** identifies and rebalances network traffic based on current and forecasted traffic needs and current network capacity.
- **Theft and revenue protection** identifies, understands, and recommends the most appropriate revenue protection actions based on theft situations across the network.
- **Predictive maintenance** predicts when network nodes are in need of maintenance, what sort of maintenance, the likely maintenance and replacement materials, and technician skill sets.
- **Network security** identifies, understands, and recommends the most appropriate actions based on unauthorized network or device/node entry or usage situations across the network.

Industries most impacted by network and operational analytics tend to be industries that run or manage complex projects or systems. These industries have to coordinate multiple vendors and suppliers across multiple sub-assemblies or sub-projects in order to deliver the end product or project on time and within budget. Some of these industries include:

- Large-scale construction (skyscrapers, malls, stadiums, airports, dams, bridges, tunnels, etc.)
- Airplane manufacturing
- Shipbuilding

- Defense contractors
- Systems integrators
- Telecommunication networks
- Railroad networks
- Transportation networks

There are many, many more examples of customer, product, and network analytics. The list above is a good starter point. And while investigating analytic use cases within your own industry is "safe," better and potentially more impactful analytic use cases can likely be found by looking for customer, product, and network analytic success stories in other industries. Bucketing the analytic use cases into those three categories helps the reader to contemplate a wider variety of analytic opportunities and best practices across different industries.

Think differently when you are in search of the analytics that may be most impactful to your organization. Don't assume that your industry has all the answers.

Characteristics of a Good Business Story

The final step in the book is to pull together the "thinking like a data scientist" results and the sample analytics to create a story that is interesting and relevant to your organization. While it can be useful to hear about what other organizations are doing with big data and data science, the most compelling stories will be those stories about your organization that motivate your senior leadership to take action.

You know from reading books and watching movies that the best stories have interesting characters that have been put into a difficult situation. Heck, that sounds like data science already. To create compelling stories, you are going to need the following components to create an interesting and relevant story that is unique to your organization (think about the process in relationship to your favorite science fiction adventure movie):

- Key business initiative (survival of the human race)
- Strategic nouns or key business entities (pilots, scientists, aliens)
- Current challenging situation (aliens are going to conquer Earth and exterminate the human race)
- Creative solution (infect the alien ships with a computer virus that shuts down their defensive shields)
- Desired glorious end state (aliens get their butts kicked, and the whole world becomes one united brotherhood)

Let's see this process in action:

- Let's say that your organization has as a key business initiative to "reduce customer churn by 10 percent over the next 12 months."
- Your strategic noun is "customer."
- The current challenging situation is "too many of our most valuable customers are leaving the company and going to competitors."
- The creative solution is "developing analytics that flag customers who have a high propensity to leave the company, create a customer lifetime value score for each customer (so that your organization is not wasting valuable sales and marketing resources saving the 'wrong' customers), and deliver messages to frontline employees (call center reps, sales teams, partners) with recommended offers to deliver to the customer if a valuable customer has a score with an 'at risk' propensity to leave."
- The glorious end state is "dramatic increase in the retention of the organization's most valuable customers that leads to an increase in corporate profits, an increase in customer satisfaction, and generous raises for all!"

This is an easy process if you understand your organization's key business initiatives or what's important to the organization's business leadership.

Summary

Broaden your horizons with respect to looking for analytic use cases. Instead of just looking within your own industry, look across different industries for analytic use cases around:

- Customer and employee analytics
- Product and device analytics
- Network and operational analytics

Since this is the last chapter of the book, put a cherry on the top of your Big Data MBA by developing a compelling and relevant story that you can share within your organization to motivate senior leadership to action. Make the story compelling by tying one of the above analytic use cases to your organization's key business initiatives, and make the story relevant by leveraging your "thinking like a data scientist" training. That way you ensure that all the work you have put into reading this book and doing the homework can lead to something of compelling and differentiated value to the organization. And heck, maybe you will get a promotion out of it!

Congratulations! For a special surprise, go to this URL: `www.wiley.com/go/bigdatamba`. And don't share this URL with anyone else. Make other folks read the entire book to find this "Easter egg" surprise.

Now you have earned your Big Data MBA! Go get 'em!

Homework Assignment

Use the following exercises to apply what you learned in this chapter.

- **Exercise #1:** Identify one of your organization's key business initiatives.
- **Exercise #2:** Apply the "thinking like a data scientist" approach to identify the relevant business stakeholders, key business entities or strategic nouns, key decisions, potential recommendations, and supporting scores.
- **Exercise #3:** Now create a story that weaves together all of these items with a relevant analytics example that can help senior leadership to understand the business potential and motivate them into action. Use your strategic nouns to help you find some relevant analytic use cases outlined in this chapter.

Index

A

B

C

D

S

Printed and bound by CPI Group (UK) Ltd, Croydon, CR0 4YY

27/10/2024

14580183-0001